Radio Ingleside; A Life On Air

John Harding

For my Mother

Virginia Paschal Harding

Foreword

Full disclosure: the author is a personal friend who mentions me several times in the following book. I worked with John Harding for 32 years. That gives me some authority to tell you the authenticity of what you are about to read.

If you are not a member of his family, the story of John's early years will be as much of a revelation to you as it was to me. But what you are about to read is also a history of one of America's great radio stations, what made it great and what led to what that station is today.

WRVA was founded in 1925 by Larus & Brother, a Richmond, Virginia tobacco company. Commercial radio was only five years old in that year. C.T. Lucy, the first General Manager, said the tobacco company thought broadcasting would be "an interesting business to get into." Within a few years of its founding, the station was broadcasting with 50,000 watts, one of only 50 stations in the country with that kind of power on the AM band. The station could be heard as far away as Oregon and South Africa. After World War II, the station *was* Richmond. It won the reputation of being the most reliable· when other stations heard about a news story, they listened to WRVA to verify it was true – and having on·air people who were, or could be, your neighbors and friends. WRVA led the ratings with the most listeners of any station in the Richmond area.

I'm giving you this bit of history as a prelude of what you are about to read. John Harding not only chronicles what made WRVA so special, but also why today that same station is no longer number 1, no longer special, and just another station on the dial.

You will meet some delightful people as you turn the pages: the people of Ingleside Avenue in Emporia, where John grew up, his artistic family, including the driving force in his life, his Mother, and his sister, the Broadway and movie star June Harding. You'll also meet the manager of WEVA in John's hometown, Will Stone who gave him his first job in broadcasting; the venerated Alden Aaroe who hired him at WRVA; the irascible News Director Joe Weeks; WRVA's Manager, John Tansey; a duck named Millard The Mallard; newshound Howard Bloom; Alden Aaroe's later partner and successor, Tim Timberlake; the highly organized Debbie Ashley who ultimately saved the history of WRVA; and stories about many others who pass into the narrative. You'll also meet and read about David Brinkley and other NBC news correspondents with whom John rubbed elbows in Washington, DC before he came to WRVA.

In the opening chapters, you will meet a young man with a vivid imagination who, like many of us, dreamed about being on the radio, talked into a make believe microphone and even set up his own (illegal) radio station. You will cheer him on as you read about his journey from hesitant teenager to becoming a great newsman with the respect of his peers, winning many awards and recognitions and becoming outstanding in his field.

John Harding has been a reporter, a News Director, a radio station Operations Manager, and my friend. Turn the page to peek in on the little kid who will grow up to give you a backstage look into the radio station I hope you had the good fortune and pleasure to hear in the days when it was a giant.

Lou Dean

Former Program Director,

WRVA

Richmond, Virginia

Introduction

It is January of 1992. I'm standing before a large crowd at the Awards Luncheon being held at the winter meeting of the Virginia Association of Broadcasters at a downtown Richmond hotel. I am about to be presented with the Association's third annual "George A. Bowles Jr. Award for Distinguished Performance in Broadcast News." Bowles was the longtime State Capitol Correspondent for the Virginia News Network.

I had been at WRVA in Richmond, Virginia 25 years at the time and it had been a great ride. I had known exactly what I wanted to do with my life since I was a kid growing up in Emporia. Not many people get to do that and I considered myself blessed, but the award I was about to receive gave me pause. It was the kind of thing that happened at the end of careers. The two previous recipients were no longer active in broadcasting. I was just 47, but I couldn't help but wonder if my selection was some sort of an omen that my career was approaching the finish line.

Those of us in broadcasting are a rather paranoid bunch. Job security has always been an occupational hazard, particularly so for those of us in broadcast news. WRVA had been one of the notable exceptions. Many of us had been there for most of our careers. While we were all concerned about our futures, we didn't go to work every day looking over our shoulder to see if the corporate reaper was on our tail. Top management at WRVA had always expected us to push the envelope, to run risks.

Perhaps that may explain the incredible success of the station over its long history, but a silent tsunami of change was slowly sweeping the business. Radio and television stations were becoming commodities to be traded like corn futures. Deregulation was the next big thing, opening the door for the huge communications conglomerates to sweep up stations as owners cashed out. We were ripe for the picking.

Across the board cuts had been ordered as our current owner circled the wagons while seeking a buyer. One sale to a west coast concern had just fallen through and we were on the block once again. Many of us were polishing up our resumes. I just hoped the VAB Award didn't stamp "The End" on my career.

All of this had been turning over in my mind as I went about preparing my acceptance remarks. After agonizing for a week over what I would say, I decided to publically thank my benefactors, those who had opened doors, spoken a word or two of encouragement or saw some molecule of potential in me along the way. A couple of them were members of the VAB and were in the audience. Their smiling faces jumped out of the crowd, but most of those who had helped me get to where I was were not present. Many had passed on. Some had been pillars of the town and neighborhood where I had grown up. A half dozen or so were very well- known. Some just occupied a line in the phone book. All were remarkable people, not the least of which were my parents. Neither was present. My father had died when I was in my 20's. Mother was 82 and not well.

My time was short that day. I only had several minutes. It was barely enough time to mention some of their names.

They deserved better. I hope this book finally gives them their due.

My story begins on Ingleside Avenue in a neighborhood straight out of a Norman Rockwell painting. It is the summer of 1949 in Emporia, a small town in Southside Virginia near the North Carolina border.

Contents

Part I

Ingleside Avenue

Emporia, VA

I

"Mama, Captain Reynolds is dead!" I screamed, stumbling up the steps on all fours. Mother rushed to the side door just off the kitchen.

"He's dead, Mama," I exclaimed breathlessly, climbing the last few steps to the small stoop. "Me and Dickie Thompson, we saw him."

"How do you know he's dead, John?" she asked.

"Because we saw his peg leg and his hat floating down the river. It was Captain Reynolds Mama, I know it was. Dickie Thompson said so."

Mother humored my daily tales of adventure with Captain Reynolds and his sidekick Dickie Thompson. She would listen in wide-eyed wonder as I described my escapades on the Captain's ship, sailing on the small creek that meandered through the dense woods behind our house. There was a creek but only a mere trickle of water, hardly enough for a toy boat let alone a pirate ship.

Reluctant to pop my imaginary balloon, Mother would go to the trouble of making the Captain and Dickie Thompson a sandwich, putting it on a plate and setting it on the steps out back. That it was gone in a few hours only reinforced their reality.

Mother wrote all of this down for posterity, perhaps with the thought that she might need to take me to a psychiatrist should I venture off the beaten path to the point of not being able to make it back to reality. I found her notes tucked away in one of the family scrapbooks.

As for what triggered this virtual unreality, I have not the slightest clue. At the dawn of the 50's, there was little in the way of pop culture to hijack my fancy. My only exposure to make-believe characters had been the few times I had watched my father's collection of 8mm cartoon shorts when I was a toddler. Mother said I would sit entranced as *Oswald Rabbit, Popeye,* and *Felix The Cat* romped in silence on the projector screen. There was no TV in those days. We wouldn't get one until 1957.

Mother told me years later she believed it was my unstructured childhood that allowed my imagination to bloom as I played alone in the backyard. Whatever the spark, Captain Reynolds and Dickie Thompson had captured my imagination and taken me along with them in the theatre that was my young mind.

Today, experts call imaginary playmates "Fabulous Fakes" and say they often morph into other forms later in life, but at the dawn of the 50's, parents were left to their own devices. After the Captain's untimely death in the Meherrin River, Mother, no doubt concerned about my sanity, came up with the idea of getting me a dog and naming him Dickie Thompson to give my surviving friend some basis in reality.

Father found him under a church in the county. A mixed breed puppy with brownish fur and a white stripe running down his nose, he must have had a little hound in him because of his signature floppy ears. We made a bed for him in the basement. Mother put a windup alarm clock nearby so the loud ticking would keep him from getting lonesome. The transference must have worked because the daily soap opera of my imaginary adventures faded beneath reality.

Dickie Thompson, the dog, had his own version of swashbuckling adventure, chasing down anything on wheels that rolled by our house. He was particularly annoyed by Donnie Tiller's red motor scooter, which was obstinately loud.

Rehabilitation was a nonstarter. Even after a lengthy stint of solitary, chained up in the backyard, Dickie Thompson remained a repeat offender until an oil company truck ran over his tail. The Vet put a cast on it and my father fashioned a caster on the tip so he could get around. Mother greased up his nose with a blob of vapor rub to make him feel better. We could always hear him coming down the sidewalk from the whirr of the caster.

Dickie Thompson would walk with me to elementary school every morning and be waiting at the door when school let out in the afternoon. When I started high school, which was in the other direction, he would never venture beyond the corner with Jefferson Street where the oil truck had flattened his tail.

Dickie Thompson had no issues with people coming to the house. He would dutifully trot off the front porch to make way for Smitty, the postman, when he came to deliver the day's mail and pick up Mother's outgoing letters, which she clipped to the mailbox with a clothespin. Dickie Thompson's wagging tail, thumping loudly against the front door, would signal the arrival of Mr. Puster, the short, elderly, white haired egg man with twinkling blue eyes who always brought a handful of dog biscuits. Dickie's favorite though was Solomon, the cheerful black man who delivered groceries for Mitchell Brothers. He always remembered to bring Dickie Thompson a large beef bone good for a week's worth of gnawing.

When I went off to school, Dickie became Mother's dog. She fretted over him constantly in his advancing age. When he went missing during a snowstorm, she was beside herself. Slogging through the snow-smothered neighborhood screaming his name, she heard him whimpering from under the Weaver's tool shed next door and summoned my father home from Swift and Company. "It was an emergency of the highest order," she recalled years later. Father eventually dug him out. They put him on one of my old sleds and dragged him to the basement where Mother nursed him back to health, no doubt smearing more greasy vapor rub on his nose, her cure-all for everything. The Vet said it didn't help but probably let him know that she loved him. She did. Dickie, the dog formerly known as Dickie Thompson, lived to be 18. When he died, Mother called me in Washington all to pieces. At first I thought my father had died. It was Dickie Thompson. Father buried him in the back yard.

II

We had moved to the neighborhood in the late summer of 1949. The two story brick house on Ingleside Avenue was similar in design and size to others on the street, but its newness made it stand out. So did the lack of a paved front walk. Wide, wooden planks bridged a moat of fill dirt brought in to level what would be the front lawn. Compared to the nondescript, single story bungalow on North Main Street we had left behind, 522 Ingleside looked like "Downton Abbey."

The houses on Ingleside were comfortable in their space with plenty of room to breathe. The lawns were all tastefully landscaped; some looked like small parks with colonies of azaleas and gardenias shaded by ancient trees. The lots on our side on the street were quite deep, reaching back to a large wooded area where the Captain and his pal Dickie Thompson would reside in my fertile imagination.

My sister's two playhouses looked right at home nestled beneath the tall pines in the far back yard. Father had crafted them out of wooden Swift cheese crates in the 30's and had them brought over from the house on North Main Street. Over the next three decades, they would embark on a second life becoming clubhouses and hideouts for a new generation of cowboys and indians, soldiers and pirates.

Most of the neighbors were middle aged and rather well to do. Most had black maids who came to work every day, often dressed in highly starched uniforms, usually blue or grey. Martha Ford worked for Mr. and Mrs. Lucas, and Levolia worked for the Harrell's. The Weaver's and the Tillar's also had maids but I can't recall their names. Mother didn't have any outside help until years later when Annie began coming two days a week to help with the housework after Mother had surgery.

Each evening in the spring and summer and on into the fall, all of the ladies of the neighborhood would gather after supper in a circle of brightly painted, metal lawn chairs in Margaret Lucas's front yard next door for an hour or so of spirited twilight chit chat. Their distant voices floated in the close, humid air, with a dreamy, sleepy quality, like a memory of some lawn party from long ago. On into the evening they would prattle, cackle and laugh until darkness descended and the lightening bugs started blinking. I dubbed them " The Chatter Society." When it rained or if the mosquitos got too annoying, they would adjourn to Mrs. Lucas's side porch.

"The Chatter Society" faded away over the ensuing decades, done in by TV, air conditioning and arthritis, but the closeness of the neighborhood never wavered. All of the families exchanged gifts at Christmas and when a kid got sick, the neighbors brought get well presents. Birthdays were always big productions. An old photograph shows most of the kids on the street lined up along our front walk, with arms intertwined, for my first birthday on Ingleside. There were thirteen of us. Even the older kids had shown up for a 5 year old's party.

My importation in the closing months of the Second World War had served to brighten my Mother's spirits. Her hero Franklin Roosevelt had died the previous day. She had been very upset; my father, who was a Republican, not so much. I had arrived just in time to net my parents, Virginia and Bland Harding, another War Ration Coupon Book with its highly prized coffee and sugar stamps. I was also something of a surprise. My sisters June Allison and Barbara Bland (we always called her BB) were 8 and 10 years old, respectively, when I made my debut.

I was tagged with the name John after Mother's father John Wesley Paschal, but my father would not buy into Wesley as my middle name. John Wesley Hardin, no "g," had been a Texas gunslinger who was said to have shot a man to death for snoring too loud. Compromise yielded the name Tisdale after my father. Tisdale was an unusual name when I was growing up and I was quite sensitive about it; so, of course, that's what many would call me.

III

Margaret Lucas seemed to know everybody who was anybody and everyone who wasn't. Ironically it was her husband Robert, owner of the Chrysler Plymouth Dealership in Emporia, who dabbled in town politics. She should have. Perpetually jolly, she presided over Ingleside from her side porch. The Lucas's had two children.

Bobby was the oldest. He had announced himself to us by signing his name in the wet cement when the floor was poured for our basement. Bobby had a pink and black 50's Plymouth with a Bermuda Chime that sounded like a very loud doorbell. He'd usually ring it several times whenever he drove home, sending all of the neighbors running to their front doors.

His younger sister Peggy was best friends with Martha Harrell, who lived across the street. Both were brains at math. Mother would later lament that some of their brilliance didn't rub off on me through some sort of neighbor osmosis. There's an endearing photograph of Peggy and Martha gracing Peggy's front yard costumed as Fairy Princesses waving magic wands. Another captures Peggy all duded up in an Annie Oakley outfit, complete with cowgirl hat and chaps, and twirling toy pistols.

My sister June would let me tag along when she, Peggy and Martha played with miniature doll house furniture on the Lucas's side porch. I could watch, but not touch, as they built outlines of rooms using small blocks of wood and arranged the furniture in each. June had a Miller & Roads shopping bag filled with doll house furnishings, everything from tiny beds to stoves. Miniature figures populated the rooms. I remember the woman wore a pink suit and looked like Blondie in the Sunday comics.

The Lucas's had the first TV set in the neighborhood, proudly advertised by the large motorized antenna attached to their chimney. We all trooped over one Sunday night to watch Bruce Davis, who lived in the apartment house down the street, sing on the *Ted Mack Original Amateur Hour*, a forerunner of the ubiquitous singing contest reality shows today. Bruce's fifteen minutes of fame came up short but his brother Mickey, who serenaded the neighborhood with fractured trumpet phrases every afternoon from his back porch, wound up on TV in Richmond as Dave Davis, a sometimes weatherman who gave voice to puppets on a children's show.

Every New Year's, Mr. and Mrs. Lucas would have all the neighbors over for eggnog. Mother, whose alcohol tolerance was between zero and none, would usually wind up sipping the spiked version "by mistake," she said. She'd come home a tad tipsy, only to suffer morning after pangs of guilt because she had signed the "no booze" pledge at Monumental Methodist Church.

In the spring of 1960, the neighborhood was stunned when Mr. Lucas died suddenly of complications during surgery. It was the third death in the neighborhood since we had arrived. The first had occurred soon after we moved in.

IV

Father had been reading the newspaper on our side porch that day when I saw him suddenly bolt upright from the glider, as though he had heard something, and run next door to the Weaver's house. I ran out behind him but Mother quickly caught me and hustled me back inside. When he finally came home hours later, he went straight upstairs to his room and closed the door. He never spoke of it. Not that day, not ever. Neither did Mother. Decades later after he had retired, we were in his studio remembering old times while he carefully went about painting spots on a giraffe he had carved. I asked him about that day. "John," he said, "It was a horrible day, let's just leave it at that."

Mrs. Weaver, an elegant, classy lady, whose name was the same as Mother's, "Virginia," took over Mr. Weaver's soft drink bottling business in the manner of a Katherine Graham. Her mother Daphne Eubank, who had a beautiful home on Peachtree Street one block over, began staying at her daughter's house during the day, looking after her three grandsons, Channing, Roly and Pete, while Mrs. Weaver was at work.

Whenever she spied Pete and me playing with toy soldiers in his sandbox, she'd raise a window and yell, "Peter Weaver, are you and John Tisdale sitting on a board?" Mrs. Eubank was convinced we would catch pneumonia through our rear ends if we sat on the bare ground.

Mrs. E, as I would come to call her, was an education. She schooled me on such things as which knife, fork and spoon was for what, introduced me to all the Ian Fleming "James Bond" books, long before the movies came out, and later taught me how to decipher stock quotes in the newspaper.

The day before I was to get married, she called my father and me next door for a toast. The liquor was smooth and the toast was memorable. "John," she said with a wicked smile on her face, "if you are fortunate enough to know when your last day on earth will be, spend it with your in-laws. That one day will seem like a lifetime. Cheers!"

Pete and I were close pals in those days along with Raynor Johnston who lived on Jefferson Street just around the corner from us, and David Tillar, who had moved into a new house across the street. We were usually involved with whatever was in season. I don't recall any of us being prodigies in any particular sport in those years but we went through the motions. In the spring and summers, we played at baseball, laying out a makeshift diamond in Pete's backyard, which had the most open space in the neighborhood, though most of our time was spent chasing down errant balls.

When football season rolled around in the fall, we all watched the Redskins on the *Amoco Game Of The Week*, then donned our shoulder pads and helmets and ran out front to choose up sides with dreams of being the next Eddie LeBaron. Mostly though, we played army. Decked out in army surplus helmets, cartridge belts, knapsacks and canteens, and armed with wooden rifles, we built forts in the dense woods behind our house using limbs from the towering pine trees. Pine cones were repurposed as hand grenades to slay imaginary battalions.

We were forever pestering Pete's older brother Channing, camping out in his room messing with his things. A paragon of composure, Channing had incredible patience with us. A tragic accident in his convertible would leave him with a broken back and a massive cast around his torso for months.

I envied Channing as he led what to me was a carefree, happy-go-lucky life. I was enthralled with his highly polished, teak stereo hi fi system he had installed in the Weaver's living room. It was where I first heard Arthur Prysock, Big Joe Turner, Ruth Brown and Lavern Baker. I was enthralled with the "Provocative and Persuasive Percussion" albums by Terry Snyder and his All Stars, straining to hear the pulsing rhythms from our side porch across the side yard.

All of us in the neighborhood drooled over Channing's red 1959 Chevrolet Corvette, constantly pleading for him to take us for rides. He'd often oblige, taking us one at a time zooming around the sleepy, staid streets of Emporia with the top down or scorching the runway at the old airport, making us Sterling Moss for a moment.

I don't remember Pete's other brother Roly being around much in those early years though he shows up in many of the group pictures at my birthday parties when I was little. Roly, short for Roland, was blond, had intense, mischievous eyes, a sharp dry wit, and a priceless Vincent Price laugh that sent chills up my spine.

V

The Harrell's house across the street was on higher ground so it looked even larger than it was. Lyman Harrell had served on the Town Council, was the County Commonwealth's Attorney and a banker. He would later be elected to the Virginia General Assembly. He and his wife Nancy had three children, Chris, Martha and the youngest Bet.

Chris always wore a sailor hat when he was a kid. He had black hair and thoughtful, honest eyes. Always understated, I don't ever remember Chris raising his voice to anyone.

There are lots of old photographs. One shows us on the porch by the swimming pool at the Slagle's Lake Road House north of Emporia with Walker Wyche Taylor, a regular in the neighborhood.

Like the Weaver brothers, Chris received a new convertible as an undergraduate gift, a white Chevy Impala with red interior. When he was home from Washington and Lee, he'd often come up to the radio station to visit and sometimes Dee Warren would come with him. *You'll have the pleasure later.* He knew I had a thing for her.

Martha favored her mother. She and Peggy Lucas cruised the neighborhood on identical Donald Duck Bicycles they got one Christmas. Summers meant trips to "Chick's Beach" at Bayside on the Chesapeake Bay where the Harrell's had a cottage. As with Chris, graduation brought new wheels: a powder blue Chevy Corvair Monza.

After college, Martha worked for a year or so as a translator at the United Nations in New York, but her passion was always math. A walking mainframe, she met Stephen Hawking at Cambridge, taught math at NYU and formed her own company. Chris often joked that Martha spoke a half dozen languages, including physics.

Bet was the only girl who participated in the cut throat, neighborhood "kick the can" games. She had a dog named Boots who had a hair for seeking his fortune away from home, triggering many a yard to yard search. Years later, Bet would be something of a referee between her best friend Cheryl and me during our on again, off again, mostly off, relationship in high school. After college, Bet followed her father into politics but as a lobbyist instead of a politician.

We were all members of the same church, Monumental Methodist, and we were distant cousins. Somewhere in the giant tree of families, we shared a branch or two with a man named Mordecai Jones. Beyond that, I never knew the precise connection until late in life. Father never, ever spoke of his side of the family, yet the annual Jones family reunion was always a "must attend." Father would pack us all up along with Mother's fried chicken and potato salad, and head back to the church, for a Sunday afternoon recital of the Jones family history, and pats on the head.

Mr. Harrell's wife Nancy died of cancer in 1956. I remember the sadness quite well. It happened right around my 11th birthday. Mr. Harrell would later remarry and bring the new Mrs. Harrell and her two daughters to Ingleside Avenue.

VI

Several years after we moved to the neighborhood, the Tillar's built a new house on the vacant lot between the Harrell's and Miss Mary. Mr. Tillar, a large man with bushy eyebrows who smoked a pipe, was a principal in the W.T. Tillar Hardware Store on Main Street. His wife, Bettie, taught World History and Geography at Greensville County High School. They quickly became regulars at the "Chatter Society." Mr. Tillar had the distinction of being the first man to be a nightly participant.

The Tillar's had three sons: Donnie, who had the motor scooter, Bill and David. I never got to know the older Tillar brothers very well but David quickly became a close friend. Every Christmas, Mr. Tillar would erect a dazzling, room-sized tinplate train layout with scores of toy trains running around the room at the same time. I promised myself that someday I would have one just like it.

I seldom saw Miss Mary, who lived across the street, but I was always aware of her comings and goings. An elderly, petite lady who looked like everyone's favorite Aunt, Miss Mary drove a robin-egg blue, 1948 Ford Sedan. She would rev it to a primal scream, then ease off in first gear. Peering through the steering wheel, she would slowly creep down Ingleside. I don't think the old Ford ever had the pleasure of second gear. You could hear the car whining in agony all the way to Main Street blocks away.

Miss Mary had an addition built onto her house for her kindergarten which was quite popular in Emporia. Little kids laughing and having fun in her backyard became a familiar sound in the neighborhood.

The Litchfield's lived next door to Miss Mary. Mr. Litchfield worked at the W.T. Tillar Hardware Store. Mrs. Litch, as we called her, was a fragile looking, wafer thin lady I remember mostly for not coming to the door on Halloween trick or treat nights. We usually resorted to a trick. I'm not proud of that.

Her daughter Dorrice Rogers and her family lived in a brick ranch next door. Mrs. Rogers taught Phys Ed in High School. Mr. Rogers was a large, jolly man everybody called "D.T." Their oldest son Ted sometimes came down the street to play with us, but we didn't go out of our way to include him. I feel bad about that too.

The Stancell's lived in a white two story traditional next door to the Lucas's on our side of the street. Willie Stancell ran a house painting outfit but it seemed he fished more than he painted. He came around most Saturdays to share the bounty of his latest catch. His wife Helen was a very friendly, soft spoken lady. I never thought of Mrs. Stancell as a big talker but she was a charter member of "The Chatter Society."

The aforementioned apartment house stood at the crest of Ingleside Hill across a narrow field from the Stancell's. Mr. and Mrs. Davidson were the owners and lived in one of the apartment units. They had a daughter Katherine, but I don't remember seeing her much when I was growing up. Mr. Davidson sold cigarettes. I remember the Camel painted on his car door.

VII

When it snowed, the hill between our house and the Lucases's next door was transformed into the neighborhood winter Olympics, mobbed by kids of all ages with sleds in tow. The steepest hill was beside our house. A fast downhill, a slight jag to the left lengthened the run all the way to the pines in the far backyard. Kids who missed the curve wound up in Mother's giant forsythia and scotch broom.

A section of the hill closest to our house had been terraced by Father into three short inclines, each anchored by a huge hydrangea hazard. It made for a beginner's "X games" thrill ride.

Mother, who fretted about her shrubs as though they were orphaned children, assumed the role of "Lord Protector Of The Bushes," keeping watch over her prized plants from the kitchen window. At the end of the day, Father went around and collected all of the sleds, gloves and hats that had been left in the yard and stored them in the basement. Every time it snowed, kids would show up asking if we had their sled? We usually did.

Summers were hell on earth in our house. The only sanctuary from the heat was the basement where Dickie Thompson and June's cat Frankie slept. The second floor was like a sauna, but, aside from the humidity-swollen windows and doors, that protested loudly when we tried to open or close them, no one ever complained. We had fans but they were of little consequence. Mother often said the only benefit of the big exhaust fan in Father's room upstairs was the loud hum of the motor. It served to mask his tooth rattling snoring. It was why he slept in a separate bedroom.

Father eventually sprang for small window AC units in the upstairs bedrooms. If they were switched on immediately after supper, the rooms would be almost habitable by bedtime. Most of the first floor was cooled by a huge AC unit in the dining room. The exception was my room in the back of the house.

I spent many a hot, sticky, sweaty summer night on the screened in side porch, sleeping on the vinyl cushioned glider. My bare, sweaty skin would stick like glue, rippling like a zipper whenever I moved, but it was better than sleeping in my room, which seldom got even a whiff of a breeze.

The upstairs bathroom had the worst of both worlds: No AC in the summers and no heat in the winter. We had to plug in an electric heater when we took showers. Even Mr. Morris, the heating and AC man who achieved God-like status with Mother, was stumped. To the day she died, Mother would grumble about the "incompetent bozo" who had installed the heating system.

If summer had a dark side, it was poison ivy. The wretched three leaves from hell always found their mark with me, often using Dickie Thompson's fur as an undercover drone to spread its misery. I was desperately allergic to the stuff, breaking out in the red itchy rash with oozing blisters like clockwork every summer. Father wondered if I was swimming in it.

Mother would mummify me with thick coats of pinkish calamine lotion she bought by the quart from Deuce Martin at Leith's Drug Store. It dried like thin plaster on the skin, cracking and peeling, leaving me looking like some decomposing ghoul in *Tales from the Crypt*.

Inevitably, Father resorted to scrubbing me down in the basement sink with his home brew of laundry detergent, bleach, and rubbing alcohol mixed with hot water. Mother fretted it would either explode, give me blood poisoning or leave horrible scars. It burned like hell but it usually dried up the blisters.

Summer evenings were often spent in the Tillar's lighted backyard playing kick the can or swinging on the enormous swing set Mr. Tillar erected using utility poles. On Saturday nights, Mr. Tillar, Mrs. Weaver, and Mrs.

Lucas took turns rounding us all up for an ice cream run to the Dairy Delight just south of town or to the Lindale Dairy Store on the Northside. When it was Mr. Tillar's turn, we got to ride in the back of his pickup truck.

The Weaver's house became soft drink heaven. Mrs. Weaver brought home a case or two of RC Cola from the bottling company every week which we freely guzzled, with crushed ice even. Mrs. Lucas's specialty was fudge, caramel and chocolate. Martha Ford would slip me extra squares of it when I delivered the newspaper. Mother's tour de force was homemade sherbet. Peach, banana and pineapple were customer favorites served up in ice cream cones she kept on top of the fridge.

It was no wonder I had rotten teeth. Our first dentist was on the north side. His wife, a severe looking woman who was grave as a vulture, would shoot streams of water on the targeted tooth to keep the drill cool, amid constant, robotic instructions from her husband to "spit that out." The high pitched scream of the belt driven drill alone was unnerving. Afterwards, as a reward for "being a good sport," we got a pass that was good for a free fountain drink at their son's drug store on Halifax Street. Father said the practice made for good repeat business.

Sometime later, Mother switched us to Doctor Tillar who had his office on Hicksford Avenue just up the street from Bruce Bowen's Livery Stable. If there was any hope he would find fewer cavities, it didn't happen.

BB and I were devoted customers. Hopelessly cavity prone, BB came home from one checkup with 14 cavities, triggering a memorable stare of disbelief from Father at the dinner table. Both of our mouths resembled US 301, completely paved. I don't think there was a tooth left in our heads that didn't have a filling. June must have gotten the good teeth gene because I don't remember her having to hedge on her checkup results like BB and I did.

VIII

Sundays began early with a trip to Patty's in White City, a mainly black neighborhood with unpaved roads just north of downtown. I was always told White City got its name from a Mr. White who owned many of the houses there.

Patty Jones, an elderly black lady with slightly gray hair who wore wire-framed glasses and a warm smile, ran a neighborhood store and also took in washing. Every week, Patty washed and ironed our sheets and pillowcases and Father's dress shirts.

Sunday morning was delivery and pickup day. Father would pick up the previous week's wash, all laundered, ironed, folded and perfectly packed into a large rectangular wicker basket, and drop off the current week's load.

Before we left, he'd give me a nickel to buy a grape soda at Patty's store and a penny for a huge oatmeal cookie. Then it was off to Sunday School at Monumental Methodist Church. Father was the Superintendent of Sunday School in those days so of course attendance was mandatory. At 10:30, we rode back to the house to pick up Mother for Church.

I was persona non grata until I was 5 years old, excommunicated after making a horrendous scene one Sunday that brought the worship service to a complete standstill. Mother said that when the Minister raised his voice and began pounding the pulpit in a very passionate, but decidedly un-Methodist foray into hellfire and damnation territory, I screamed, "I CAN'T STAND IT!" so loudly it echoed in the sanctuary.

After the service, the Minister told Mother, "That's the most unruly child I've ever seen in a Church." She never forgave me.

Sunday afternoons were spent at Grandma and Mernie's house. My sisters and I couldn't pronounce "Myrtle" when we were little. It came out "Mernie," so that's what we always called her. Our Sunday visit, commanded to never be before 2PM or after 3PM, was a rather formal affair. We'd sit elbow to elbow on the steel framed, flowery slipcovered couch in the sitting room while Grandma presided over our visit as though it was some sort of family board meeting, mostly cross examining Mother about the past week's doings. Each of us sat at rapt attention, only speaking when spoken to, including Father, who always sat off to the side in one of the room's platform rockers with hat in hand wisely keeping his own counsel.

Because they lived "over the river," (southside slang for the northside and downtown) I was seldom farmed out to Grandma's and Mernie's. It was June who invariably got stuck looking after me, probably because she was usually available, easily drafted by Mother for brother minding. I was the devoted puppy, always tagging along behind her; whining outside her closed bedroom door, "June, can I come in....pleeeese".

In the evenings after supper, June and I would listen to the radio serials on the small radio in her room. June clipped the radio logs out of the *Richmond News Leader* every week so we could keep track of our programs. Just about every night, one of our favorites crackled through the little speaker: *Gunsmoke* with William Conrad as Matt Dillon, *Johnny Dollar, Gangbusters, Mr. Keen, Tracer of Lost Persons,* Orson Welles' *The Shadow* and *The Inner Sanctum* with the ghoulish host Raymond. We'd laugh until we hurt listening to *Jack Benny* and *Burns and Allen.*

I got my own table top set for Christmas that year. It had an earphone jack on the back allowing me to listen in private after everyone had gone to bed, but it was never as much fun as when I listened with June in her room.

I would sit for hours watching her make puppet heads out of paper-mache' or paint scenery for her puppet shows she put on for all of us in the neighborhood. On my 8th birthday, she invited the neighborhood to a wiener roast and puppet show: *How The Easter Bunny Lost His Tail.* Later, she managed to talk me into donning a leopard skin to play the giant in *Jack and the Beanstalk.* My favorite was *Murder In The Graveyard,* complete with glowing tombstones, lightning and thunder.

In the summers, June and I would venture down to Swift and Company at Briggs and South Main Street. Father let us chill out in the big freezer along with the watermelon he would bring home for us that evening. Cooled to perfection, we'd rummage in the company supply closet, making off with a few writing tablets, pencils and clips. We called it "School Stuff." Between Mother's poetry and lists, Father's drawings for projects in his studio and June and BB's endless sketching, tablets were a staple of life at our house.

June and BB both had part time jobs at Leggett's Department Store and the "5 and 10." They were both cheerleaders in high school and both attended Mrs. Myrick's Dance School in the Virginia Hotel. Every year Mrs. Myrick staged a dance recital at the Emporia Auditorium, the prime venue for everything in Emporia, from band concerts and high school graduations to the Miss Emporia beauty pageant and the yearly Lion's Club Minstrel with its black- faced "End Men."

June auditioned for the lead in the Senior Class Play *Cupid In Pigtails;* but Miss T. I. Johnson, the history teacher who produced and directed the play every year, told her she was too tall and cast someone else, only to come back to June just before opening night. The girl who had gotten the part had also gotten pregnant and was beginning to show. There was no time to learn the lines so June carried the script disguised as a book she was always reading as part of the role. She followed BB to RPI in Richmond (now Virginia Commonwealth University) where she majored in Dramatic Art, then went to New York to pursue her dream of making it on stage.

IX

In the summer of 1951, we went to Nags Head on the North Carolina Outer Banks on vacation. It was the only vacation I remember when I was little. Mother often talked about the happy time at Buckroe Beach in Hampton in 1947, but it's lost in the black hole that is infancy. I have no memory of it.

The Outer Banks seemed to go on forever in those days before it was invaded by runaway development. Father snapped a slightly overexposed photograph of Mother, BB, June and me in our swimsuits sitting on the deserted beach, June striking a pose that carried a hint of flirtatiousness, an indicator, perhaps, of her future in front of the camera. The high key lighting and low contrast gives the picture a hazy fragility as though we were living a dream and were about to wake up.

The following year, Father was diagnosed with tuberculosis. He was forced to take a leave of absence at half pay from Swift and Company where he was Manager of the Emporia branch house. He was sent to the Blue Ridge Sanitarium near Charlottesville where he stayed for just over a year. Uncle Paul and Aunt Mernie drove Mother and either BB, June or me to see him every month.

I was not allowed in the building and could only see him through the window of his room. At first, I didn't recognize him. He had shaved off his moustache and had put on a lot of weight. Mother said the doctors were building him up for major surgery. He began sending me postcards with drawings of himself in pajamas. Most were done with colored pencils. In the drawing, he was always holding up a sign wishing me a Happy Birthday or counting down the days to Christmas. He sent dozens of them over the year he was there.

He underwent surgery to remove the infected lung and most of the ribs from that side. Mother said it was a horribly bloody operation that lasted for nearly 12 hours. She had not expected him to live through it. It foretold a long, slow, steady slide in his health.

All of us had to wear patch tests to see if we were infected. It didn't take long for other kids at school to find out what the patch was and when they did, many kept their distance. The county health department burned our mattresses in the backyard, transforming the lawn between Mother's flower beds into a scene from an Audie Murphy war movie. The lady who had been the health department nurse in those days later moved into the apartment house down the street. She was very nice, but she would forever be a reminder to me of that awful year.

Somehow Mother made do on Father's half-pay. She got the Emporia Building and Loan to allow her to pay just the interest on the home mortgage. Mr. Bloom, who sat on the board and owned Bloom Brother's Department Store where my Aunt Mernie worked, promised Mother he would never allow us to lose our home. Mother called him "her knight in shining armor." So did scores of others. Mr. Bloom was a beloved figure in Emporia. He helped many families through difficult times. When he died, the town lowered flags to half-staff and most businesses closed to allow their employees to attend his funeral.

It fell to my oldest sister BB, short for Barbara Bland, to help with the heavy lifting. The only driver in the family other than Father at the time, she wheeled his prized 1937 Chevrolet sedan with floor mounted stick shift around town like Junior Johnson, once scraping by another car on the single lane, "Old River Bridge" on Hicksford Avenue, tearing the chrome edge off the running boards.

BB, who was just 16 at the time, had to grow up before she was grown up. She drove Mother on all of her weekly rounds, cut all of the grass, weeded the flower beds, and helped Mother with cooking and cleaning the house. She still managed to find time to paint and draw, which was always her passion, and for her boyfriend, an angular faced boy, whose sole talent aside from camping out on our front porch, seemed to be dancing the jitterbug with her at a joint BB called the "Fall and Run."

BB won the Miss Emporia Beauty Pageant in the early 50's. Forty years later the color picture of her in a red gown wearing the "Miss Emporia" sash was still prominently displayed in Mother's living room photograph ensemble of great Barbara-June-John moments. June would soon run the table with stills from Broadway, TV and the movies, but if 80 percent of success is just showing up, there was hope for me. The only picture of me was a snapshot in the hospital after my arrival.

Mother was always yelling for one of us to do something or another. If she wanted me, she would, by force of habit, scream "Barbara" first, then "June" before finally getting down to me. It came out "Barbara-June-Jooohnnnn." Mother's voice ripped the sky like an F-22 making a low pass at Mach 3, reverberating up and down the street like a sonic boom. She did it so often it became a self-characterization. One afternoon when I had gone over to see Mrs. Lucas on her side porch about cutting her lawn, Mother let loose with her blood curdling call just as I opened the screen door. Mrs. Lucas yelled back, "He's over here, Virginia." Then looking at me with a big grin said, "Well come on in Barbara-June-John!" Old habits die hard though. Long after both of my sisters had left home for college and careers, Mother would still call me "Barbara-June-Jooooohn."

After graduation in 1953, BB enrolled at Richmond Professional Institute (now Virginia Commonwealth University) where she majored in fine art. She won a fellowship at the Virginia Museum of Fine Arts and received her degree from RPI in 1957. She married Martin Sant from Pittsburgh her senior year. They had two children but a decade or so later, went through a nasty divorce. BB and the boys, Martin and Paul, returned to Emporia where she taught art in the public schools. Later she went back to school and began teaching on the college level. She eventually moved to North Carolina where she painted full-time for the rest of her life.

X

When Father came home from the sanitarium, he was in deep depression, lying on the glider on the side porch day after day, week after week, never speaking, as though he were in some kind of hypnotic trance. Finally, his pal Clyde Euell, who worked for Swift in Richmond, drove down to talk some sense into him. We all loved Clyde. Relentlessly jolly, he brought us gifts when he came to Emporia. He adored Mother, always remembering to bring her flowers.

Clyde went out on the side porch and closed the door. There were loud voices. Angry words. I don't know what Clyde told my father that day, but he snapped out of his depression and eventually went back to work.

For years, he had to take massive doses of streptomycin, a powerful antibiotic. He had an injection every day. Mrs. Weaver, who had been a nurse, came over to administer the drug. He also took it in pill form, a handful twice a day. Within a year, he suffered a massive hemorrhage at home. There was little doubt the powerful drug had eaten his stomach lining away.

It had happened just before I got home from school. I had spotted Mrs. Weaver out of the corner of my eye as

I approached our front door. She was running across the side yard toward our house yelling and waving her arms, trying to stop me from going inside. She was too late.

I stepped into a pond of dark red blood oozing into the carpet in the foyer. Bloody footprints were smeared on the stairs and hardwood floor down the hall and over into the dining room. It looked like the scene of a massacre. Just as I yelled for Mother, Mrs. Weaver put her hands over my eyes and hustled me over to her house until Mother got home that night.

Father had been rushed to St. Luke's Hospital in Richmond in a hearse from Echols Funeral Home. There were no ambulances in Emporia and no hospital in those days. He underwent emergency surgery that removed two thirds of his stomach. He had lost a massive amount of blood but he had survived. Painfully frail and thin when he came home, he eventually went back to work

XI

Never one to sit in front of the TV, Father seldom watched at all until June started showing up on the networks. His evenings and weekends were spent in his studio and workshop. He had taught himself to paint and draw in the 20's, but the Great Depression and family responsibilities had nixed any thought of accepting an invitation from the Disney Studios to come to California and study animation.

He had begun repairing antique furniture during the Depression as a way to make extra money. Our basement was like a furniture hospital waiting room with injured chairs and other pieces awaiting his attention. He designed and built all manner of projects, including an elaborate portable puppet show stage for June, and later, a merry go round in the backyard.

Mother had her own "below the waterline talents." She dreamed of being the first in her family to go to college. She wanted to be a Librarian, but her father's death when she was sixteen scuttled any thought of higher education. She went to work at Bloom Brothers and, a while later, Joe Turner recruited her to sell tickets at the Pitts Theatre.

She became a voracious reader and wrote poetry throughout her life; some of it was published. She also had an eye for design and decorating and sold many of her ideas to American Home and other national magazines.

She and Father were a good team. Her designs of a table centerpiece carousel and a table top Christmas tree made of pine cones were both brought to reality by Father in his studio. Miller & Rhoads, the huge department store in Richmond, purchased the prototypes and sold replicas in their store.

Christmas was Mother's favorite holiday, her biggest production. She started making her lists right after the previous Christmas, stocking up on wrapping paper and ribbon at the post-holiday sales. By April of every year, she had already begun to salt away gifts in the upstairs hall closet. God have mercy on your soul if you were caught sniffing around.

The Christmas traditions that developed at our house were mostly dictated by Mother, beginning with the Christmas tree. It was always a cut cedar. Never Spruce!

Mother insisted. When my Aunt Louise put a shiny aluminum tree in her home, Mother was appalled. It was as though the sacred covenant with "Father Christmas" had been forever broken.

The opening of gifts on Christmas morning was staged like a Broadway Show. Despite our groans, the script never changed. Presents were distributed one at a time with each of us opening one gift when it was your turn. Just one! It was Mother's way of stretching out her favorite day.

When we were little, she would move heaven and earth to find what we had on our Santa Claus lists. Her all day search in downtown Richmond for a blond "Sparkle Plenty doll" for June was a family legend. ("Sparkle Plenty" was a character in the Dick Tracy comic strip.)

When we were older, the gifts became more personal; usually something special that was an antique or something handmade or a painting. Mother had a special knack for coming up with something she knew you wanted but had never mentioned. Father, of course, almost always gave us something he had restored, carved or painted. So did June who had Father's talent for carving and painting.

We all coveted BB's art work. I wasn't above lobbying her for what I wanted. In the 70's, my begging went beyond the pale. I shamelessly pressed her for an enormous Nags Head Seascape abstract she had placed in a large gallery on the Outer Banks at a price well beyond my meager means. I even stooped to getting Mother to intercede on my behalf. BB was furious at me, but she gave me the painting. From then on, I always paid full price for her work though she often would grant me the brother discount.

When I was in Washington, my assignment every Christmas was to pick up June who flew in to Dulles Airport from Los Angeles. Our nighttime trips down I-95 to Emporia were always a highlight of the holidays for me. It was the only time we got to talk face to face in private. Once June opened the front door at home and yelled "Yoo Hoo," Mother went into her one on one full court press.

The house glowed at Christmas time with spotlights on the front door announcing Father's latest creation. In the early years, he and Mother put together some incredibly elaborate productions involving the entire front of the house.

Subsequent efforts were limited to the front porch. He began painting a Christmas scene in oils every year on a large, door sized canvas and entered it in the annual Christmas door decorating contest. We would watch through the front windows with eager anticipation for the judge's car to stop in front of the house and listen for the tell-tale rap of a ribbon being tacked on the door. It was almost always blue.

Christmas took on added significance after my sisters left home for college and career. It was the only time we were all together, and Mother would work herself into a frazzled frenzy trying to make it perfect.

I don't know why we didn't drop dead of artery strangulation from all the fat we consumed in those days. Father brought home big tins of Swift's "Jewel" Lard every week. The sight of the white globs melting in iron skillets was as familiar as a sunset. Mother always choreographed her fried entrees to include healthy sides like her prized Harvard Beets, which I refused to eat because they looked like sliced blood clots. "Vampire food," I protested. She was not amused.

My other "hate food" was boiled okra. Father loved it. I thought it looked like slimy green eels. Sweet Potatoes were also on my despise list. I would probably have eaten them if she had thought to fry them. It seems odd she never did. Regular potatoes were cool. They were June's major food group. Uncle Paul brought bushels of them to the house from his garden every summer. I don't ever remember a meal that June didn't have a potato, but it was BB who always got drafted for potato salad prep on Sundays while Mother fried the chicken.

I loved Mother's "Simlins," sliced up summer squash and onions fried in bacon grease. Mother would often fry some up to go with her fried pork chops. God made pork chops to be fried!

Aunt Mernie was the Queen of Collards in our family. Her secret was to cook only late season collards. "Cold collards," she called them, seasoned with a ham hock in the pot. She would often bring giant bowls of steaming collards to the house hot off the stove, served with a splash of vinegar. I wouldn't touch them with a ten foot fork, but I was a big fan of her butterbean pastry. It was my Great Grandmother's recipe. Grandma said it was often all people had to eat in the years after the "recent unpleasantness," which was what she called the civil war.

Mother had several signature dishes I will always associate with her, but none more so than her homemade sausage biscuits. Not the fast food knockoffs of today,

Mother rolled fresh maple flavored sausage into the handmade dough, which was then sliced, baked and served with a choice of mustards.

Once a year Father, would fire up the small, green tile wood stove in the basement and cook up a mess of chitterlings and turnips for the gang at Swift. Mother never allowed chitterlings to be cooked upstairs in the kitchen because of the smell, which even Dickie Thompson couldn't handle. He moved out into June's playhouse until the "all clear" in the basement.

XII

I first met Aileen, Mother's younger sister, one Christmas when she had been allowed to spend the holiday at Grandmother's house. She had been institutionalized when she was a teenager. Mother said Aileen had come home from school one day very upset, locked herself in her room and refused to come out. Nothing more was ever said about it, but I always thought Mother had Aileen in the back of her mind when she would caution us about getting too angry. "It can go too far," she said, "and ruin your life."

Aileen called Mother "Sissy." I was struck by how much they favored; but Aileen had a distant look in her eyes as though she was seeing beyond us. She became violent during a subsequent holiday visit and never came home again.

Mother, Mernie and Paul visited Aileen at Eastern State Hospital in Williamsburg regularly for decades. The visits took a toll on Mother who was always visibly shaken when she came home. Years later, when the hospital was closed, Aileen was relocated to a facility in the Richmond area and I took over for Mother as guardian of record. My wife and I visited regularly. It was always a sobering reality check and a quick cure for those times when I thought life had dealt me a lousy hand.

We had busloads of relatives. Most were on Mother's side of the family. My maternal Grandmother had five sisters and four brothers. Mernie, of course, was our favorite. She was a regular at the house. Pearl, who lived in Rocky Mount, came up every year to regale us with her latest ailments.

Mamie Lou and Mattie Lee were my twin Great Aunts. Or, was it Mamie Lee and Mattie Lou? They were identical with bright, mischievous eyes and, even in old age, dressed alike. Mother said that growing up they would switch off on dates. They were like scripted, twin female TV news readers, each contributing part of a sentence at a time when telling a story. Enormously fun to be with, both lived in Burlington, NC but made the trip to Emporia quite often.

We seldom saw Florence, except when we went to Littleton, in North Carolina. Thin as a string, she pulled her hair back into a tight bun and wore dark, print dresses that draped on her boney figure like a shroud, giving her a look that was straight out of American Gothic

We always perked up when Spurgeon came by to visit. One of Grandma's four brothers, Spurgeon, his middle name, was a sometimes inventor who was said to have barely lost out in getting a patent on some kind of high efficiency propeller for fighter planes. Raspy voiced, no doubt from the cigars he constantly smoked, we thought of Spurgeon as an adventurer, like "Smiling Jack" in the Sunday Comics.

Father's sister Katherine and her husband, Gene Vincent, the always jolly salesman with the throaty voice, usually came by at Christmas time when June was home. Mother said June was living Katherine's dream of being an actress. Their youngest daughter Beverly was a frequent guest when her parents went out of town. "Aunt Virginia was always my favorite," she said.

Father was never close to his brothers, Vance and Norman, so visits from them and their families, even at Christmas, were fleeting at best. Some sin from the past I gathered, but no one ever talked about it. Like so many things about Father's family, it was locked away in the closet of unmentionables.

Vance's wife Louise, on the other hand, was a regular at the house. She and Mother were tight, talking on the phone for an hour or more every night after Mother returned from "The Chatter Society."

Louise, who taught third grade in elementary school, came by often in the summers to cut some of Mother's flowers when it was her turn to put an arrangement in church. One day I noticed her out by Mother's middle flower bed cutting daisies and cosmos, carefully laying each stem on a newspaper broadsheet. Each time she would cut a flower and put it on the newspaper, "Jim," a very large pet crow belonging to Bobby Jean, who lived around the corner on Jefferson Street, would swoop down from his perch in the pines, steal the flower and fly back to the clothesline where he dropped the flower with the others in a nice neat pile.

When Louise went to collect the flowers and found none, she dropped her clippers and ran to the house screaming, "Virginia, I have lost my mind!" Mother, wise to the ways of "Jim" the crow, walked a thoroughly shaken Louise back to the clothesline where, there on the ground, were the flowers she had cut.

XIII

When I was little, Mother often dragged me along when she and Louise made their weekly rounds "over the river." It wasn't so much about shopping, though there was shopping to be done. "Keeping up appearances" was the phrase Mother used; a little face to face diplomacy with Emporia's retail elders.

First stop was usually R.E. Callahan and Sons Department Store where Reggie Pruitt held sway. Reggie was among the permanent fixtures at Callahan's, usually anchoring the men's counter, which was always a caution with its racks and racks of brightly colored Rep Ties.

Reggie's buying trips to New York with his pal, Charles Baker Harding - our cousin - provided "CB," as we called him, with endless stories about mingling among the expensive people in Manhattan. One tale had it that after paying a "King's Ransom" for a potato and a pork chop at a five star restaurant in New York, CB told the hat check girl to just keep his Callahan's fedora because the expected tip was more than he paid Reggie for it new.

Mother made it a point to speak to Mr. Dunn, the tall and elegant, always dark-suited "Shoe Czar" at Callahans. Formal and deferential, Mr. Dunn (I never knew his first name) was the quintessential shoe salesman, back in the day when your feet were actually measured for proper fit.

The State ABC Store on Halifax Street never got a visit from Mother, just a sort of walk-by wave to Mr. Griffin behind the counter. He and his family were members at Monumental. The closest Mother ever came to liquor was that "mistaken" sip of Mr. Lucas's bourbon spiked eggnog on New Year's.

And so it went store by store all the way up Halifax Street as Mother said her weekly "hellos" to Mr. Rice at Leggetts, Mr. Leath at his drug store, all the Mitchell's at Mitchell Brothers and so on, regardless of whether she needed anything from a particular store. The point was, sooner or later she would.

The last stop was always Bloom Brother's which was synonymous with Emporia. Everyone in town seemed to have worked there at one time or another, including Mother. Mr. Bloom was usually "floating" on the floor greeting customers along with his son Eugene, who would follow in his father's footsteps. There was always a chat with the ladies in "The Rose Room" and of course, with Mr. Novey in the Men's Department.

"Over the river " notwithstanding, Mother's heaven on earth was Miller & Rhoads, and its competitor Thalhimers, the big department stores in Richmond. She made untold pilgrimages over the years. Dressed to "A" list specs and armed with her charge plates, the forerunner to credit cards, she would wear Father and I completely out checking out every item on every floor of both stores as though she was taking inventory.

Lunch was always in the very formal Tea Room at Miller & Rhoads where ladies were treated like Queens, seated in throne-like, upholstered chairs at tables dressed with starched tablecloths, linen napkins and fresh flowers. Pampered to the max and re-energized, Mother would head for Berry Burk and the May Company and, if time permitted, a quick blitz through the G.C. Murphy Company, the mother of all dime stores.

The day long jaunts prompted Father to muse, "Old ladies never die, they just go to Miller & Rhoads and Thalhimers." When he could not take her (Mother never learned to drive), she would hop on the bus to Richmond. Never cowed by strangers, she would quickly know everyone on board on a first name basis, including the driver, before the bus got out of town.

XIV

I was usually packed off to Grandma's and Mernie's when Mother and Father went out of town. My upstairs room at the front of the old stucco house had a view through the leafy maples to Virginia Avenue below. The sensation of being in the trees was enhanced by a forest of huge Boston Ferns in front of the windows. They thrived in the always cool and very quiet room that was bathed in soft, filtered light during the day. Sleeping often required a light quilt, even in the summers and when it rained on the tin roof, it was like a lullaby, softly serenading me into a thick sleep.

Their backyard was like a small farm. Grandma raised chickens, there was a huge garden and Paul had a smokehouse where he cured hams. Mernie's huge hydrangeas s lit up the landscape and there was always a cat or two on patrol. The Emporia Bus Station which was on the street behind the garden was like another universe.

Before TV and Air Conditioning killed conversing with neighbors, spring and summer evenings after supper were usually spent on Grandma's front porch. Heavy oak rockers painted hunter green and fitted with bright, multicolored canvas seat covers and backs shared the space with more of Mernie's ferns. She and Grandma would while away the early evening nursing their sweet tea, chatting with a steady stream of passersby out for an after dinner stroll.

A nightly visitor was Trixie Rose, a petite lady with pure white hair who lived in a small brick house across the street. Of course, Trixie ran a beauty parlor; it's what women named Trixie do. When the passerby traffic was slack, Trixie, who had a reserved rocker on the porch, was an unending source of Northside scandal.

Words and phrases I wouldn't hear anywhere else entered my limited vocabulary: "Nome" for "No Ma'am," "Turn" for personality, as in, "She ain't got a lick of "turn," "Close," which described the thick summer humidity, and my favorite, "Caution," to describe a showy dresser or a very bright color, as in, "She's a real caution in that yellow dress."

After dark, Grandma would sometimes walk me up to the Atlantic Coast Line Passenger station on Halifax Street to watch the crack streamliner *The Champion* roar through town at 100 miles an hour, streaking through the night to Miami from New York. My grandfather had been an inspector for the Coast Line and the engineers all knew "Miss Lucy," saluting her on the platform with three short toots on the big diesel's horn.

The day after my 11th birthday, Father took me to see Mr. Woodruff, the agent for Richmond Newspapers in Emporia. I was quickly signed up as a carrier for *The Richmond News Leader*. I had to earn my spending money. There would be no more "tips," (the word "allowance" was verboten) for cutting the grass, sweeping out the basement or feeding Dickie Thompson.

The *News Leader* was an afternoon daily except Sundays. I had eighty or so customers on my route, which was south of the river. It took an hour or so to deliver them after school, longer if the weather was bad. When it was beyond awful, Mother would shame Father into taking me around in the car.

Saturday was collection day. My customers had unique places they would hide their change so it would be readily available when I came collecting. Most left it in their mail box but Mrs. Palmer on Jefferson street always buried her change in a huge geranium plant on her porch. I'd have to dig to China to find it, penny by penny.

I usually started at the Lassiter's big, white brick house on Jefferson Street just around the corner from us. Mrs. Lassiter (her first name was "Charlie") was my biggest tipper. Dressed to the nines in bright colors and decorated with dangling earrings and glittery bracelets on both arms, Mrs. Lassiter was a "caution" when she came to the door, always with the exact change plus a dollar. At Christmas time, she upped it to a five dollar bill. "For exceptional service," she said.

Depending on how collecting went, I usually made around ten bucks a week. It funded my constant search for a Jackie Robinson baseball card to finish out my Brooklyn Dodgers collection, (I never found it) and a Rawlings "Stan The Man Musial" infielders glove I bought on time from Mr. Tillar at the hardware store, paying 50 cents a week for an eternity.

I had become a rabid Dodger fan at Grandma's and Mernie's listening with Paul to Red Barber and his sidekick Vin Scully call the games on WOR in New York. The Dodgers had a propensity for losing the World Series to the dreaded Yankees in the early 50's, but in 1955 they finally beat their cross-borough rivals. Even Buddy Ferguson, the die-hard Yankee fan at the Greensville barber shop on South Main Street, had to tip his cap. The team moved to Los Angeles in 1958 but I lost interest. By then my scout troop had toured the local radio station and my whole world had changed.

Part II

Radio, Rock n' Roll & The Girl Across The Street

I

The small white cinderblock building on Washington Street was almost overwhelmed by the bright red, three dimensional call letters that spelled out "WEVA" on the flat roof. The front door opened into a small lobby graced with gun metal chairs and a Sun Drop vending machine, but the place was rockin'. A wall mounted loudspeaker the size of a kettle drum was booming Bo Diddley's 12 bar blues song "I'm A Road Runner" so loudly the plaques on the wall were dancing.

With one of the long tremolo licks in "Road Runner" chasing us, we were led down a narrow hallway lined with floor to ceiling racks holding thousands of 45 RPM records in green sleeves. The red "on air" light went out above the door and we crowded into the small control room.

Will Stone, a young man with a flat top haircut, who wore black framed glasses, wheeled around from the big control console. "Hi, welcome to WEVA," he smiled! We moved around behind him, standing in front of a wall filled with audio equipment, the red, green, and white indicator lights blinking and meters dancing, all in time with the music.

"Road Runner" began to fade, and, just as it did, there was a click and a very quick, up-tempo WEVA Jingle jumped on the air, instantly followed by the opening screams of Jimmy Forrest's classic "Night Train" with its distinctive stop-time rhythm. A rush of adrenalin spiked. It was my conversion, my "Road to Damascus" moment.

For hours on end every night, I'd lock myself in my room and pretend to be on the air like the DJ's on the big AM powerhouse rock stations in the northeast that boomed in after dark like a local. Father, no doubt concerned that I was embarking on another trip to fantasyland, brought it up with Mother one night in the kitchen while she cleaned up after supper. "He's just dreaming of being on the radio, Bland," she said. "It's what he wants to do."

"I know that Virginia," he said. "We got him a dog to replace his pirate friend, but we can't buy him a radio station."

He didn't have to.

Using money from my *Richmond News Leader* paper route, I ordered a wireless broadcaster kit and a cheap crystal microphone from a Chicago mail order electronics store. I had seen their ad in a magazine at the drug store. I was waiting on the front stoop when Smitty brought it to the door.

The box was filled with all kinds of things I had never seen before. I had no idea what they did and I was absolutely clueless as to how to decipher the schematic diagram, let alone how to put the thing together. But my uncle did. Vance was Father's older brother and he was a radio junkie, a sort of leading edge Geek. His house was filled with cool audio stuff: tape decks, citizen's band transmitters, short wave and police radios and turntables.

I hopped on my bike and took the kit over to Vance's garage workshop one Saturday afternoon after taking papers. A big grin slowly crawled across his face. "Well, well, what do we have here, John!"

He fired up his soldering iron and with running commentary on circuits, antennas, frequencies, and stuff, painstakingly went about applying heat sinks, installing color coded diodes, resistors and sockets until the tubes glowed. Radio Ingleside was on the air.

I wasn't the first kid to discover that radio gave them a voice. The attraction for me was its anonymity. My skinny frame, bird-like chest, cowlick, goofy snaggletooth smile, along with the rest of my truck load of stored fears and insecurities remained safely hidden while giving my personality a get out of jail free card.

Using June's old record player, slightly modified, and a stack of 45's, I was on the air just like the big guys. Linda Harrell Bachman remembers coming across the street to watch and announce tunes. "You'd put an LP record on the record player," she recalls, "then hop on your bicycle with a transistor radio and ride to see how far you could pick up the station." It wasn't far, but my pal Randy Grigg, who was sharing the announcing chores, helped me tweak the antenna I had strung in the pines behind the house and soon the kids at the high school football games were picking us up on their car radios. It never occurred to me that I was operating an illegal, pirate radio station.

Father made me a cabinet to house the wireless broadcaster and my prized VU (Volume Units) meter I had ordered from Radio Shack. I didn't know exactly what it measured but I thought it was cool, jumping in time with the music. Everything fit snugly in a corner of my room, but I soon moved it to a small walled off corner of the basement. I could turn the volume way up without Mother yelling at me and it was more private, away from her prying eyes.

I began hanging around WEVA rifling through the trash pulling out outdated beer and soft drink jingles that were on LP records and running them on my station. They sounded so cool, especially the beer jingles. I tapped my paper route money to buy new 45's from Mr. Slate at the Music Shop.

Then one day, the phone rang.

II

Icy chills streaked down my spine when I heard the familiar voice on the other end.

"Hello John, this is Will Stone at WEVA!"

"Yes sir."

"John, I just heard you on the radio."

"Yes sir."

"John, you know you can get into some very serious trouble broadcasting without a license."

"Yes sir." Mother had come out into the hall from the kitchen. I could feel her laser-like stare burning the back of my neck.

I quickly volunteered to shut down my Wireless Broadcaster.

"Good idea," said Will, who then popped the question that would change my young life and set the stage for everything that came afterwards.

"John, I'm looking for a student to train to work weekend afternoons here at WEVA. Why don't you come up to the station after school one day this week and we'll talk about it?"

I don't think I have ever been as excited in my life, not ever, as I was at that moment! Being on the radio was something I wanted to do so badly it seemed implausible, so far-fetched as to be impractical. Now in an instant, it was within my reach.

As soon as I hung up the phone, Mother was on my case. "Who was that?" she demanded.

"It was Mr. Stone at WEVA," I said, so excited I could not stand still.

"What kind of trouble are you in John Tisdale?" Mother always used my first and middle names when I was on thin ice with her.

The scowl on her face quickly became a big grin. In a nanosecond, I had gone from the outhouse to the penthouse. I never told her, and certainly not my father, that I had been running an illegal radio station. Will never spilled the beans either.

I rode my bike up to WEVA every day after school when I finished delivering my papers to practice reading copy. Randy went along too at the beginning. We recorded everything on a portable tape machine. Will and Eddie Anderson, the morning personality at WEVA, would listen to the tape and critique our performances. I was obsessed with getting on the air, but Randy was drawn to the technical side of radio and went on to obtain his First Class FCC License.

After months of practicing and critiques, Will told me he would put me on the payroll and start me on the air as soon as my "Restricted Radio Telephone Operators Permit," a small wallet sized card, arrived from the Federal Communications Commission in Washington. When it showed up in our mailbox, I took it up to Will who included it in a big frame on the wall in the control room with all of the other "tickets" for everyone on the air at WEVA. I was in.

Mother was ecstatic that I had gotten the job but Father was, as usual, skeptical, inquiring at the supper table, "Is this just for fun John?" He could not accept the fact that radio was real work. I had to get Mother to intervene before he allowed me to quit my paper route.

III

My first actual on the air tryout came on a Sunday morning running the big control board console for black gospel groups from 6:30 AM to 9 AM. Most of the programs were a quarter hour in length. Some ran for thirty minutes. Will was there to collect their payment for the time prior to going on the air. After he counted the cash, no checks, the groups would move their guitars and amps into the station's only studio, a rather large room which contained a sofa, chairs, a table, an upright piano, a very large clock on the wall over the window to the Control Room, a loudspeaker and, of course, microphones.

The Starlight Gospel Singers, The New Jerusalem and Rising Sun Holiness Church Choir, The Gospel Tones, Reverend T.J. Thomas and other groups would all take their turns. Most of the programs featured requests for specific hymns and dedications which had been mailed in.

The cast of characters included a very large black woman. I cannot remember her name, but I clearly recall her waddling into the studio wearing a flowery dress and a huge hat. She would carefully balance her bulk on the tiny piano stool and begin pounding the keyboard with a ferocity that would have made Oscar Peterson smile.

My favorite was the Reverend T.J. Thomas. A towering black man with a velvet voice and an infectious personality, T.J. worked for Belmonte Motors, a used car lot on North Main Street in Emporia. I presumed Danny Belmonte paid for the time because T.J. would weave a Belmonte commercial into the body of his sermons with, shall we say, impressive Biblical creativity, "For God so loved the world, he gave his only begotten son a used Buick from Belmonte Motors." Amen!

Everything became very official when Barbara Little, who was the traffic director along with other duties, showed me the weekend program logs she had just finished preparing. There, in all capital letters was *The John Harding Show,* one o'clock until signoff, every Saturday and Sunday. There's nothing like seeing it in print to make it real. I had to play the current hits on the weekly *Billboard Hot 100* music chart, but I was free to choose old hits from the station's massive record library. The first few weekends, Will came in and worked in his office right across the hall from the control room while I was on the air.

After about a month of weekend babysitting, he cut me loose, coming by only once each Saturday and Sunday afternoon to check on things and see how I was doing. Soon, I was totally on my own. I don't ever remember him having a cross word with me. His mother was a different story. Elizabeth Stone could not countenance James Brown. When "Please, Please, Please" would hit the air, she was on the phone in a flash demanding to know what that awful noise was on her radio station! Will told me to humor her.I did but always with respect. She would later become one of Mother's good friends.

I was alone in the radio station, but I was never lonely and never ill at ease. I only remember being frightened once. A summer thunderstorm spawned a lightning strike on the tower, which conducted the surge into the building triggering the dummy load, a huge wall of very high wattage light bulbs normally used to test the transmitter at night after the station was off the air. When it happened, the entire building erupted in an eerie, blinding, Biblical glow. In a flash, it was over.

There really wasn't time to be nervous. Aside from cueing the next record to play, I had to keep the program and transmitter logs up to date, which included going outside to the tuning shack near the tower once an hour to take antenna current readings. There were commercials to pull, run and log. And every ten minutes or so, I had to run down to the tiny wire room to see what was coming in on the printer, clear the copy and peg it according to subject.

Records in those days ran maybe two to two and a half minutes tops so there wasn't a lot of time during tunes. I remember a Hayley Mills record "Let's Get Together," which ran all of a minute and 10 seconds or so, not even enough time to grab a cold delicious from the Lobby.

Not to be indelicate, but long tunes were a godsend when one had to use the bathroom. I think the first single to break the four minute "barrier" was Dave Brubeck's "Take Five" with its 2 cord piano vamp in unusual quintuple 5/4 time. It became a huge hit in 1961. A few years later, Columbia Records released Bob Dylan's "Like a Rolling Stone" as a six minute single. They were the gifts that kept on giving.

IV

After dinner on school nights, I would retreat to my room and, after homework, or often in lieu of it, switch on my radio to take note of how the big time DJ's did their shows, checking out their banter, technique, and slogans. Pretty quickly, I picked up the vocabulary of top 40 radio. It was an exciting time. I literally could not wait for weekends.

I grabbed a few mentions in the papers. *The Richmond Times Dispatch* ran a lengthy feature article with a picture but they misspelled my name, tagging me as "John Haring." Bummer! *Billboard Magazine* gave me a mention in their radio column, and they spelled my name right.

An upstart local paper *The Greensville Mirror* ran a multi-page spread about WEVA along with pictures, no doubt a trade for on-air commercials. Inside was a large ad with my picture promoting my weekend shows! Looking at it today is painful. I looked like the sickly, skinny kid getting sand kicked in his face in the old

Charles Atlas magazine ads. Will joked I had a face made for radio.

I was the only part-timer. There were six full-time staff members, Will Stone had succeeded his late father as President of Stone Broadcasting, which owned the station, when he was only 22 years old. He was also the General Manager, and went on the air to sub when someone was ill or on vacation. Barbara Little was the Traffic Director in addition to Office Manager and Receptionist. In other words, Barbara was indispensable. I had enormous respect for her. She was also a hell of a poker player. "Deal the pasteboards" was a familiar refrain in her office when things were slow.

The Chief Engineer was Elton Short. A friendly, easy going man who had a flat top haircut. He and his family were members at our church Monumental Methodist. My Uncle Vance worked in his radio TV repair shop on Baker Street.

Don Collins was the Sales Manager. A classy guy and a natty dresser, who always had the perfect tan, Don was a fashion plate, but he was one of those people who never met a stranger. A born salesman with a booming voice, the slogan he used for L.W. Mitchell's grocery store still rings in my head: "Make your food budget a winner at L.W.'s Food Center."

There were three full-time air personalities. Eddie Anderson was a fixture in the morning. Enormously popular, Eddie had a huge following in Southside Virginia. Other than local politicians, he was probably the town's only widely known celebrity.

Dick Phillips was the Program and Music Director. A very deliberate and meticulous guy, Dick did a show in the late morning and another in the early afternoon. When Eddie left the station to head for Richmond, Dick took over mornings.

Every week, I looked forward to sitting with Dick when he auditioned the new record releases that arrived in the mail from Schwartz Brothers, the big record distributor in Washington. One day he plopped a 45 on the turntable by an unknown group on the Swan label. As soon as the speaker blared out the first few bars, we looked at each other. Kids today would say "No Brainer." The tune was "She Loves You" by a group called the Beatles. It quickly shot to the top of the music charts.

Afternoon Drive, such as it was (WEVA went off the air at sunset) was Skip Lyndon's slot. A very soft spoken and laid back guy, Skip's style reminded me a bit of the legendary William B. Williams on WNEW in New York. I always thought he would have been more at home spinning Sinatra and Ella than Chubby Checker and the Beatles, but he had a loyal and devoted following in the afternoon.

V

Without WEVA, I'm not sure what would have happened to me. I was a skinny kid with a towering inferiority complex; school had always been traumatic. I had never excelled at much of anything, certainly not grades. In elementary school, I had trouble reading. Mother enlisted a tutor, Mrs. Bagwell, an elderly woman who wore little pillbox hats with flowers growing out of them, who, if nothing else, made it her mission to shame me into comprehending what I was "reading." Her story of the kid who got paint all over his trousers because he couldn't read the wet paint sign on the park bench must have made an impression.

In today's world, I would probably be on drugs for ADHD. I had the attention span of a goldfish. I remembered every detail of my teachers' mannerisms and peculiar traits but little of what they taught.

I was always being compared to my sisters, who were both brains and made straight "A's." A few of my teachers had taught both June and BB and would often remark about how smart and sweet they were and, "What on earth happened with you?" The implicit implication being, I had the IQ of a bed spring. My elementary school music teacher, a latter-day Margaret Thatcher look-alike with flaming red hair and a screeching, high pitched voice, told me in class one day I had no sense of pitch and should never try to sing. I never did. My self-esteem was always circling the drain.

Away from school, I was the typical Emporia kid. We checked out the comics and snuck looks at the Playboy Centerfold at Jones Drug Store, messed with firecrackers, guzzled "cold deliciouses" (R.C's and Pepsi Colas) shot BB guns, choked on cigarettes, stole pumpkins at Halloween, walked the trestle, climbed the town water tower, and joined the scouts: Troop 7 at our church, where the main activity was selling Chicken Muddle (a very thick and gloppy chicken stew) by the quart, the go-to fundraising foodstuff in Emporia.

Three of us, David Martin, Butch Little and I, had a go at scout camp one summer, heading for Camp Waters on the James River across from Jamestown. Given our proclivity for nicknames, Butch was automatically destined to be tagged as "Big" Little. "Big" managed to sneak out of our camp one night after taps and walked the beach to Scotland Warf, a tiny community several miles away, to buy a candy bar. He was caught trying to sneak back in but, of course, had eaten the evidence.

I think I made the rank of First Class before I quit; radio, rock and roll and the girl across the street become higher priorities. My Aunt Louise was quite miffed about my not making Eagle Scout as cousin Bobby had, but it was never a big deal for Mother. She was more concerned about my grades in school.

Every year, I sweated out the final report card to see if I was being "retained in" for the next term. I was always skirting disaster. High school only amplified my insecurities.

There was no middle school in those days. Eighth graders were lumped in with much older kids in high school, easy prey for upper class tough guys who ran a protection racket. Twenty five cents a day or suffer the consequences in the boy's restroom. I was slapped out of lunch money several times before the wanna-be wise guys were busted by the powers that be.

I spent school days lurking in the background of the ebb and flow, sitting in the rear of my classes hoping to avoid attention. Somehow I managed to sliver by. I dreaded every day and prayed every night for the school to burn down.

Things went south at breakneck speed when I slithered into the 10th grade. I was a miserable failure in Betty Wiley's Algebra class. I could not grasp the abstraction of it. I also failed English and Biology. The only course I passed was Mechanical Drawing, and I got a "D" in that.

The long and the short of it was I had to repeat the 10th grade. It was the single most humiliating episode of my young life. Everybody knew I had flunked. A permanent thought balloon with "FAILURE" in big block letters hung over me like a black cloud. I was the older kid who couldn't learn. I hated myself.

Mother quickly imposed house arrest: no more going to the radio station after school or anywhere else, including Jones Drug Store, a four star hangout for the after school crowd in Emporia. A TV blackout was imposed. None, not even *My Three Sons* after homework. I was placed on suicide watch. Mother would explode into my room unannounced, like some Gestapo agent, demanding "PAPERS," checking my work and grilling me on any reading assignments I had.

My grades began to snail upwards. Even a blind squirrel finds a nut now and then, but the voyage from "F's" to "D's" and "C's" was glacial. I was petrified of failure. My biggest fear was that my parents would force me to give up my job at WEVA. They never made the threat, but I knew it was lurking in the background. It was a powerful motivator.

I clawed my way into "D" territory and, later, "C's" and a B in English, I had finally mastered the art of diagramming sentences, but the "suicide watch" continued. My father, the enforcer, joined the evening shift. Even cutting the radio on after dinner was a felony. Somehow I managed to make it the rest of the way, graduating a year late in 1964.

Mother would later remark that repeating the tenth grade had been a blessing in disguise for me. Perhaps, but it was very well disguised at the time.

VI

As I settled in at the radio station and gained some self-confidence, I began to emerge from the wallpaper. Girls became more than participants in neighborhood kick the can games. One afternoon at the dawn of the 60's, one of Dee Warren's girlfriends ran across the street to tell me, "Dee Warren likes you!"

Dee Warren and her younger sister Linda had come to live in the Harrell house across the street when Lyman Harrell married their mother Duane. By any standard, Dee Warren had won the genetics sweepstakes - she had staggering looks, but she didn't act like it, which made her all the more appealing. Not surprisingly, she quickly had a boyfriend, a pouty faced boy who walked her home from school every day. When the news arrived that their romance had run on the rocks, it was beyond fabulous.

Our juvenile infatuation consisted of sitting on her breezeway looking moon eyed at one another and holding hands in the Pitts, the movie theatre on South Main Street. She "broke up" with me after returning from the beach that summer, but she remained entangled in my thoughts like a permanent mental sticky note.

We dated other people through most of high school. Dee Warren says she had "attention deficit" with boys in those days which, she added, is probably how it should be at that age. Her class was filled with cute girls and I went out with a lot of them and had great times; but I was always captivated by Dee Warren.

I ginned up enough courage to ask her to go to the Junior Senior Prom with me. Convinced I was pushing my luck and the cosmos would intervene, I was blindsided when she said "Yes" and floated home on Cloud 9. But when prom time rolled around, she was going steady with someone so I figured our date was off. When word got back to her that I wasn't going, she marched across the street.

"What's this about you not going to the Prom?"

When I told her that since she was involved with someone else, she should go with him, she gave me a shove.

"I'm going with YOU JOHN. WE ARE GOING!"

Her mother made her dress and snapped our picture before we left. For once, the planets had finally lined up correctly.

We hung out a lot my senior year in high school. "Come ride with me to take Levolia home," she would call, or, "Can you come over, I need to ask you something." I always did, never wanting to miss an opportunity to be in her company even if it meant going one on one with a bat.

Dee Warren and her sisters had ventured over to my backyard in the wee small hours one summer night and began tossing pebbles against my bedroom window to awaken me. Dumb with sleep, that fuzzy moment between dream and reality, it took me a few seconds to come around.

I staggered out of bed and raised the window that looked out on our backyard and saw them all wrapped up in bathrobes with huge curlers in their hair. Their silhouettes in the misty moonlight gave them the look of space aliens. My services were needed to remove a bat which had invaded Martha's bedroom.

Without the slightest clue as to how to catch a bat, I pulled on some clothes and followed them across the street. There were still no lengths to which I would not go to impress Dee Warren.

The bat was clinging to the ceiling over Martha's bed. The TV was on. Barry Goldwater was delivering his speech accepting the Republican Presidential Nomination to the GOP National Convention at the Cow Palace in San Francisco. I always wondered if the bat had somehow jinxed his campaign. I fetched a bag and a broom from the Harrell's kitchen, and by sheer luck, managed to bag the bat.

Decades later, Duane wrote me that the bats had finally extracted their revenge. The family that bought our old house across the street had to call an exterminator to remove a colony which had taken up residence in the basement.

As that summer of 1964 began to melt away, the white haze of wishful thinking faded and the cold stare of reality came into focus. I had been chasing a shadow. Dee Warren did not share the depth of feeling I had for her. The prickly heat of embarrassment raced up my spine as

I realized what a clueless bonehead I had been, unable to discern friendly indulgence from attraction. The signals were all there. I had just missed them. I had no antenna. Dee Warren was just too nice to tell me to buzz off. Even as a teenager, she was a class act.

Mother had never intruded in my romantic life, such as it was, other than to repeatedly tell me to stop wearing my feelings on my sleeve. I only recall her being complicit in one fix-up. One of her friends had called to enlist her help in getting me to escort a visiting niece to a dance at the Episcopal Parish House. Of course, I resisted. My fear genes ranked blind dates well ahead of public speaking and certain death, but, as always, Mother's around the clock full court press prevailed. When she wanted me to do something, she was like a bad cold that never let up.

I approached the front door that night harboring a bottomless pit of dread. Perhaps, I thought, at the very least, she would have a good personality. All blind dates at least have that, right?

When the door opened and I met Susan, my jaw clanked on the floor! We had a great time and wrote each other a few times that summer, but college quickly intervened and we lost touch.

Her brother, Sam Adams, later bought the old Lankford house next door to the Weavers on the corner with Jefferson Street. He went on to become one of Emporia's longest serving mayors.

VII

In the fall of 1962, Mother and I took the train to New York to see June on Broadway. Her career had taken off when she was cast as a delinquent on the CBS soap opera *As The World Turns*. After she left the show, (the writers banished her to reform school) she went on tour with *Under The Yum Yum Tree* which later opened on Broadway. She spent summers in New England doing summer stock theatre in New Hampshire and upstate New York. In 1961, she won a Theatre World Award for her role in the off Broadway play *Cry Of The Raindrop* and had just snatched a plum role on Broadway in *Take Her She's Mine* with Art Carney and Elizabeth Ashley. The entire cast was on *The Ed Sullivan Show* one Sunday night in March 1962. Mother was beside herself.

Opening night for *Take Her She's Mine* was over the holidays in December of 1961. Mother and Father had driven up for the premier. A year later as we prepared to catch the train for New York, Mother was still gushing about the "after opening night party" at Sardi's in New York.

It was my first visit to New York and the "then grand" Penn Station. The ornate building would inexcusably be demolished a year later to be replaced by the current underground, cave-like facility beneath Madison Square Garden.

From the moment I walked out onto 34th Street, I was hooked. Everything was larger than life. The pulse and the vibe were like a B12 shot to the soul, intoxicating and addictive. I would make scores of trips to the city over the ensuing decades and every time I left, it was always tugging me to come back for another dose. I have never gotten enough of it; but that first exposure to big time Broadway remains wired in my thoughts like no other subsequent visit, not NBC at 30 Rock, the Knicks at the Garden, or Flushing Meadows.

It was a dreamlike experience, vaguely familiar yet unfamiliar, sitting with Art Carney in his dressing room, chatting like we were old friends catching up. The actor George Peppard popped in. Carney introduced me as though I were an equal. "George, this is June's brother John; he's in radio." Peppard was having a fling at the time with Ashley, who would be his co-star in the movie *The Carpetbaggers*. They would later marry. Ashley, who had a husky voice I thought was sexy as hell, would scurry off stage to light up and chat with Peppard, then hand me her cigarette to nurse while she ran back for another scene.

After the curtain, stars, the well connected, the beautiful people, politicians, musicians, the arts crowd, and fans all poured backstage, stopping at June's dressing room with smiles and hugs, telegrams, flowers and cards. I was completely mesmerized by it all - the dazzling, bright lights that surrounded June's vanity mirror, the sound of champagne corks popping, the laughter and gaiety. I was a visitor loitering on the edge of the big time. It was a different world. Then, overnight, I stepped back into mundane reality as the train rolled into Emporia. Father met us in his "new" white Chevy Impala hardtop. I had totaled his Plymouth in the spring.

The first casualties of the "learning to drive" trauma had been two galvanized trash cans I had flattened in front of our house trying to master the art of parallel parking. One belonged to Mrs. Lucas, who dismissed it in her usual delightful way, "It needed killing, John." I bought her a new one.

The unsanctioned "test track" for kids learning to drive in Emporia was the huge parking lot behind the high school. Coupled with the vacant physical education fields, there was plenty of room to accommodate off road misadventures.

My father's 1952 Plymouth had a manual transmission, and I discovered I was a bit of a klutz at syncing my left foot on the clutch with my right hand on the gearshift, thereby transforming the car into a mechanical bull on wheels, simultaneously grinding the gears and my father's clinched teeth. Eventually, I was able to drive around a city block and parallel park between two sticks without jumping the curb or hitting anything. I got my license. I would keep it for only a couple of weeks.

VIII

Driving home from the radio station one afternoon in the late-spring, I lost control. The heavy little Plymouth veered off the road and smashed into a large sycamore tree. To this day, I have no clue what happened. There were no seatbelts then, and the impact sent me crashing through the windshield head first, putting a good sized gash in my forehead and inflicting deep cuts in my face that took dozens of sutures to close. My left thumb was fractured in the joint when it smashed through the steering wheel and windshield. I had three broken ribs, a busted up knee and a badly chipped front tooth. I looked like a thoroughly beaten flyweight. The car was totaled.

Doctor Allison told Mother I would have no joint in the base of my thumb but that, over time, some flexibility might return. Very little ever did. Mostly, Mother fretted over the huge facial scar that left me looking like some kind of lesser Teutonic Knight who had come out on the short end of a duel. But, within a year or so, the scar had all but faded away, testament to Doctor Allison's reputation as the best stitch man in Emporia.

Amazingly, I was not given a ticket. Even so, Father took my license, and I was not permitted to drive again until I was 19. He admitted to me years later that it had been one of the worst decisions he ever made about me. It was! Not being allowed to drive hamstrung me all through high school. Weekend nights were the worst. If I managed to get a date, I had to double up with a friend; but it was more than just dating.

Driving to the Emporia Diner on a Saturday night was a rite of passage for teenagers in those days. I got there, but only with friends. Riding my bike would have been uncool. So was walking, though I swallowed my pride and did more than once.

The Diner was more than just a hangout. It was the great social equalizer, the showcase for youth in Emporia, and THE place to be seen, to get noticed and, to that end, we were all willing to supply the antics. Silly stunts abounded. Probably the most memorable: stashing ducks in the men's room to send the post Friday night high school football crowd into hysterical laughter when they waddled out. Even the owner, Catherine Whitley, who was always wise to us, had a good laugh.

The Diner was always the post-date, post-dance, post-game show, a stanza in every teenager's story in

Emporia, and, as the late Robin Williams said in *Dead Poets' Society*, "we all contributed a verse." When it closed and was later torn down, Emporia lost part of its soul. I never thought the town was the same again.

IX

There were six of us: Randy Grigg on guitar, Tinker Williams on bass and saxophone, Rick Brothers on keyboards, Wayne Kei on trumpet and most anything else he chose to play, me behind the drum kit and Bobby Lee was the vocalist. We called our group "The Elektras." I think it was Randy who came up with the name.

At the beginning, we sounded like six teenagers making noise in a large metal trash can, but my cousin Hamlet sat in with us once or twice and helped us to begin polishing our act. Hamlet was the "Boneman" (trombone) with "The Weejuns," a white soul band out of Elon College formed by Don Miller. The band was named after the Bass Penny Loafer that was all the rage in the 60's —Weejuns were de rigueur for dancing The Shag. The band had drawn big crowds at the Emporia Armory Dances put on by the National Guard. We were green with envy.

I had learned drum rudiments in the elementary school band but had quit because I didn't like the marching. I used my pay from WEVA to buy my first drum kit, a cheap, off brand set with sky blue pearl finish. Father lettered my initials on the kick drum head, and, with some of Mother's old sheets, I muffled the kick and snare to where I could get some good tones out of them.

I'd set up the kit in my bedroom, put some 45's on my Magnavox portable stereo and play along. After I had wrapped up one afternoon, Mrs. Lucas saw me in the kitchen and hollered over from her side porch perch, "John, I don't know what you're playing on those drums but you're sure beating the hell out of them." Soon, I moved the kit to the WEVA Studio where the band started holding practice sessions after the station went off the air, much to the delight of my parents and Mrs. Lucas.

Our first gig came through my weekend radio shows on WEVA. The high school in Conway, North Carolina, wrote and offered to pay my expenses plus fifty dollars if I would come down and spin records for their high school prom. I countered that perhaps they might like to have a live band play at their prom for an additional hundred bucks. It was our first paid performance.

I began promoting the band's upcoming appearances on WEVA. Soon we were playing dates around Emporia and the surrounding area. Early on, we made several appearances at a local teen club that two young guys were trying to get up and running in a vacant building next to Vogue Cleaners across North Main Street from the Diner.

We had repeated gigs at the Cotillion Club Dances at the Emporia Country Club. I had never been there before. My parents were never members. I had always imagined the clubhouse as a magnificent Ritz Carlton-worthy palace with ornate, gilded mirrors in a grand ballroom reflecting the glow of Emporia's old money. The comedown was epic. It was just a big room with a fireplace.

We soon graduated to higher paying venues. We picked up our first big prom date at Stony Creek High School. "The

Elektras" became the house band for the National Guard Dances at the Emporia Armory. The Guard hung huge, billowing parachutes upside down from the cavernous ceiling, which transformed the enormous space into a cozy, acoustically friendly, dance club that had a custom made two-tier bandstand and a bar that must have been twenty feet long. We played at a string of dances deep into the summer and quickly learned to pass the hat to keep playing after midnight. The well lubricated crowd was always more than generous.

The tunes we performed are still in heavy rotation in my head. Many had R & B roots like Jimmy Reed's "Baby What You Want Me To Do." We did several James Brown sides including my favorite, "Good, Good Lovin," with its opening snare rim shots. Mainstream stuff in those days included Jerry Butler's "He Will Break Your Heart," Ray Charles "What'd I Say, The Drifters "Up On the Roof," and the original "Shout" by the Isley Brothers.

Hank Ballard's "Let's Go, Let's Go, Let's Go" with the big bass line usually pried the wall flowers lose as did Eddie Cochran's 1958 teen anthem "Summertime Blues." Chuck Berry was huge in those days. "Johnnie B. Good" was a mainstay along with "Nadine," "Maybellene" and the original version of "Memphis." So was "Stay," the Maurice Williams classic, the Animals monster hit "House of the Rising Sun," with its towering organ riffs, and the Kingsmen's "Louie Louie" with its indecipherable, or were they indecent lyrics. The FBI investigated but even the G Men couldn't decode them.

Several instrumentals were in the stack including James Brown's "Suds," the all-time rock band classic. Every band I ever played with had it on their list. So was Mongo Santamaria's classic "Watermelon Man," Another was the Markeys' "Last Night," Lonnie Mack's "Wham," with its squalling lead guitar and the rollicking Phil Upchurch original version of "You Can't Sit Down," with the barking Sax line. By far the most energetic instrumental was the Safaris "Wipe Out," a 12 bar tune with a simple but fast drum solo based on a high school marching band's drum cadence. It was pounded out on table tops across the country that summer of 1963.

"The Elektras" big break came in the mid-summer of 1964 when we were booked at the legendary Top Hat Club on the oceanfront in Virginia Beach. We followed a set by one of the beach's big name bands "Bill Deal and the Rondels."

The place was rockin'! The jam packed, beer saturated, standing room only crowd went into a frenzy when we lit into the Contour's "Do You Love Me" with Bobby Lee belting the title with the intensity of Screamin' Jay Hawkins. The tune had a false ending - a four-beat pause before the sock line blasted through the big amps, sending the crowd into a near seizure.

There's a photograph of all of us standing around my father's white Chevy Impala just outside the club holding beers after our set. (My father had finally given me my driver's license back.) Clearly, we thought we were hot stuff.

Later, when I was in school in Washington, I got on with a couple of bands in the DC- Baltimore area and made some respectable money, but I knew my limitations and never had any illusions about making a living behind a drum kit.

X

The news that President Kennedy had been assassinated in Dallas that infamous Friday in November, 1963, came over the intercom at school. When we were dismissed from classes, I immediately went up to WEVA.

Nothing like it had happened before in broadcasting and no one knew exactly what to do. Will had rushed back to the station when the news broke and immediately pulled all of the commercials off the air.

Almost from the first "Flash" from Dallas, we started playing the somber organ music we normally broadcast during a program called "The Obituary Column of The Air," which featured funeral announcements from the area funeral homes. It seemed far more appropriate than continuing to play the pop and rock and roll music the station usually programmed.

WEVA was not affiliated with any network at the time so it fell upon us to keep breaking in to relay the running Associated Press dispatches that were moving constantly on the wire. Every single one was a "Flash" from Dallas, accompanied by a string of jarring bell alarms triggered on the teletype machine down the hall. Will quickly got us hooked up temporarily to one of the radio networks, and we began carrying wall to wall coverage.

If you were old enough to understand what had happened, you will remember how completely stunned and on edge the country was. For more than a week, it was the total focus of the nation.

It was a watershed moment for me. For the first time in my short career, I realized there was another side to radio, a higher calling. From that point on, I began treating the newscasts I was reading each hour as more than just an interruption, an irritant to get out of the way before I could go back to having fun and playing tunes. My whole reason for wanting to make broadcasting a career would slowly evolve from entertainment to broadcast journalism.

More than 25 years later, I used a free afternoon during a company meeting in Dallas to visit the 6th Floor Museum housed in the former Texas School Book Depository where the fatal shots that killed President Kennedy had been fired. Standing at the very window where it happened with Dealey Plaza laid out below and beyond sent a cold chill up my spine. I almost expected to see the President's motorcade come into view.

By the summer of 1964, weekend afternoons at WEVA had become an impromptu flash mob. Carloads of kids would congregate in the station's parking lot with radios blasting wide open. I usually kept the station's doors locked but kids I knew, mostly girls (lucky me), would call and ask if they could come in to watch, hang out, and often dance in the adjoining studio. Will would drop in from time to time, but he never said a negative word to me about the kids in the parking lot or those I allowed inside.

My swan song came over the Labor Day weekend that September. I turned the weekend into a three day oldies extravaganza, playing nothing but hits from the past. It took days to pull all of the records from the library. Will took out several ads in the local papers promoting the show, which became something of a tradition at the station after I left.

Leaving was difficult. Will Stone had rescued me from the shoe molding of high school. I came of age at WEVA and I had the time of my life there.

In the Spring of 2007, I went back to Emporia to speak at a banquet honoring Will for his long service to the community as owner and manager of WEVA. I was grateful for the chance to publically thank him for opening that door way back in 1959. I shudder to think what might have happened to me if he hadn't. Will died in 2009.

John, Barbara and June Harding. Emporia. 1948

Listen To The
John Harding
Show
1:15 To 5:15
Sat. & Sun.

Over
W EV A
Radiant Radio
860
On Your Dial

The Greensville Mirror. Emporia. 1962

At WEVA Emporia. 1963

With Dee Warren Harrell,
Junior Senior Prom May 1963

"The Elektras" at The Top Hat. Virginia Beach. 1964

Part III

The Road to Washington and NBC News

I

Life after high school began to dominate the dinner table talk in the fall of 1963. As usual, it was Mother who drove the conversation. Other than demanding I take typing and accounting, my father left just about everything concerning me to her. It was probably a safe assumption he would consider me a huge success if I simply finished high school, got a job to support myself, though he still did not consider radio a real job, and got out of the house. But I really didn't know what he thought because we never talked about it; and frankly, I hadn't thought much about it either. I just assumed Will would give me a full time job at WEVA once I graduated. I must have considered the fact that since it had taken me a second time around to pass the 10th grade, what feasible chance of success could I expect to have in college if I could even get accepted anywhere? And that was a very large IF!

One night after supper (the word "dinner" was never used unless we ate in the dining room), the subject came up. Mother had gathered her lists · she always had lists · and was arranging what wonks today would call "talking points." I volunteered that I'd be more than happy to just stay in Emporia and work at the radio station. As soon as the words were tumbling out of my mouth, I regretted opening it.

Mother froze, stunned into shell shocked silence. A cold, furious stare washed over her face. The moment seemed to linger as though she was trying to comprehend how my brain had been sucked out by some other-worldly force that had left me dumb as a garden rake. "THAT," she finally said, so forcibly I winced, "IS NOT GOING

TO HAPPEN! ABSOLUTELY NOT!" I started to say
something else but thought better about it.

Off she went, her usual reserve unmasked, reminding me
of the trainloads of things I had no clue about, and never
would, unless I got out of Emporia and exposed myself
to other ideas, races, and cultures. "I will not grow old
in this town watching you hanging out with provincial
know nothings who have not one scintilla of ambition,
guzzling beer, shooting pool and flirting with high school
girls at the Diner, all the while degenerating into a
lecherous, ignorant, middle aged flunk out!" she shouted.
" IT WILL NOT HAPPEN...PERIOD! YOU ARE GOING
TO COLLEGE JOHN TISDALE or I will DIE trying!"

I was hammered into meek silence. Father, stunned by
Mother's completely off the hook tirade, dropped his fork
and gave her a stunned look. He quietly resumed eating
his pork chop. He was staying out of it.

After what seemed an hour, it was only a minute or so,
she pushed the dinner dishes to one side, whipped out a
Virginia road map she had retrieved from Father's car,
and unfolded it on the kitchen table. "You are going to
college. I don't know where yet, but you ARE going, and it
will be beyond an easy trip home on weekends." She drew
a circle on the map roughly 100 miles around Emporia.
"Somewhere outside of that circle," she said.

My high school guidance director John Krebs (we called
him Maynard G. after the TV character), probably
thought I was a lost cause. It wasn't a difficult diagnosis
given my sterling record. Undeterred, Mother wrote off
for college catalogs. Some of them would have left the
impression that I had aced the SAT's · The University
of North Carolina at Chapel Hill, Syracuse University

and so on. Mother knew where the good communication schools were and was checking on the courses offered to compare with less exclusive and less pricey schools. She immediately struck RPI, Richmond Professional Institute (later VCU) off the list. It was too close to home, never mind that both of my sisters had gone to undergraduate school there. I started to make an issue of it, but in deference to my continued mental health, I kept my thoughts to myself.

As she reviewed her back of the Swift and Company envelope list, I remarked that perhaps I could go stay with June, who was then living in Los Angeles, and go to UCLA. Mother made no effort to even acknowledge I had said anything. My words lamely floated, uncaptured by intended ears, until they faded from thought, like the tree that falls in the forest with no one around to hear it.

Finally she looked at me and said, "I think the best fit for you, John, is American University in Washington." She pushed the AU catalog across the table to me opened at the School of Communications Broadcast curriculum.

AU had a very highly regarded broadcast and journalism department and the school was affiliated with the Methodist Church. Not that the church affiliation would put any shine on me; I hadn't been to a service for so long, our minister, Reverend Herbert A. Moyer, who had been at Monumental Methodist for two years, was not aware Mother even had a son. Deftly setting him straight, she prevailed upon him to arrange a visit to the University one weekend.

A student volunteer met us for a tour of the campus in Northwest Washington and a detailed walk through of the Communications Building with its radio and television studios. As Mother had figured, I was transfixed. It was as though I had gotten a glimpse of broadcasting's promised land. I wanted to be there, but I had no chance. My only hope was to attend a Junior College, build up my grades and transfer.

Mother turned to our neighbor, distant cousin and family lawyer, Lyman Harrell, Dee Warren's father, to try to find some way to get me shoehorned into Ferrum Junior College, another Methodist affiliated school, in Southwestern Virginia.

Lyman had some serious juice. A former Commonwealth's Attorney and member of the Town Council, he was Chairman of the Board of Trustees at our Church, President of the Citizens National Bank, and a ranking member of the Virginia House of Delegates.

What screws he turned or arms he twisted or favors he called in, I never knew, but it worked. That April, I was accepted for the fall semester at Ferrum Junior College.

He called me one night in the early spring and asked me to come over to his house. When I walked in the den, he congratulated me on my acceptance.

I thanked him for helping me.

"You're welcome," he said. He then proceeded to tell me in no uncertain terms that he had stuck his neck out for me, that failure was not an option, that he expected me to graduate from Ferrum and go on to graduate from American University.

I told him I understood and I would not let him down.

"It's not about me," he said. "Don't let yourself down, John."

There is absolutely no doubt whatsoever that without his intervention, I would not have gotten a shot at a college education. It simply would not have happened. I was forever indebted to him and to his wife Duane, who Mother said, had lobbied fiercely on my behalf.

II

Ferrum Junior College, now a four year institution, is located in the foothills of the Blue Ridge Mountains, about 10 miles from the small town of Rocky Mount and 35 miles south of Roanoke. Downtown Ferrum, at the time, consisted of a pool hall attached to something loosely called a restaurant and a hamburger joint called "The Panther," named after the school's mascot. Other than that, there was nothing to do at Ferrum except go to class, which of course, was the whole idea. I told Mother it was like going to school at Alcatraz! She was not amused.

Ferrum was coed. It was essentially a large high school. The only difference was that it had a campus and dorms, and students were required to attend chapel. Even the high school cliques seemed to have been scooped up and transplanted intact to the wilds of Southwestern Virginia. The majority of kids were from the DC suburbs in Virginia, the Roanoke Valley and the Richmond area.

On my first day, I was slammed by roommate shock. I had no advance notice of who my roommate would be and for the first two days, I didn't have one. When he finally showed up, we didn't hit it off. Whatever it was that made for a good roommate match, we didn't have it. Within a couple of months I split, moving in with a friend whose roommate had gotten married and moved to the married student's quarters.

I kept noticing a girl in the cafeteria line who seemed chummy with a pale, painfully thin boy with blond, almost white hair. I thought they were a couple but her roommate said those magic words, "just friends." A petite "Jane Wyman" look-alike, she seemed to know many of the clique set but didn't appear to hang out with them, a big plus on my score card.

The actress Jane Wyman, Ronald Reagan's first wife, had never been on my Hollywood hot list but this "Jane" pushed my buttons. She had short dark hair, soft eyes, a pale complexion and a quiet, *Mona Lisa* like smile. I found her irresistible. We started talking in the cafeteria line, going to campus events and double dating with my roommate.

Soon her parents drove down, I presume to look me over. I must have passed muster because a short time later, she asked me to go home with her over a weekend. We wound up at a party somewhere in Alexandria or Arlington.

Mother reciprocated, giving me the okay to invite "Jane" to come home with me for a weekend that spring. Mother and Father were exceedingly polite but I remember it as a rather chilly weekend. I thought it was a case of the "not good enough for the only son" malady. Mother later said that was never the case; that I had simply been caught up in a "pool of exuberant hormones," as she put it, that blurred the goal of getting a degree

I had my own car by then. Father had found a used 1959 Austin Healey 3000 roadster in British Racing Green at the Chrysler Plymouth dealership on South Main Street. My heart melted, but the electrics were all bad and replacing all the wiring would cost more than the price of the car. I was crushed.

I settled for a used 1962 Ford Falcon, with a chronic squeaky valve from Watkins Ford. Father said I would have to make a good faith effort to pay him back. I did, in full. Will had hired me to do weekend mornings and fill in during vacations at WEVA that summer of 1965. He had recruited another high school kid to do weekend afternoons.

"Jane" had not done well grade-wise that year and was in summer school at Ferrum. That August, I drove up to spend a weekend with her.

As I entered the final year at Ferrum, I was completely under her spell. When I called home and told Mother I wanted to give "Jane" a ring, she was blindsided, stunned into what for her was a remarkable silence. Then, with dripping disdain, she said, "I would have hoped you would have better judgment, John Tisdale." She ticked off all those little, always annoying virtual boxes: how difficult it had been to get me in school, that Lyman had stuck his neck out for me, how they were skimping to send me, having already educated my two sisters, and now, she said, "you're ready to chuck everything to get engaged to someone you could not possibly know who has charmed you into giving her an engagement ring!" I started to say something, but the line had gone dead. My own Mother had hung up on me.

Within an hour, there was a rap on my dorm door. "Your Father is on the phone!" I cringed. The phone booth took on the mantra of the gas chamber as I dragged myself to my final comedown. That he had called, from work no less, was extraordinary. He never, ever called me about anything, always doing what little business he had with me face to face where there was no exit.

Using his best, barely under control, drill sergeant tone, he quickly put an end to the ring talk with one simple question: "How exactly were you planning to pay for this ring, John?" Pointedly, his emphasis was on the past tense. I stammered that I was hoping he would lend it to me. "Over my dead body," he barked. Then, like General MacArthur addressing the vanquished Japanese on VJ day, he announced, "This conversation is closed." Game, set and match.

III

I was summoned home that April for "June Harding Day" in Emporia. Duly proclaimed by the Mayor, it kicked off a celebration marking one of the two East Coast Premiers of Columbia Pictures *The Trouble with Angels,* starring Rosalind Russell, Hayley Mills, Gypsy Rose Lee and "Introducing June Harding." Directed by Ida Lupino, the film was shot on location at St. Mary's Home for Children in Ambler, Pennsylvania and at the Columbia Studios in Hollywood. The World Premier had been held earlier that month in San Francisco. June had written Mother a long letter filled with details of the glittery affair.

It was the blue hour when I drove into Emporia that evening, the uncertain time between dusk and dark when the sun has dropped below the horizon and the residual sunlight takes on a decided blue hue. It was a dramatic backdrop for the dazzling lights chasing one another on the Pitts Theatre Marquee on South Main Street, which proclaimed, "June Harding starring in *The Trouble With Angels*."

I parked in front of the Presbyterian Church across the street and walked over to the front of the theatre. Movie posters and black and white stills of June, Hayley Mills, Rosalind Russell and Gypsy Rose Lee were encased in the glassed-in metal frames. Since the days of putting on puppet shows for neighborhood kids when I was little, she had always dreamed of being in the movies. Now it had come true. What were the probabilities?

Our house on Ingleside was a madhouse. VIP's, TV people, newspaper reporters, politicians, PR people from Columbia Pictures, neighbors, friends, and relatives we didn't even know we had were everywhere throughout the house and yard. Columbia Pictures had catered everything. There were enormous spreads of food and wine. June waved at me from the living room as I squeezed into the foyer. She was being interviewed by a reporter from the *Richmond Times Dispatch*. Another was waiting for his turn. Mother was so wound up I thought she would start zooming around the house like a runaway balloon losing its air. The talking and laughing went on into the wee small hours. I don't think any of us slept that night.

The next day, we were all awakened by the high school band drumming its way down the street. They were practicing for the parade that afternoon in June's honor. She rode in a convertible with "June Harding, Emporia's Star" printed on a sign on the door. Mother, Father, my sister Barbara and I piggybacked on her fame, following in a convertible under a banner proclaiming "The Harding Family." Behind us was a car filled with Cheerleaders from Greensville County High School. It didn't seem that long ago that June was one of them.

The parade ended at the Courthouse on South Main Street. It was a mob scene. People were everywhere. The Mayor made a speech and presented June with the key to the city. Afterwards, she climbed on top of a fire truck for the ride home. That night, we all went to a local restaurant, I think it was "The Sportsman," for a special dinner, then it was on to the freshly painted Pitts Theatre where we all sat in a special ribboned section.

Dwarfed by the huge screen behind her, June went up on stage wearing the blue suit she had worn in the movie and thanked everyone for coming. Then suddenly, there she was on the screen, bigger than life itself, with Hayley Mills and Roz Russell. Mother cried.

Afterwards, June was mobbed by children who wanted to touch her. There were hugs and kisses and autographs. I finally managed to clear a path for her to get outside. The Police Chief drove us back to the house on Ingleside where Mother and Father were hosting a huge party, but I had to leave to get back to school.

In 2011, Dick Parker, a family friend, put his collection of my late sister Barbara's art on display in Emporia. (Her career had been cut short by emphysema in 2000 and she died five years later from congestive heart failure.) My wife and I drove up for the opening. Included in the exhibit was BB's signed and numbered colored pen and ink of the old Pitts Theatre with the marquee as it was for "June Harding Day" all those years ago. The theatre had long been torn down to make way for the Emporia City Government Building which, in an ironic twist, was the site of the exhibit. Almost every person who saw me that evening mentioned the artwork and said they had been there for "June Harding Day." One lady remarked, "It was the most exciting weekend I can ever remember in Emporia."

June went on to appear in scores of network television series and TV movies in the 60's and 70's, including *Doctor Kildare*, multiple episodes of *The Fugitive*, the Emmy and Golden Globe winning *Richard Boone Anthology Series, Mr. Novak, The Doctors, The Nurses*, and *The Defenders*, among others. She retired to coastal Maine in the late 70's.

IV

The non-stop thrills of the weekend soon plunged like the roller coaster at Ocean View. I floated back onto campus stoked by the excitement of "June Harding Day"; but, when I walked into my dorm room, the air was heavy as though someone had died. My roommate's face was strained. "Jane" had cheated on me, going out with the guy I had ditched as my assigned roommate when I first got to Ferrum. I felt a chill as the highs of the past two days were sucked out in an instant. I was slammed, like the cowboy who gets blasted as he walks into the saloon, his body hurled backwards through the saloon doors into the street.

I didn't see her until the next day. Amid sobs, she begged forgiveness. When I asked why, she shrieked something unintelligible and began crying, heaving between sobs like a cat trying to bring up a hairball. Looking at me with bloodshot eyes, she suddenly collapsed onto the pavement. She was as white as a gardenia bloom. I picked her up and carried her up the hill to the College Infirmary. The nurse brought her around and gave her a mild sedative. Her eyes opened and she mumbled something before drifting off to sleep.

We continued to see each other the remainder of that last semester and into the summer of 1966, but the bloom was off the relationship, and we soon went our separate ways.

In late April, I was accepted for transfer to American University in Washington, conditioned, of course, on my graduation from Ferrum. My parents came up for the ceremony early that June.

Father had told me that, while he and Mother could help with spending money and perhaps a bit with tuition at AU, I would have to work while attending classes. Staying out of school in order to earn enough to pay my way later wasn't an option because my student draft deferment was contingent on staying in school. Mother and Father quickly bought the idea of my staying in Washington that summer so I could get a head start finding part-time work, putting away some money and getting familiar with the city.

The cheapest place I could find to stay on the Virginia side, from scouring the *Washington Post* classifieds, was a basement flat in Falls Church. It had one room with a bed, a metal desk, and a lamp. There was an alcove with a wash basin, a toilet and shower. A black, floor-length curtain separated it from the living area. There were no kitchen facilities, but I had a hot plate. It was a place to flop and take a shower, nothing more; and it was dirt cheap. It also leaked. One morning after a storm, I awoke to three inches of water on the cement floor. After some badgering, the landlord made good on my ruined books and record albums, including my prized Brubeck collection.

"Jane's" father had gotten me a summer job with a defense contractor in the district where he worked. The money was fantastic; but, after "Jane" and I split, I didn't feel right about continuing to work there and I quit. Working at WEVA got me in the door at several DC area radio stations where I got on as a part timer running taped programs and doing production work. I began to put away some decent money for school.

The cost at AU worked out to 63 dollars a credit hour or 189 dollars for every three-hour class. Carrying a five class load that first semester would total just short of a thousand bucks - a tidy sum in 1966. I wrote the number on a piece of paper and stuck it on the wall in my flat, a stark reminder of what I was up against. Then one day in August, it didn't seem to matter anymore.

V

I opened the letter slowly, as though I was hand cranking my own Zapruder-like film strip, frame by frame, depicting my descent, in all likelihood, into the black tar pit of Vietnam. The infamous "Greeting" had caught up with me. Like every other able bodied American male, I had been living under the threat of the draft and Vietnam ever since I had graduated from high school. It had been a powerful incentive to stay in school. Now, reality was staring at me in crisp, black and white print. There was no lottery then. My student deferment had been summarily revoked. I had been reclassified 1A and was ordered to report to the Draft Board Office at the Emporia Post Office to board a bus to the Military Induction Center in Richmond to undergo a physical for entry into the armed forces.

Numbly, I went through the motions of packing my stuff in the Falcon, calling my landlord and where I worked, telling them I had been drafted. Somber "Good Lucks" came in reply. I tried thinking about pleasant things as I navigated the maze of streets around the Pentagon heading to Interstate 95, anything to ease the mounting dread of what was ahead.

I went by the Kaiser-Allison clinic on South Main Street to pick up my medical file to take with me. Father had gone back to work. Mother made me some dinner and sat with me at the kitchen table. I just picked at my food. Neither of us said much of anything. The next morning, we said our goodbyes. Father drove me down to the Post Office. We shook hands. He told me to take care of myself.

There were about 50 or 60 of us on the bus that day. We had all been in high school together. There was a lot of nervous joking, but every one of us knew we probably would not be coming home anytime soon; and the odds were high that we would wind up in Vietnam. 1966 was not the year to be a 21 year-old male in America.

We had to strip, bend over, spread cheeks, turn your head, and cough, all the stuff you hear about. There were vision tests and hearing tests, then chest X-rays, and, of course, the pee in a cup routine. The orderly checked our fingernails before we went into the tiny restroom. One of the old tricks was to scrape sugar under your fingernails to dump into the cup when you peed which would signal diabetes. When Jack went in, he stayed and stayed. Finally the orderly asked if he was okay. Jack screamed, "I can't go. I need a cold delicious!" We all cracked up laughing, breaking the strain of the moment.

After taking an aptitude test in which one had to match things like a pipe wrench to a pipe, we arrived at the last checkpoint where the Doctor, a Navy Captain, reviewed our individual medical files. He snatched mine from my hand and was quickly flipping through it when, suddenly, he stopped and lingered on one piece of paper for what seemed like an eternity. He studied an X-ray film for a moment, then scribbled something on a small form, which he folded and handed to me. I was to give it to the orderly on the second floor. The wooden stairs had dips in the treads worn by God knows how many souls who had trudged on them before me, unsure of what was coming next.

I assumed I had passed the physical. The orderly at the top of the stairs grabbed the form the Navy Doctor had given me. I cursed myself for not having looked at it. He walked me over to a small, glass enclosed office and handed the form to a wisp of a woman behind an old wooden desk piled high with folders and papers. She smiled and motioned for me to sit. She glanced at the form, then looked at me over the top of her reading glasses and announced, "Mr. Harding, you have been declared medically unfit for military service." She rattled on, explaining she was with the Virginia Employment Commission. I zoned out, not hearing anything else she said. A hazy, mental fog smothered my brain. I had the sense of being in some safe, anxiety-free upland and, for the first time in a long time, I knew I was going to be all right.

"Mr. Harding, are you okay?" she bellowed, jerking me back into the moment. I was given a folder filled with pamphlets, brochures and forms and sent to a very large room filled with nothing but rows upon rows of hundreds of scuffed, wooden folding chairs. The folder was about the services the employment commission offered to disabled people to help them find work. I had never thought of myself as disabled. Out of the corner of my eye, I saw Jack coming into the room. We were the only ones of our group who had not been inducted into the Army or the Marines that day.

When I walked into the house, my parents looked as though they had seen an apparition. There was a moment of stunned silence. Both were dumbstruck. I learned later that I had flunked the physical because I was deemed two thirds disabled in my left hand. I had broken it in the wreck when I was 16.

VI

A week before registration, I was back in Washington looking for a place to live in the District. The flat in Falls Church was okay for the summer but I'd freeze to death there in the winter. There was no heat. Besides, Falls Church was too far from school; but living on campus was only a pipedream. There was no way I could afford it.

I settled on McLean Gardens, a complex of nine privately owned brick dormitory buildings at 39th and Wisconsin Avenue, not far from the AU campus at Ward Circle. McLean Gardens had been built during the Second World War to house defense workers, but in 1966, most residents were day students at nearby schools.

Each room had a bed, a bureau, a desk, and a wash basin. There was no cafeteria; but the rent was within my meager means. A large, open shower room and a wall of toilets were located at each end of the hallway on each floor. There were no stalls, meaning no privacy. The dorms had a few rules: no booze and no women allowed in the male dorms and vice versa; but enforcement was pretty much nonexistent and, every now and then, I would see a girl coming out of a guy's room. Once, when I walked into the bathroom, I ran into a girl in the shower. She smiled and waved as though being naked in front of a strange guy was perfectly normal. I was a long way from Emporia.

Several of us who were short on money took up eating at the Waffle Shop, a tiny eatery on Wisconsin Avenue that only hired ex-cons. Everything was fast and fried. The food wasn't bad, and best of all, it was cheap. I would sometimes venture over to the new McDonalds on Connecticut Avenue and splurge on a Big Mac and a vanilla shake. When money was really low, which was usually the case, I'd dine on those staples of college kids everywhere · peanut butter, crackers, sardines and canned ravioli.

The two daytime radio stations on the Virginia side, where I had been working before the draft notice arrived, gave me my part-time jobs back, just on different days. I was jockeying religious tapes on one and "rip and reading" news wire copy on the other.

When school started, I got on with the University station, WAMU-FM. Aside from running the control board and running taped programs, I engineered a weekly chamber music recital one night every week at a venue on Massachusetts Avenue. It was easy enough. All I had to do was show up, cut on the equipment, which was already in place, cue the announcer and stay awake.

Sunday nights, I did an old hits program on WAMU AM, the student run station at American and actually had a few listeners in the dorms. There was no money but it was fun and a break from the work and class routine. I would later be elected Program Director on an "all top 40" ticket, the first and only time I ever ran for anything.

I managed to get the courses I had to have at times that fit with my work schedule. Thanks to my years at WEVA, I did not have to spend time preparing for the radio courses, which gave me more time to do the work for the material which was new to me, including several television and film production courses and still photography, which would lead to a lifetime of joy with a camera. I was hooked from day one.

That November, I was the Virginia Anchor for WAMU-FM's Election Night Coverage. WAMU's coverage area included not just the District, but also the Maryland and Virginia Suburbs. It required a huge staff to cover. Twenty five student reporters were assigned to critical field locations. Each hour's fifteen minute national election wrap- up alone took a staff of 14. My part of it went smoothly enough until I had to introduce a field reporter whose first name had escaped me. "Here's Hamilton," I said. Then, turning to the main anchor Steve Chamides, I asked "What's his first name?" My gaff was preserved for posterity in the AU Newspaper *The Eagle.*

Home for Easter, I went up to WEVA to sound out Will on the idea of setting up a local news department that summer. I needed a steady job for several months, and staying at home would be less expensive. We'd cover the doings of local government plus police and fire calls and so on. He loved the idea and said he wanted to do some of the reporting himself. We agreed to get started as soon as I was done with classes that semester.

It was the perfect time to go into news in Emporia. The town was in the midst of a campaign, spearheaded by the Mayor, to transition Emporia to city status. It required a ballot question in November. If approved, Emporia would become a city and thus a separate entity from Greensville County. It was a hot issue and dominated the local news all summer. That fall, Emporia voters gave it a thumbs-up.

Will and I divided up the local government and school board meetings and took turns responding to fire and police calls. I would usually do the 8AM newscast. Will handled most of the afternoon newscasts. WEVA, being a daytime station, freed both of us to cover night meetings. When I left in late summer, I was sure Will was in it for the long term and would hire somebody to replace me. He did.

VII

After classes got underway that fall of 1967, I was summoned to see the head of the Communications Department. No reason was given for the requested meeting so my usual premonition of disaster settled in, which always left me in a perpetual state of dread. But Doctor Donald Williams was smiling when I walked into his office. He was recommending me for the NBC News Internship for the winter/spring semester of 1968.

Convinced I had no chance, I thanked him and promptly forgot about it.

Much of my free time that semester was spent on a documentary project for a radio production class. Assignments were made to teams of three. Our team settled on the upcoming March on the Pentagon, a massive anti-Vietnam war protest that was scheduled for late October in Washington. A million people converged on the National Mall. Armed with tape recorders and lots of enthusiasm, we fanned out across the area near the Lincoln Memorial where the demonstration began with an address from famed baby doctor, Benjamin Spock. He called President Lyndon Johnson "The Enemy," but the rally was peaceful.

All hell broke loose when the marchers reached the Pentagon across the Potomac River in Arlington. A radical element clashed with the soldiers and US Marshals, who were guarding the huge building. By the time order was restored, hundreds had been arrested, including two reporters. Covering the march, doing the interviews and collecting natural sound had been easy. The hard work was just beginning.

We adopted a production technique which used opposing points of view throughout, beginning with long clips of sound from each side followed by shorter and shorter clips until, toward the end, the effect was that of a rapid staccato of still shorter and shorter opposing views as though people were shouting at one another. We spent days sorting through the sound, dubbing and editing specific sound bites, and weeks more splicing the program together. It was all done by hand with a razor blade and splicing tape, an art form lost with the advent of digital editing on a computer. We called the documentary *Profile of a Peacenik.* We got A's for our work and the program was broadcast on WAMU FM.

Four of us who lived on the same floor at McLean Gardens decided we could save some money by going together to rent an apartment and splitting the rent and expenses. We found a place just off route 29/211 in Arlington about a mile from the Key Bridge. The only downside was 8 AM classes, which would necessitate a very early wake up in order to beat the nightmarish rush hour traffic; but we could come and go as we pleased.

Furnishings were sparse. The living room consisted of a sofa we had scrounged and a chair or two. I brought a coffee table from home that Father had built. My bedroom had the look of a squatter's lair: a mattress on the floor, a footlocker that doubled as a desk, an old desk lamp and a *Cool Hand Luke* movie poster on the wall.

I was seldom there except to sleep. When I wasn't in class, I was working. Making tuition money was always clawing at me, and I had little time for anything else.

My last date, actually an escort job, had been arranged by, of all people, Dee Warren's mother.

VIII

Duane Harrell had subpoenaed me to come home and escort the reigning Miss Virginia to several Emporia Peanut Festival Events, which Duane was coordinating for the city that September. I could never say no to her.

Miss Virginia was 19. A brunette, she had sparkling eyes and, as one would expect, was quite a head turner. She was also a bit of a flirt. I accompanied her and her chaperone, a middle aged woman who seemed devoid of humor, to the Miss Peanut Festival Beauty Pageant, which was held at the Emporia Auditorium. The contestants were all beauty queens from peanut growing areas.

The default MC for such major productions in Emporia was George F. Lee, the Mayor. Lee, who owned a jewelry store in Emporia, had been an announcer at WEVA in its early years. He cut a rather dashing figure in his tuxedo. Very polished, with good looks and a booming voice, Lee had the manner of a lesser Bert Parks as he went about the business of introducing and interviewing the contestants. The winner, of course, was crowned by Miss Virginia.

The Festival Dance was a ticketed event attended by Emporia's movers and shakers. Having played at countless similar affairs, I always found it mildly amusing to watch middle aged and elderly adults gyrate to rock music. It was also something of a challenge for Miss Virginia, who wore a straight cut gown and high heels. My brief weekend soiree with "Royalty" was crowned with a sweet kiss at her hotel.

I was carrying a full course load that winter and spring. Two stuck with me · Advanced Photography and News Writing, taught by the legendary Ed Bliss.

Bliss was the longtime Editor of *The CBS Evening News With Walter Cronkite*. Regarded as the best of news scriptwriters, Bliss left CBS to found the Broadcast Journalism Department at AU in 1968, just in time for me to get in his first class. It met at night for three hours once a week. I loved it.

The class always created a bit of a stir on campus because of the "who's who" of broadcast news Bliss brought in as guest lecturers. That semester, we were treated to the likes of Walter Cronkite, Eric Sevareid and David Brinkley, among others. I would soon get the opportunity to meet and talk with Brinkley quite a bit, and his methods became ingrained in me, but I was also powerfully influenced by Sevareid, whose commentaries on *The CBS Evening News* planted a burning desire to write opinion that I would later exercise at WRVA.

There were only about 30 of us in the class so the instruction was intense. Bliss was always very polite, but he took no prisoners on words and copy. All mistakes were equal opportunity offenders. A factual error, a grammatical error or a mispronunciation were all unacceptable. None was worse than the other and that included misspelled words. Saying it didn't matter because it was radio would get you his ultimate signal of disdain - a slow shake of his head.

With the finish line finally in sight, my cloistered lifestyle opened up a bit. I ventured down to the Cellar Door on M Street to catch the Cannonball Adderly Sextet. The group was then charting with "Mercy, Mercy, Mercy," a 20 bar tune with a distinct blues flavored chord progression that pushed my buttons. After years of pounding out medium to quick tempos in 4/4, I was drawn more and more to the freedom of Jazz.

I even had a date. I had met Tracey at a mixer. Dangerously cute with riot prone blonde hair, an infectious laugh and a free spirit, we began hanging out a lot that spring.

On the rare weekend when I wasn't working, we'd just rent a boat at Fletcher's Boat House in Georgetown and float around Fletcher's Cove, a park area on the Potomac River between the Key and Chain Bridges in Washington. Tracey went to flight attendant school after graduation. She wanted to fly. I thought that was it for us but we'd hook up again for a time later in Richmond.

IX

Sensing that it was something I might want to preserve for posterity, I opened the letter very carefully with a kitchen knife, taking pains not to tear up the envelope which hinted at its importance.

Dear Mr. Harding:

This won't exactly be news, but it will make it official on behalf of NBC News. We're happy to confirm that you are one of the two successful applicants for the internship program at NBC News, in Washington.

We congratulate you on your success and hope you will profit substantially by the period with us.

It was signed: Len Allen, Director NBC News Operations

I was floored. I had no thought of winning and had forgotten about it. The letter was clearly a case of the confirmation arriving before the news. The School of Communications had been trying to get in touch with me for a day or so.

When I finally saw Doctor Williams on campus, he told me that setting up a news operation at my hometown radio station had been the clincher. Will Stone had written a glowing account of my efforts.

NBC's headquarters in Washington was just up Nebraska Avenue from the AU Campus at Ward Circle. It was home to NBC News' Washington Bureau and NBC's owned and operated stations in Washington, WRC, WRC FM and WRC TV Channel 4.

I gave my name to the guard in the lobby. Within seconds, Len Allen's Secretary, a pretty woman named Mary Warren, came out to take me to his small office, located just off the network newsroom. Len Allen was a thin man who wore wire framed glasses on the tip of his nose. He had the demeanor of someone always in a hurry, and our meeting was predictably short. He congratulated me on my selection and said it would be an invaluable experience that I would remember for the rest of my life. It was all that and more.

I would be spending most of my time in the network newsroom, which was a long, narrow, incredibly noisy room along the front of the building, dominated by a huge desk. Next door was the WRC TV Newsroom.

The network's Washington Bureau Chief was Bill Monroe, a local news legend from WDSU-TV in New Orleans. Mary introduced me that first day, but I only caught glimpses of him afterwards.

My immediate supervisor was George Cheeley, the News Desk Supervisor at NBC. Nearly bald, George was a chain smoker, wore glasses and looked a bit frumpy. My first take of him was as a "hard ass," but when he found out I was working my way through school, he lightened up.

George would eye me in the newsroom and wave me over. He communicated by cryptogram, scribbling on a scrap of paper while talking on the phone: "Got time? Goralski at the Pentagon. Grab a cab and turn in the chit." Cheeley was totally plugged in to Washington, Capitol Hill in particular. He had a handle on just about everything that was going on or would go on. He nearly always assigned me to shadow the correspondent who was on the major story in Washington that day.

The news editors at NBC worked at the same huge desk as Cheeley. I had a lot of contact with two of them. Herb Brubaker was a Managing Editor and Producer who occasionally went into the field for the radio network. He took quite a bit of time with me during my time as an Intern, and I was not surprised to learn later that Herb had gone on to become President of the Television News Center in Washington, where anchors and reporters are trained.

George Burlbaugh was a Producer and Editor. He worked with Russ Ward in the mornings to put together the World News Roundup on NBC Radio. George would later become one of the "Princes," meaning he worked for *The Huntley-Brinkley Report.*

The only female on the News Desk was Christie Basham. An extremely attractive but no nonsense woman, Christie was the Network News Film Assignment Editor. She ran a tight ship, more than holding her own with the network film crews. They were some pretty tough customers, including George Sozio. It was said that Sozio was *Huntley-Brinkley's* ace cameraman having never shot a bad frame. He would test her patience, but Sozio and all of the crews had a load of respect for her. Christie went on to several executive positions with NBC News including Producer of *NBC Nightly News* and *Meet The Press.*

Getting the exposed film back to the processing lab in the basement from shooting locations and the airports fell to the NBC Couriers. They crisscrossed Washington like human buzz bombs on their motorcycles. There was a huge demand for them in those days and I suppose the pay was pretty good.

Many had deals with flight attendants on airlines coming into DC area airports, including Washington National (now Reagan National) across the Potomac in Virginia. The courier would sit on his bike, with the engine gurgling, waiting for the jet to roll to a stop on the apron. A flight attendant would open the cabin door and toss down an "onion bag" filled with cans of exposed film to the leather clad courier who then blasted off across the Potomac back to Nebraska Avenue for processing in the "Soup Factory."

Molly Sharpe booked guests on *The Today Show.* A striking woman with white hair and a distinctive British accent that commanded attention even in the ear numbing racket of the newsroom, she had come to NBC from the BBC in London. I was never formally introduced to her, but she knew who I was. Always flitting about the newsroom, she was usually looking for Charlie Jones, who directed Washington segments of *Today.* "Allo luv, have you seen Charlie this morning?" she would croon, as she breezed by. I suspect they were a formidable team · Jones with his reputation as a perfectionist, personally scouting remote locations, dictating camera placements and shooting angles, and Molly, who was like a bloodhound tracking down anyone who was anybody in Washington. Her cache of phone numbers was said to be a sort of Rolodex version of J. Edgar Hoover's private files.

X

Mary Warren gave me a quick tour of the building. Studio "A" was the heart of the complex. It was just off a long hallway that ran along the front of the building just behind the lobby. It was where David Brinkley did his half of *The Huntley- Brinkley Report,* and it was home to *Meet The Press.*

Each correspondent had a private office off a long hallway, a sort of correspondent's row, which connected to the newsroom. There resided the elite of the elite. Their names jumped off the doors: John Chancellor, Elie Able, Sander Vanocur, Herb Kaplow, Robert McCormick, Frank McGhee, Edwin Newman, Robert Goralski, Carl Stern, Charles Quinn, Neil Boggs and Paul Duke, among others. Mary introduced me to all who were in their offices.

At the end of the hall was a glass door with *The Huntley-Brinkley Report* lettered on the glass. For anyone at NBC News, "HB" was the absolute pinnacle. No one applied to work for the news broadcast; "HB" recruited them.

David Brinkley had a large office in the "HB" complex with large windows that overlooked a small park-like scene. Huntley was based in New York. Some found Brinkley arrogant and unapproachable but when Mary rapped on his door and we walked in, he came around his desk with a big smile as she introduced me. He shook my hand and asked, "Where's home?"

"Emporia in Southside Virginia on the North Carolina Line, Mr. Brinkley," I said.

"Just call me David, John." Brinkley insisted people use his first name. "I'm from Wilmington, North Carolina."

"I know," I replied. "If it helps, I was born in North Carolina."

Brinkley laughed. "It does," he said, and added, "I look forward to working with you." Our brief conversation was the first entry in my Journal, which Mother had suggested I start keeping after winning the internship.

I asked George one evening if it would be possible for me to sit in the studio while Brinkley was on the air with his half of *The Huntley-Brinkley Report*. I was given a chair by one of the floor crew just off the set in Studio "A," which consisted of a high gray draftsman's desk and a black background. The desk was custom fitted with a shelf hidden from the camera that held an ash tray with a built-in fan that dissipated tell-tale cigarette smoke. I had heard that Brinkley had made the desk himself. He was an expert woodworker and cabinet maker. He was also regarded as the best writer in the business.

He gave me a nod when he walked into the studio, maybe five minutes before air, with several assistants trailing. There was always an open line between him and Huntley so they could see one another on monitors. When a film piece or a commercial was running, he and Huntley would often chat. Seeing Huntley nursing a cup of coffee,

Brinkley remarked, " Chet, you need to stop drinking that stuff; it's bad for your kidneys."

Huntley replied, "It's not my kidneys that I'm worried about David." Huntley was a heavy smoker.

The Huntley-Brinkley Report wasn't simply two anchors alternating stories or sentences as the ubiquitous male-female pairings do today on local TV. Each had specific things they did. Brinkley, who wrote his own copy, only covered Washington News. Huntley covered everything else and handled most of the intros to field reports so Huntley had the most camera time. Even so, Brinkley's commanding presence led many to believe that he and Huntley split the half hour 50/50.

There was a second feed of the program for the West Coast. When that ended, with the famous sign off "Good Night Chet, Good Night David and Good Night From NBC News," which both of them hated, Brinkley started to gather his script, then glanced in my direction.

"Where's your interest?" he asked. I said that all of my experience was in radio but TV seemed very exciting. "It can be," he said. "But once the thrill of being recognized wears thin, you find you have no privacy. I can't even go to the hardware store and buy a bag of nails without it becoming a media event," he complained.

An assistant had come in with papers. Brinkley headed toward the studio door asking in passing if I had a class that night. I said I was working. He stopped, reached in his pocket and peeled off the first of many 20 dollar bills he would give me.

"Don't forget to eat," he said. Twenty bucks went a long way in 1968 Washington. I recounted our give and take in my Journal that night at the apartment.

Brinkley was filled with wonderful anecdotes. My favorite was about the woman in a big flowery hat who ran up to him at Washington's National Airport shortly after he had gotten off the Eastern Airlines Shuttle from New York.

"Are you Chet Huntley?" she asked with a determined look on her face.

Brinkley said he started to say no but hesitated, thinking that she would be embarrassed and follow with profuse apologies, and he was in a hurry, So he just said, "Yes Ma'am, I'm Chet Huntley. "She quickly smiled and said, "I'm delighted to meet you Mr. Huntley, but I can't stand that damn communist David Brinkley!"

Years later, two of us from WRVA were attending an ABC Network meeting at the ABC Headquarters in Washington when we ran into Brinkley in an elevator. He was then doing *This Week With David Brinkley* on Sundays. I thanked him for putting up with me at NBC all those years ago, dispensing the wise advice and for all the twenty dollar bills he had pressed in my hand to help me with school.

"It was my pleasure," he said. Then, eyeing my ID Badge which read "John Harding, Operations Manager and News Director, WRVA Richmond, Virginia," he said, "That's a fine station. You've done very well for yourself. Congratulations and Good Luck!"

XI

I had set hours at NBC three days a week, but I often came in after classes when I wasn't working. I didn't want to miss anything. That was the case in early April when Doctor Martin Luther King Junior was assassinated. I was sitting at the news desk when the call came in from Memphis just after 7 that evening that King had died in the hospital.

As word of the assassination spread throughout Washington, crowds started gathering downtown. Soon there was trouble. Riots broke out along "U" Street. Bob Goralski, who normally covered the Pentagon, was preparing to go downtown with a camera crew. I begged George to let me go along with them, but he said "No, it's just too dangerous."

There was nothing for me to do; but I couldn't leave. Like news people everywhere, I had a terminal case of needing to be wherever the action was, an obsession to do something when something happened.

Later, when I saw the initial film frames from downtown, I understood why George had kept me in the bureau. Downtown DC had the look of a war zone. Goralski, who had been a combat reporter in Vietnam, said it was like being caught in a firefight. Businesses were firebombed, houses were ablaze, scores of people had died. Many had burned to death in their homes. Federal troops would soon move in to restore order.

My first spot news assignment had me shadowing Max Robinson, a tall, young, outgoing and erudite black man, with an easy going, cool manner. Max was a Richmond native. He and Paul Duke, who was also from Richmond, were probably the only two people at NBC who had ever heard of Emporia.

I went along with Max to cover a large civil rights protest in West Potomac Park. Located just below the Lincoln Memorial between the Reflecting Pool and Independence Avenue, it was one of the most picturesque spots in Washington. Protestors who were part of the "Poor Peoples Campaign for Economic Justice for the Poor in America" had chosen it as the perfect site to erect their tents and shacks. Their encampment had been dubbed "Resurrection City." From the looks of many of the protestors, they might have been homeless had they not taken up residence in the camp, which many days of rain had turned into a sea of mud and trash.

I spent several days there in a tent with Max noting the goings and comings of major political and civil rights figures, many of whom arrived like potentates in shiny, black limos wearing tailor made suits. The disconnect with the protesters in the mud was startling. After a week or two, violence flared and began to spread out of the Park onto Independence Avenue. Police moved in and cleared the area.

Max went on to co-anchor the ABC Evening News and became a pioneer for black journalists in broadcast news. He died in 1988.

Elie Able had been recruited by NBC as its State Department Correspondent in 1961 from the Detroit News where he was the newspaper's Washington Bureau Chief. He had had a long and distinguished career with *The New York Times*. As the Times' Bureau Chief in Belgrade, he had contributed to the paper's Pulitzer Prize winning coverage of the Hungarian Revolt of 1956 and had served as the Times' Bureau Chief in India. Working out of New Delhi, he covered the Chinese takeover of Tibet in 1959.

Cheeley introduced me to him one Friday morning and told me to wear a suit and a tie the following Monday. I was to follow Able around Foggy Bottom, the old Washington neighborhood West of downtown that was home to the State Department. I had one suit. Appropriately, it was a dark pin stripe from "Bloom Brothers," in Emporia.

Tall and distinguished looking, Able himself was the very picture of a diplomat. I was always inclined to call him "Mr. Able." His formal nature and demeanor seemed to command it, though, like Brinkley, Able insisted I use his first name. I did, but I wasn't comfortable with it. I suppose it was the Southerner in me.

Watching him as he worked his contacts and picked through his notes, while delicately crafting a nuanced piece for air, was like observing a master watchmaker. Able carefully explained the need for subtlety in diplomatic reporting, or as he put it, "the careful shading of words," making the point that everything can turn on one badly chosen phrase.

Over the next 33 years, I would often find myself using one of Able's trademark phrases in a script. It was always a privilege to be in his company. Elie was the recipient of the "George Foster Peabody Award for Outstanding Radio News" that year (1968). He left NBC in 1970 to become Dean of the Columbia University Graduate School of Journalism.

Robert McCormick was one of the broadcast news pioneers at NBC. He had joined the network in 1942 and became NBC's Central Pacific Correspondent during World War II, followed by stints as Washington Bureau Chief and then on to Paris and Germany before coming back to Washington in 1955.

In addition to covering the Congressional beat, McCormick originated the noon hourly newscast on NBC Radio from the Senate Radio Gallery. He did not write a script as such but scribbled a few notes while reading the wires and the papers. The news desk would phone him with the taped inserts he would have in his newscast, the run time on each clip, and the out cues. Duly noted, McCormick would then ad lib the entire newscast looking only at the clock on the wall, signing off with his signature lockout, "Rrrrrrrobert McCormick, NBC News at the Capitol." It was amazing to watch

Most of the NBC Radio Network's hourly newscasts in the morning originated from a small radio booth just off the newsroom. Chief among them was Russ Ward's *World News Roundup,* a 15 minute newscast that went on the radio network at 7AM.

Russ would arrive around 5 AM to begin putting the broadcast together. Watching as Russ and his producer and editor rushed to get the last possible update in before deadline was exciting to me. At WRVA I would come to thrive on deadlines, doing my best work as air time approached.

After the newscast, Ward would usually head down to Capitol Hill to cover some hearing or a vote that was coming up that morning. I was often allowed to go along with him. Russ was almost strictly radio with NBC so I identified with him more than I did the other correspondents who were primarily concerned with television.

Russ left NBC News in the 80's when NBC sold the radio network to Westwood One in Los Angeles. He retired to his sailboat and bought a marina on the Chesapeake Bay.

The WRC TV Newsroom was just across a divide from the network newsroom so many of the Channel 4 people became familiar faces and made time for me, Neil Boggs in particular. Boggs, a soft spoken man with not a trace of ego, was a workhorse at NBC. Boggs was a network correspondent and anchored many of the evening hourly newscasts on NBC Radio. He also co-anchored the 11 PM newscast on WRC TV with Glen Rinker and was also Moderator for Meet The Press for a time. Neil was among those who stepped up to write recommendations for me at the end of my stint at NBC.

XII

I hadn't been as excited since Dee Warren said she would go to the prom with me. George was sending me to the White House for a Presidential News Conference. I was to shadow NBC's White House Correspondent Ray Scherer. I grabbed a cab to the West Wing Security Gate to begin the security clearance procedures. It went quickly. I was already in the system, having undergone a security clearance to work at the Defense Contractor on Wisconsin Avenue.

Armed with my Photo ID, I walked up the driveway everyone has seen on television. Scherer was waiting at the door. He had covered every President since

Harry Truman. In 1956, he became the first reporter to broadcast live from the floor of a Presidential Nominating Convention and among the first to broadcast live from the White House.

We went back to Scherer's "cubbyhole," as he called it, in the White House Press Room. The air was electric as correspondents received instructions from their respective news desks. Most of the TV crews were busy setting up for live shots of "scene setters" from correspondents who would preview the upcoming Presidential News Conference. After Ray wrapped up his live, unscripted preview of what was likely to come, it was time to head for the East Room of the White House, where President Johnson would meet reporters.

Lyndon Johnson was a big man and tilted the room when he walked in. Whatever it was he had, he had a lot of it. He made a short statement and then began taking questions beginning, according to custom, with the Associated Press White House Reporter. Most of the questions were about Vietnam and the upcoming Presidential Primaries. The rest has been blurred by time but I do remember picking the same lead as Ray.

President Johnson shocked the nation that March with his announcement that he would not seek another term as President. By sheer luck, I was standing in the NBC Control room watching Edwin Newman as he anchored the Presidential Address. There was stunned silence when Johnson dropped his bombshell. It was a complete and total surprise. Suddenly, the way seemed clear for Senators Robert F. Kennedy and Eugene McCarthy, both of whom had mounted formidable opposition to Johnson's re-nomination.

The wide-open presidential race dominated the Republican Governor's Conference, which was meeting in Washington that spring. George had assigned me to tag along with Carl Stern and a camera crew. We were bird dogging Nelson Rockefeller, the Governor of New York.

Rockefeller was in the running for the GOP nomination but he was behind in the polls, and when he saw us in the Lobby of the Washington Hilton Hotel, he ducked into the men's room. When we got to the restroom door, we all looked at Carl.

Carl had joined NBC the previous year. A licensed attorney, he covered the Supreme Court for the network but on this day, politics had called.

"Lights up guys," he ordered, "we're going in." With high intensity lights blazing and the camera rolling, we barged in and caught the Governor of New York, in all his glory, standing at the urinal. Exasperated, Rockefeller said something akin to "Holy Christ Fellas, a guy can't even go to the bathroom in peace," whereupon he flushed the toilet.

The clip made *The Huntley-Brinkley Report* that night. David Brinkley made a quip about Nelson Rockefeller's Presidential Campaign being in trouble. And, of course, then came the sound of Rockefeller flushing the toilet.

My internship was done in mid-May, and my focus turned to finding a full-time job. NBC's Editors knew a lot about where the really good local news shops were, so my list of prospective employers was largely based on their suggestions. All were television stations. I had probably aimed too high. Most never replied to my queries. I decided that if I were ever in a position to hire people, I would respond to every person who applied.

A few politely informed me they had no openings. The only promising response I received was from WRVA TV in Richmond. Bob Griggs, the Program Director, wrote and requested that I come down for an interview; but when I met with him, Griggs had nothing to offer me other than a strong suggestion that I drive up to Church Hill to WRVA Radio.

At WAMU American Univertsity Washington 1967.
Brad Huffman Photo

Sitting on David Brinkley's Desk.
The Huntley Brinkley Report NBC News 1968

Father, Mother, Aunt Louise, June and I. Christmas 1960's.

Joe Weeks. News Director WRVA 1969

Election Coverage. John Marshall Hotel Richmond. November 1969

Part IV

WRVA Richmond, VA

The Larus Years

I

WRVA Radio shared the same call letters with WRVA TV and for years both been wholly owned by Larus & Brother Company. By 1968, Larus was beginning to unwind its holdings, but it still owned a piece of the TV station. By design, both stations had been operated separately with no overlap of personnel. That spring, WRVA Radio had completed its move from the Hotel Richmond to a brand new, ultra-modern studio building on the brow of historic Church Hill, which overlooked the city.

Joe Weeks was the News Director. Pencil thin, brittle and gruff as a troll, he gave a quick glance at my resume and grimaced when I volunteered that Bob Griggs at WRVA TV had referred me. Joe had no love for the sister TV station.

"Got time for an audition?" he barked. I did. I was given a small portable tape recorder, a microphone and a "Reporter's Notebook" and told to go down to the Virginia State Capitol where the Student Model General Assembly was meeting. The Student Governor was to address the Model Assembly and Weeks wanted me to file a piece on it. "Not a second over a minute," he demanded. Afterwards, I was to go to the State Capitol Press Room, where someone from WRVA would help me feed my story back to the station, after which I was to report back to Weeks. He wanted my piece in house by noon. It was my first working audition, and I found that to be to my advantage. There was no time to be nervous.

When I walked into Weeks' office, he gave me a nod and said, "Go see Aaroe." Alden Aaroe was the Program

Manager and Weeks' Supervisor. He said he wanted to check my references and talk more with Weeks and my parents but added that he thought I had a pretty good lock on the position. "I'll call you the first of the week in Emporia," he said.

Mother was pretty excited when I gave her my news, Father even more so after Alden called and told me I had the job. I think, for the first time, my father was finally sold on the fact that I could make a living in radio.

I was back in Washington June 9th for my graduation. My parents drove up for the ceremony, but they got lost. My father, who hated Washington with a passion, transposed his aversion to the city into a refusal to look at a map. They were supposed to meet me at the apartment in Arlington, but somehow they had crossed the Potomac and wound up in the District at the Lincoln Memorial, where he called me from a pay phone.

I drove across the Memorial Bridge and saw the familiar white Chevrolet parked on Independence Avenue. They followed me up to Massachusetts Avenue and the Jewish Community Center, which had been selected as the rain venue for the ceremonies. It was pouring. We made our way inside and I showed them to their seats, then, went to sit with my class.

No diplomas were handed out. We just walked up on stage and shook hands with the President of the University and the Dean when our names were called. Diplomas had been mailed to our homes. Mother had mine framed, museum mounted in fact, by the time I got back to Emporia. She was as proud of it as I was.

Toward the end of June, after I had started working, a letter from the Dean's Office at American arrived in Emporia. I had made the Dean's List for the Spring Semester. I had graduated on a high note. Mother said it was sweet revenge for my having flunked the 10th grade in high school.

Alden Aaroe sent me a list of possible apartment locations to check out. At the top of his list was River Towers Apartments on the south bank of the James River near the Robert E. Lee Bridge. It was an impressive address. I liked it right away, but the only apartment within my slim window of affordability was a small efficiency.

A visit to a "scratch and dent" store netted the bare necessities, including an ugly green sofa bed with a strategically placed steel bar which served to rearrange my lower back. I also had a small black and white TV my parents had given me for graduation. After the cold water flat in Falls Church, it was the Ritz.

II

WRVA was actually two stations, WRVA and a sister FM. The AM station was a 50,000 watt station at 1140 on the dial. WRVA FM duplicated WRVA AM most of the broadcast day. Both had monster signals, the AM station in particular. My sister "BB" would later listen to my 8AM Newscast on her counter-top kitchen radio in Chicago.

I was as intimidated by the WRVA Building on Church Hill as I had been with NBC's Headquarters in Washington. Designed by legendary architect Philip Johnson, the single story cast concrete building with a full basement had very large punched windows with a concrete tower behind it that replicated the building as though it were turned on its end. It was an ultra-modern temple to radio.

The lobby ran from the glassed front with two glass doors to the glassed back wall with double glass doors leading to the back lawn. It afforded an extraordinary, unobstructed view of the city below and beyond. The WRVA News Studio and all of the Air Studios were located across the back of the building. Each had a large, floor to ceiling window that overlooked the city. At night, the scene was breathtaking. The contrast with the neighborhood was dramatic.

Church Hill was the oldest section of Richmond. St. John's Church where Patrick Henry had delivered his famous "Give Me Liberty or Give Me Death" speech was only a few blocks away; but by the mid twentieth century, the once prominent neighborhood had descended into poverty becoming a virtual "No Man's Land" of slums and crime. Over the next 30 years, the WRVA Building would serve as a catalyst for the restoration of much of the area.

The station was owned by the Larus & Brother Company. Two old Richmond families controlled the company, which dated back to 1877. It had put WRVA on the air in 1925 and initially ran it commercial free as a service to the city.

I would later meet several of the senior family members at a fund raiser for American University at one of their homes in the genteel Windsor Farms neighborhood, one of Richmond's gilded zip codes. They were very polite, but there was a reserved formality about them like that of old film stars. They always referred to WRVA as "Tha Station."

I gave my name to the receptionist and told her I needed to see Mr. Aaroe. "We've been expecting you Mr. Harding," smiled Virginia Jordan, a very attractive lady who had an elegant air. "I'm certain you will love it here."

No sooner had I thanked her than Alden was shaking my hand, saying "Let's go meet the boss."

John Tansey had been a boxer in the Navy and he looked the part. He had come up through the ranks as a reporter before going into management becoming the Vice President and General Manager of the station in the mid 50's. It was said that no one was hired in News at WRVA without his expressed approval.

He said he was delighted I was joining the station and that I had come very highly recommended. I thanked him, said I was thrilled WRVA would have me and that I would do my best to live up to expectations. I would be paid the princely sum of 106 dollars a week. Journalism was not where the money was.

III

If there was anyone who epitomized WRVA Radio, it was Alden Aaroe. A large man who wore glasses, his size was more than eclipsed by his personality. His title at WRVA when I arrived in June of 1968 was Vice President and Program Manager, which in those days included supervision of the News Department. He was also the patron saint of Richmond Radio. For hundreds of thousands of Richmonders and untold numbers of devoted listeners across Virginia and beyond, Alden was the first thing they heard in the morning. "Did you Aaroe this morning..." was a WRVA jingle in those days. Most everyone in Richmond did.

Alden P. Aaroe, the "P" was for Petersen, was born in Washington, DC, in 1918. His father, George Aaroe, was stationed in the city with what would become the Army Air Corps. Alden's mother Anna had a job as a secretary in the government. They divorced after the war, and Alden grew up on his maternal grandparents' dairy farm in New Jersey. His mother commuted home on weekends from her job as a school teacher in the Jersey suburbs of New York.

After graduation from high school, Alden enrolled at the University of Virginia where he majored in economics. The money ran out during his senior year so he left school and went to work for a Charlottesville radio station, WCHV.

After Pearl Harbor, he joined the Army Air Corps and spent the war "flying milk runs out of Iran and the Azores," as he would tell it later. After the war, he got a job at WRVA in 1946 as a staff announcer. When John Tansey became General Manager of the station in 1956, he made Aaroe WRVA's voice of the morning.

Almost immediately, Aaroe in the morning became the gathering place for Richmond. There was an easy familiarity about Alden. Farmers, sportsmen, teachers, stock traders, car dealers, bankers, attorneys, housewives, and tradesmen all claimed him as one of their own. Alden was WRVA's everyman.

To listen today to recordings of his program over the decades (the word "show" somehow seems inappropriate) is to marvel at the absence of platitudes, bromides, half-baked thoughts, mindless slogans and the other consultant customized nonsense that corrupts the airwaves today.

Hearing him now is a reminder of all that radio has lost. Alden was almost poetic, lyrical when he described his tomatoes, his travels and misadventures. Even later, when sparring with "Millard The Mallard," there was a subtle sophistication about him that was both charming and, at the same time, endearing. By the early 60's, he had already become something of a legend in Richmond Radio.

Thanks to WRVA's 50,000 watt night time sky wave which reached the Caribbean, South Africa, Western Europe, Chicago, the Northwestern United States and the Canadian provinces, as well as much of Virginia, Lou Dean was probably WRVA's most widely known personality.

A native of Chicago, Lou came to Virginia in 1956 after a hitch in the military. Following a short stay at WEAM in Arlington, Lou joined WRVA in 1957 and succeeded Frank Brooks as host of the all night *Music Till Morning* program.

Lou's signature theme song, "Devotion," by Otto Cesana with its distinctive three chimes followed by the swell of a full orchestra, would begin five hours of overnight pop music, show tunes and chats about everything from Lou's camping adventures across the country to Japanese pancakes.

Lou quickly became Richmond's Ambassador-At-Large, spreading the richness of the city across the continent and beyond. Hopping a cab in Hamilton, Bermuda, late one summer night in 1974, I was surprised to hear WRVA blaring on a small transistor radio hanging from the cab's rear view mirror. "Oh, yes mon," the Jamaican cabbie said, "Lou Dean, W R V A, listen every night." Lou's precise, crystal clear voice seemed to be tailor made for night listening, cutting through the darkness like a laser from his studio on Church Hill.

When his all night show ended in the 70's, Lou embarked on a second career at WRVA on talk shows, as Program Director, Community Services Director, and as host of the long running *Newsroom* Program. In 1994, he was recognized by the Virginia General Assembly for his long service to the community.

IV

Every week, one of the Larus tractor trailer trucks would pull up in front of the studio building to unload free samples of the Company's cigarettes and pipe tobacco. Each employee received two cartons a week of either "King Santo," "Domino," "Half and Half" (half pipe tobacco), a menthol brand "Yukon," or two tins of "Edgeworth" pipe tobacco. I can't speak to the pipe tobacco, but the cigarettes were horrible.

The manager of a Semmes Avenue convenience store near my apartment had told me of his fondness for "Domino" cigarettes. There's no accounting for taste. We had a standing deal: one carton of "Salem" for two cartons of "Domino's." I considered it a fair trade. Word of my weekly transaction somehow got back to Miss Bertha Hewlett, in the business office, who was not pleased at my "disloyalty."

Miss Bertha, who never married, was a sort of WRVA Godmother. She was there at the station's beginning, bringing table lamps from her home to help light the studio when WRVA went on the air in 1925. She was nearing retirement when I arrived and spent her days in the business office, where among other things, she gave pedantic attention to dispensing office supplies from a small, toy-like, grocery cart that she pushed around the building. When I would ask for a replacement "Reporter's Notebook," Miss Bertha would insist on seeing the old one to make sure all of the pages had been used. She seemed a bit out of place in the new modern building. So did Harry.

Harry Wood was among the initial programming personalities I met when I started at WRVA. I had been put on the evening anchor shift one night a week for four hours to cover for the regular anchor, who always had a night off every week to stay home with his children while his wife went to choir practice. Sounds quaint, but such were the criteria taken into consideration when weekly work schedules were made out in those days. Young singles, such as I, were given short shrift. I'd work four hours one night, then four hours the next day, then 8 hour days for the next 4 days, which totaled a six-day work week with no overtime.

Harry's deep, soothing voice tranquilized Richmond's high-brow set during two evening semi-classical music programs, *Music Room* followed by *Gaslight*. The nightly musical seduction was almost atmospheric. Harry's calming, reassuring tones coupled with the symphonic strains was like some kind of palliative mist wafting through the Richmond twilight.

A thin, gentle, soft spoken man who wore glasses, Harry was polite almost to a fault. His only vice was a fondness for the spirits. One evening, Harold, the always stressed out Production Manager, rushed into the newsroom in a frenzy and shoved an LP at me. "Mr. Harding, put this on the air when the network news ends at 7:05," he ordered. Harry had been a no show for *The Music Room.*

Twenty minutes and a few commercial breaks later, a well lubricated Harry was dragged into the studio and propped in the chair at the control console. When the red "On Air" light popped on, Harry miraculously perked up and, in his best pear shaped, dulcet, Northeast commercial tones, bellowed, "Hello Richmond, this is Harry Wood! Welcome to *The Music Room.*"

V

The aforementioned Harold (not to be confused with "Harry") was the ever present Harold Phillips. Easily spotted by his beet red face and permanent stub of a cigar planted in the corner of his mouth, Harold was WRVA's Production Manager extraordinaire, self-appointed protector of the King's English, Godfather of pronunciation, minder of talent, proctor of WRVA's torturous announcer's audition and frequent sparring partner for Joe Weeks.

Harold never seemed to go home. He was always around, busying himself to the point of nervous exhaustion reminding all within earshot that "you are announcers, not disc jockeys." He was constantly in the newsroom lying in wait for anyone who dared to pronounce "News" as "Nooze" or "strength" as "strinth." Even when minding his grandchildren he was at the station, corralling the kids in the spacious Studio A with their toys while he went about the never-ending task of speech cleaning and punctuality preaching.

In the early evenings, Harold could be found in one of the studios previewing the night's scheduled episodes of the recorded religious programs, chief among them Garner Ted Armstrong's *The World Tomorrow*. Harold would sit for hours meticulously splicing out "unsavory" words and editing for time. "WRVA has standards, G** damn it," he growled. He was mortified to learn one Friday night that the station had been running the same *The World Tomorrow* program every night for a week. The Garner Ted people had forgotten to mail current episodes. There was no harm. No one had noticed until Harold saw the date on one of the tape cans.

Because he was always around, Harold was witness to most of the legendary pranks that were played out during the "Larus years" of WRVA; and he often found himself as the target.

Howard Bloom, Traffic Reporter, Anchor, fire chaser and incurable prankster, had spied Harold indisposed one evening with pants down in one of the men's restroom stalls. Bloom rushed back to the equipment room with its racks and racks of audio processing gear and switched off the building's monitor speakers. Harold, believing the station had gone off the air, hauled himself from the throne, catching a pants pocket on the stall door mechanism, ripping them to his shoes, then went barreling down the hall with trouser leg flapping when suddenly the speakers came back on and Howard walked out of the equipment room with a big grin on his face. Harold, knowing he had been "had," spewed some very un-Christian invectives and vowed to send Howard the bill for his ripped trousers.

Lou Dean recalls another Bloom Classic - "It's midnight. Harold is still working at that hour, as usual. NBC News is on the air prior to my show going on at 12:15 AM. Then, over the NBC News, Harold hears Howard and me talking and telling dirty jokes. Absolutely convinced that we accidentally left the microphone on while the network news was on the air, Harold comes flying out of his cubicle, and dashes down the hall to the on-air studio, flings open the door and sees...... nothing! Howard had patched the other studio into the building monitor circuit. The on-air news was as pristine as ever."

Pranks notwithstanding, Harold was relentless in his never- ending crusade for perfection on the air. His legacy endures. To this day, whenever I hear someone on the air mispronounce the contraction "didn't" as "did dent" or, God forbid "Nooze" instead of "News," I think of Harold, defender emeritus of the King's English.

VI

Walt Smith had the title of Operations Manager in those days but the position did not have the same cachet as it would 20 years later when I would be given the same title. Smith's job seemed to be more along the lines of an efficiency expert. He constantly bombarded the staff with official memos covering everything from parking to trashcans.

He had incurred the wrath of Weeks over trash cans. Smith had large, tall, rectangular metal trash cans placed at both ends of the main editor's desk in the newsroom. Because the cans were the exact same height as the desktop, one supposes Smith reasoned they would be more efficient to use. In reality, they were constantly being hit and toppling over. Dozens of times a day, the ear jarring clang of the metal trashcan hitting the floor would startle everyone in the newsroom, even penetrating the supposedly soundproof news air booth.

Weeks was not pleased. He and Smith went nose to nose in the newsroom yelling at each other like a baseball manager getting in the face of an umpire. Weeks had his way, sort of. The metal cans were replaced with plastic versions. They still tipped over but there was no clang.

Smith's memos wallpapered the bulletin board in the downstairs snack room with detailed regulations, procedures and instructions for everything imaginable. There were loud groans when the following memo was posted in late June of 1968:

To: The Staff

From: Walt Smith

Subject: Restroom Procedure

Because of our large staff, and the limited facilities in our WRVA Rest Rooms, effective this date, the following procedures will be instituted.

Those who work in the rear half of the building will use the downstairs restrooms, and those who work in the front half of the building will use the upstairs restrooms, with the following exceptions: Those who work in the basement will use the upstairs rest rooms between 9 and 10AM, and the downstairs rest rooms between 3 and 4 PM. At all other times, these assignments will be reversed.

In order to make maximum use of the existing spaces, check in and out on the sheet provided, so that it will be known how many spaces are available at all times. Should anyone wish to make reservations, application forms are available in the Operations Department, and should be turned in to the Operations Manager no less than three hours before intended use.

If there are any questions about this matter, see me.

It was signed Walt Smith.

It was a prank of course but that so many staffers took it seriously is testament to the climate that existed at the time. Shortly after the memo came out, I spied one of the older members of the business office staff walking by the upstairs men's room heading for the stairs to the basement with memo in hand. He was precisely following the instructions in the memo.

The repercussions were immediate. John Tansey ordered all copies of the bogus memo confiscated and destroyed and all but promised a public execution of those responsible. Many of us had a good idea who had posted it but the powers that be never found out. Smith later left the station.

Tom Parker's job description was "Porter," a sort of hybrid messenger, mail clerk, janitor and "go'for." In today's world, Tom might very well be an air personality.

A middle aged black man with the sunniest of dispositions, Tom kept the place spic and span, got the mail twice a day, ran errands, tipped us off when the suits were in the building, and served up the booze after election night broadcasts all the while dispensing front porch wisdom. "Always keep your pencil sharp and cut a lot of grass," he counseled. Translation: Raise a lot of hell "so you'll have something to reminisce about when you're old." We all tried our best to follow his sage advice.

Tom, I recall, worked two jobs. When he finished up at WRVA, he was a driver for executives at Reynolds Metals Company in Richmond. When he died, Alden and I were among dozens from WRVA who attended his funeral.

VII

A month after I arrived at WRVA, the station sent Harvey Powers and me to Roanoke to cover the State Democratic Convention for three days. It was my first assignment on the road out of town, and I was on edge about it; but once we got a handle on the factions at work and identified the power brokers, I had confidence in what we were doing.

The Byrd Organization, which had dominated Virginia politics since the 1920's had begun to crack in the mid 1960's and by 1968, moderate and liberal factions of the party seized control. The upheaval opened the door for Virginia Republicans, who would prevail a year later in the 1969 contest for Governor.

Upon our return, John Tansey sent us both a memo, saying our "reporting conveyed very well the competition, color and uncertainty of the convention." It was my first

"Tanseygram." I felt as though I had passed my first big test in the field. Harvey later went into the Army and would go on to a distinguished career at Channel 12 in Richmond.

My first assignment from the network came late that first summer in Richmond, interviewing University of Virginia Professor Ian Stevenson for an upcoming NBC News Documentary. Stevenson was the Founder and Director of the UVA Division of Perceptual Studies, which investigates the paranormal. The NBC Documentary *Man and Himself* would be an in-depth look into reincarnation, the idea that emotions, memories and even physical injuries in the form of birth marks, can be transferred from one life to another. Stevenson was internationally known for his research into the subject.

It was pretty deep stuff, and I knew little about it. I went to the Richmond Library and checked out several books that Stevenson had written and took copious notes. The Producer Harry Mantel, who worked out of WMAQ, the NBC Owned station in Chicago, called the week of the interview to remind me that Stevenson was very sensitive about criticism of his work. "Be delicate," he said, "We need him."

I interviewed Stevenson in his office on the UVA campus in Charlottesville. Tentative and a bit suspicious at first, Stevenson seemed to warm to me when he became convinced I had done my homework. Most of the interview made the program.

NBC Second Sunday; Man and Himself aired on the NBC Radio Network late that summer. It was my first assignment for the NBC Documentary Unit. I would get several more assignments before, sadly, NBC pulled the plug on the Peabody Award winning series.

VIII

Joe Weeks, the news director, was a self-described "Retired Catholic." He had come over to WRVA from WRVA TV. "They went out of the news business," he grumbled.

Weeks was a journalism war horse. He had earned his stripes in print: *United Press* in Europe during the war and a string of big city daily newspapers, including *The Detroit Free Press,* where he said he was fired for writing the headline, "There's No Hope We're All Going To Die" for a page one, above the fold story about a prolonged summer heat wave that was cooking the Motor City.

A skeptic straight out of the H.L. Mencken mold, Weeks' 8AM broadcast of biting, sarcastic commentary with a side order of news was, in newspaper jargon, a "ripper," a story so compelling the reader rips it out of the paper. In broadcast terms, Weeks daily requiem for the state of the commonwealth was a "must listen" for any official or politician or would-be politician in Virginia, if for no other reason than self-defense.

His daily ritual began precisely at 5AM. The heavy oak, soundproof, door to the newsroom crashed open with a kick, and Weeks scurried in carrying a large cup of coffee with plastic lid, a runny egg sandwich wrapped in wax paper, and the morning papers tucked under his arm. His pockets bulged with notes scribbled on small scraps of paper, the result of his working the phones the night before.

He precisely arranged each scrap of paper across the top of his desk, then smashed his adjustable, spring loaded desk lamp down on the plastic lid of the coffee to keep it hot, which of course melted the thin plastic into the coffee. He'd pack his pipe with Edgeworth Pipe Tobacco, light it with his pipe lighter, which had a blue flame like a blowtorch, puff enough white, billowing smoke to choose a Pope and say to no one in particular, "How the hell are ya!" Then he'd address his antique, open frame, Underwood typewriter.

The engineers had rigged a roll of two carbon teletype paper under the typewriter stand so Weeks would not have to bother with inserting individual sheets of paper. He'd take a slurp of coffee, bitch about it tasting like plastic, have a bite of his runny egg sandwich, most of which dripped onto his permanently stained, paisley print necktie, and start pounding out copy for his broadcast. He was the embodiment of *The Front Page.*

I was often assigned to the same early morning anchor shift. Joe handled the two major news strips at 7 and 8 AM which ran for 10 and 15 minutes each, respectively. I did the others. All were five minute strips, but the major and minor commercial positions reduced the news window to three and a half minutes. It demanded tight writing to keep the story count up, which was always the order of the day.

Weeks was wise to my brevity, and when he would come up short on his own strips, he'd boom out of the studio in a panic and help himself to my copy to use as filler, which of course left me short. Tired of his thievery, one morning I moved my finished script to the floor beside me and put some national wire copy I had rewritten on the side of the desk. Weeks barged in, grabbed it and ran back to the studio.

A few minutes later he exploded into the newsroom yelling about me "sticking him" with national copy! "I didn't stick you with anything Joe, you just took it," I replied.

I thought he was going to throw his typewriter at me, but he just said, "Right," went back to his desk and lit his pipe. It didn't cure him of the habit, but he did start asking. Knowing Joe, I considered that in itself a large victory.

Weeks had come to Richmond in 1962 from WQMR in Washington. He had previously worked in Indianapolis where he said he was all but run out of town. Joe had written a novel, *All My Yesterdays*. Like most writers first books, it was autobiographical.

Weeks was always on, juiced every morning with his usual bracer: a headache powder in a bottle of cola filled with salted peanuts, shaken, not stirred. He swore like a sailor, soaked up "Old Fashions" like a sponge and drove like a maniac. He had torn the engine from its mounts in one of the WRVA news cars while gunning it up the steep hill beside the Monte Maria Convent on Church Hill.

He was prone to vicious tirades with inanimate objects. His antique, open frame typewriter was a frequent target. It misspelled words! So was his car. I had once come across him beating the hell out of it with an umbrella one afternoon on Monument Avenue. It had run out of gas.

Joe's ongoing refrain was that journalism was not aggressive enough. He prowled the newsroom like a panther, constantly haranguing us to "come up with something," to look for the real story after getting the official version, which he always dismissed as nothing but spin.

He was like a hawk spying a field mouse as he went about uncovering buried leads and "history lessons." "This isn't TEE VEE," he would rail, "You don't sit on the lead until your face is on camera."

He ranted daily about us being clerks and stenographers practicing recycled journalism." Or, another favorite, "You're all just being spoon fed by PR flacks," as he called Public Relations people.

Most of us would walk through fire to bring back a story to him, and if we managed to kick somebody's ass, or take a pompous CEO, bureaucrat or politician down a notch in the process, he loved us.

At home, he was a lamb in the care of his extraordinary wife Mid. A lovely woman with twinkling eyes, she doted on Joe as though he was a fragile prince. Dinner at their home was always an adventure, with Joe supplying the war stories as Mid tweaked the atmosphere with perfectly prepared "Old Fashions" with the precise dash of bitters.

IX

Joe seemed to have sources in every nook and cranny of Richmond and Capitol Square, and he worked them like a beat cop, constantly on the phone, making the rounds at the State Capitol or holding court at his table at the Raleigh Grill in the Raleigh Hotel across from Capitol

Square. Weeks was a human depository of political rumor, intrigue, gossip, and scandal. I supposed he knew far more than even his rather loose interpretation of required sourcing would allow him to put on the air.

He took great pleasure in needling the powerful players at city hall, the Virginia General Assembly, and throughout state government · none more so than Richmond State Senator Edward E. Willey. Many believed Willey and the Speaker of the House, John Warren Cooke and later A.L. Philpott, were the most powerful men in Virginia. It was said Willey and Philpott let the governor occupy the Executive Mansion, and they did the rest.

Willey was the Senate Majority Leader and also Chairman of the powerful Senate Finance Committee. He and Weeks were almost constantly at loggerheads, often over legislation which involved the health insurance giant Blue Cross and Blue Shield of Virginia. Weeks called the company's ornate headquarters building in Richmond the "Taj Mahal."

He also had an on-air handle for the Virginia State Penitentiary. He called it "Peyton's Place," a twist on the Superintendent's name, C.C. Peyton, and the prime time soap opera *Peyton Place,* which was then running on ABC Television.

The prison, which was torn down in 1991, was then located on Spring Street in Richmond. The most violent criminals in Virginia were housed in a dungeon-like basement cell block below the prison building. Death Row was also located at the prison, along with the state's electric chair. Weeks never let a prison story pass. Everything from lawsuits to executions was grist for his broadcasts. Not surprisingly, he and Peyton had a long-running feud.

Peyton's wrath was on full display at a news conference following an inmate demonstration in the prison yard. Located out of public view behind the tall concrete prison walls, Weeks had asked for a reporter to be admitted to the yard. The answer was a predictable "No!" Joe then ordered the WRVA Traffic Helicopter into the air to hover over the prison yard to report on what was going on. Peyton was livid.

Most of us were used to being dressed down by officials like Peyton because of Joe's commentaries. I resented it at first but later came to view it as a combat medal. Weeks, of course, loved it.

Then Governor Mills Godwin always held his own with Joe. Their friendly, albeit adversarial, relationship was often on public view at the Governor's Press Conferences. Weeks often sat with Mel Carico of *The Roanoke Times,* himself quite the character, with his Southwestern Virginia drawl and trademark red baseball cap.

After the Governor had answered the last question from reporters, Joe would invariably raise his hand. The Governor would grin and recognize Joe, who would always say, "Thanks for nothing, Governor," to which Godwin would reply, "You're most welcome, Mr. Weeks."

Godwin was nearing the end of his term when I arrived at WRVA. That fall, I was putting together a documentary on his four years in office, and Weeks and I had scheduled an exit interview with the Governor at the Executive Mansion.

We were sitting around the table in the formal dining room recording the interview when the Governor asked if we were hungry. Lunchtime was nearing, and he wanted a sandwich. "Can I get you fellas something?" The Governor led us into the kitchen where, to my surprise, he grabbed the mayonnaise out of the fridge and proceeded to make us all a chicken salad on white with a glass of sweet tea. Godwin, who was a Democrat, would run again for Governor in four years as a Republican and win a second term, becoming only the second Virginia Governor since 1830 to serve two terms. Virginia's governors cannot succeed themselves.

X

In early 1969, Weeks had begun reporting tidbits which were highly favorable to J. Sergeant Reynolds, a young, handsome State Senator from Richmond. Reynolds was the son of Reynolds Metals Magnate Richard S. Reynolds. "Sarge," as he preferred to be called, the "J" was for Julian, was an up and coming star of the Virginia Democratic Party.

He had declared his candidacy for Lieutenant Governor in the upcoming election. It seemed a forgone conclusion that in four years, Reynolds would be the next Governor and who knew what next. It was said that Reynolds' father had remarked that if he was paying for this campaign with Bill Battle, the son of former Governor John S. Battle, at the top of the ticket, "his boy was going next." Many thought of "Sarge" Reynolds as Virginia's Jack Kennedy.

I was pretty sure Reynolds was leaking favorable internal poll results to Weeks, who was a closet supporter. Soon I found myself embroiled in the Reynolds Campaign. He had called to ask if I would be willing to voice some of his campaign ads. He quickly picked up on my dilemma, squaring what he wanted me to do with my position as a reporter.

We met at "Chicken's" snack bar at the State Capitol for a sandwich. I paid. As long as I knew him, Reynolds never had any money with him. "I want your vote, John," he said, "but I'm not asking for your endorsement." He said I would not have to use my name and the spots would run only outside the Richmond market. It still felt sticky to me, but Weeks was all over me to do it and, of course, he prevailed. As Mencken had noted, journalism is an inexact science.

A must stop on the Virginia political circuit was, and no doubt still is, the Wakefield Shad Planking in Wakefield, Virginia. Sponsored by the Wakefield Ruritan Club, the Shad Planking is a large, very wet party held in the woods just outside of town. It was a command performance for anyone with any idea of running for office, statewide or local. It was said more deals were made under the tall pines in the woods of Sussex County than in the Virginia General Assembly.

Weeks loved it. He'd walk around for hours sipping bourbon and hobnobbing with the well lubricated crowd, sniffing around for political gossip. His first stop was always former Governor Bill Tuck's big Lincoln with the single digit license plate, number "6" I seem to recall. It looked like the Queen Mary docked in the shade of the tall pines.

Weeks said Tuck had a soft spot for WRVA because of Sunshine Sue, who was one of the big stars of WRVA's *Old Dominion Barn Dance* in the 40's and 50's. The WRVA Theatre, the old Lyric Theatre on Broad Street, which was home to the program, was within shouting distance of the Governor's Mansion. Tuck was a big fan.

Tuck Stories abound. One tale had it that while Governor, he had held up an RF&P Redskins' Booster Train to Washington so *Richmond News Leader* Reporter Carl Shires could run up Broad Street to fetch a "church key" to open a six pack of "National Bo Beer." "Tab Top" cans were yet to be invented. When Carl returned to Broad Street Station with church key in hand, he found the Governor standing under the train shed in the middle of the track in front of the big RF&P E8 diesel locomotives with his hand up yelling to the engineer, "I'm the Governor of this damn state and this train ain't going anywhere 'til I say it can!" I never knew if the story was true but if it wasn't it should have been.

Tuck, who was elected to Congress after serving as Governor, was always a regular at the Shad Planking. When the trunk lid on his Lincoln was up, it signaled rivers of bourbon were flowing with abandon.

A speech by the sitting Governor who spoke to the crowd from the bed of a flatbed tractor trailer lined with folding chairs for the old guard always got top billing, but the Governor seldom said anything of substance, making the main event just being there. It was a see and be seen thing. I always showed up to show the flag for the station.

The highlight in my book was a stop at the Virginia Diner just up the road in Wakefield on the way back up US 460 to Richmond. Dinner there with owner Bill Galloway was always a memorable experience. The Diner's battered and fried onion rings and country ham biscuits were worthy of a "James Beard Award." Galloway, who became a life-long friend, died in 2009 at the age of 76. It was said he built an empire from peanuts, which the Diner shipped worldwide. His family carries on the legacy.

XI

The center of the news universe in Richmond in those days were the two press rooms at the Virginia State Capitol. Both were tucked away along the south hall on the ground floor near the famous "Chicken's" snack bar. Just down the hall from "Chicken's," *Times Dispatch* inkers went about meeting their daily deadlines.

When things were slack, and a quorum of rank and file "Mullets" could be rounded up (a group of politicians, lobbyists, journalists and, of course, lawyers), out came the cards for a round of "Mullet Gin," a peculiar translation of gin rummy based on Virginia politics and politicians. The Jokers were named after prominent state politicians such as A. Willis Robertson who served for 20 years in the U.S. Senate. In later years, the Jokers would be named "The Byrd" for Harry F. Byrd Junior who was elected to the U.S. Senate as an Independent and still later, one would be named "The Wilder," named for L. Douglas Wilder, who was Virginia's first elected African American Governor in 1989.

When the "foreign press," i.e., an out of town paper, blew the whistle on the gambling, the proceedings were shelved, but only temporarily. Traditions die hard in Mr. Jefferson's Capitol.

At the far end of the hall near a tribe of vending machines, those of us on the broadcast side went about preparing and filing our "Voicers," a voice report, "Wraps," a voicer with an "actuality" (taped sound of a newsmaker) in the middle, or just a stand-alone actuality. The term "actuality" would later be ditched in favor of the more hipster term, "sound bite," which, in time, would come to define broadcast news.

WRVA maintained a small booth-like studio in the press room that was tied in to the Church Hill Studio Building via a broadcast line leased from the phone company. When we covered happenings downtown or at Richmond City Hall, which was nearby, we went over to the broadcast press room at the Capitol to file rather than having to go back up the hill to the station.

Often politicians and other nascent actors and contestants looking for their fifteen minutes of fame, would pop in for an impromptu "news" conference, many of which got covered the same way a mountain gets climbed - because it's there. The well-worn blue curtain in the press room became a familiar backdrop for talking heads on the local TV newscasts.

The legendary "Chicken's" snack bar was the domain of Louise "Chicken" Oliff, the delightfully crusty proprietor. The name came from the chicken salad, which had always been on the menu at "Chicken's." Appropriately, it was outstanding, particularly when washed down with "Chicken's" home brewed limeade, made with fresh squeezed limes and a homemade syrup that generated the mother of all sugar highs.

"Chicken" was a virtual gold mine for what was going on at the Capitol. Quite often, the governor himself would venture down to "Chicken's" to find out what was what. Suffice it to say, "Chicken" was plugged in. She'd sometimes spy me walking by on the way to the pressroom and holler, "John, in here!" and proceed to clue me in to some closed door "pow wow" going on in the Speaker's Office or another brewing upheaval in the ongoing game of political one-upmanship that trumped even "Mullet Gin" as the dominant pastime in the hallowed halls of the State Capitol.

XII

News tips were the primary medium of exchange in the news trade in those days, and every now and then I'd go off the record with one or two colleagues to pass along a tip, hoping they would respond in kind. Often they did - a little journalistic quid pro quo or "calculated indiscretion," as Weeks called it. The State Capitol press room was a hotbed of rumors and whispers that summer of 1969, mostly about the upcoming Virginia Democratic Primary Runoff.

State Senator Henry Howell, a liberal progressive from Norfolk, had become a household name in Virginia with his tirades against the Virginia Electric and Power Company, VEPCO, which Howell said stood for "Very Expensive Power Company." Constantly hammering that "there's more going around in the dark than Santa Claus," Howell's rants about VEPCO and large banks propelled him into a rematch with William C. Battle for the Democratic Gubernatorial Nomination. Lt. Governor Fred G. Pollard, who had been elected in 1966 with Mills Godwin at the head of the ticket, had polled a distant third in the July 15th Primary and thus was out of the running.

I was trying to schedule an interview with Howell for the documentary I was putting together on Governor Godwin's term in office, which was coming to an end, but Howell was laid up in a Norfolk hospital awaiting surgery.

Desperate, I phoned his hospital room. Political candidates were quite accessible in those days before straitjacketed handlers became part of the establishment. Howell's wife, Betty, answered. When Howell heard her talking to me, I heard him yelling, "Betty, give me the phone, give me the phone!" Declaring there was no way he was going to miss the opportunity to talk about Mills Godwin, he agreed to an interview before he was wheeled into the OR.

The Godwin Years; Four Years of Change was broadcast on WRVA in December of 1969.

Battle prevailed in the August Democratic Runoff, which we covered wall to wall from the Roof Garden of the Hotel John Marshall downtown. After Battle claimed victory over Howell, we filed all the overnight sound and packaged pieces for use the next morning in drive time, then, headed across 5th Street to Michael's Restaurant for a nightcap. When I left the restaurant in the wee small hours of the next morning, it was raining harder than I had ever seen. 5th Street was awash in a torrent of water. Hurricane Camille was beginning to bear down on Richmond.

The News Desk rousted me out of bed just after 5AM. Flood warnings had been posted for the entire James River Basin from the Blue Ridge down to the 14th Street Bridge in Richmond. The worst damage was occurring in Nelson County along the upper James River, but the high water was also threatening Richmond's Shockoe

Slip and Fulton Bottom areas. There was no floodwall in those days and the low-lying areas of the city were at the mercy of the river.

Weeks had dispatched us to various locations on the river as it wound through the city. I went down to the City Pumping Station in Shockoe Slip. Normally, the huge pumps forced storm water from the low lying streets into the river, but as the river rose, it roared into the outflow pipes backing up through the sewer system flooding the area.

When I arrived, the pumps were buzzing loudly, but it wasn't long before crews had to shut them down as the river began to flood into the pumping station. Within minutes the order to evacuate was sounded.

I had started my cassette machine on record amidst all the yelling. The sound of the pumps grinding down, the gushing of the water, the dinging of alarm bells and, the clanging of heavy metal manhole covers being upended by geysers of river water, conveyed, better than I could describe, the alarm and pandemonium of the scene. I was running to stay ahead of the oncoming water as manhole covers bubbled up with flood water.

I made my way to the 14th Street Bridge, where the water was lapping against the underside of the bridge deck. I lowered my microphone down to the water's edge to record the roar of the angry river. I used all of the sound I had collected in my lead report on the six o'clock news that night, letting the sound tell much of the story.

The next day, I was in Columbia, a tiny river town in Nelson County west of Richmond. From early accounts, the county appeared to have sustained some of the worst damage from the hurricane and flooding. More than 120 people were missing and feared dead.

I pulled into a service station not far from the river's edge. The floodwater had shorted out the signal at a nearby C and O Railroad crossing and the bell was dinging constantly. Two elderly gentlemen in bibbed overalls and straw hats were sitting in rocking chairs on the flat roof of a trackside building, smoking pipes and watching the raging James River tumble toward Richmond. An NBC camera crew was there. "Are you fellas okay up there?" someone yelled. "Yes sir," one answered, "We're just fine, but that dammed bell is driving us crazy!"

I grabbed some passable sound and packaged a piece for WRVA and WRC in Washington. It made for great radio, but the flood was a huge tragedy. Scores of people were killed. Many more had lost everything they owned in the disaster.

Alden Aaroe came up with the idea of organizing a car caravan for Nelson County Flood Victims. He convinced car dealers throughout the metropolitan area to donate used cars in good running condition that had passed state inspection. Relief agencies in Nelson County would distribute the cars to those who had lost their vehicles in the flooding. Soon, the entire WRVA parking lot on Church Hill was filled with donated cars. So was 22nd Street in front of the studio building. The trucking companies, which transport new cars to dealers, volunteered to take the vehicles to Nelson County.

Huge signs were made up and affixed to each side of the "Nu-Car Carriers" reading "WRVA Nelson County Car Caravan." To this day, the faces of those who were given vehicles are still etched in my memory.

Alden and John Tansey collaborated on numerous "Good Works" as Tansey would later call them. The "Nelson County Car Caravan" joined a list that included a critical fund raiser for Crippled Children's Hospital in Richmond, the predecessor to today's Children's Hospital at Virginia Commonwealth University; a campaign to save the Carillon, the World War One Memorial in Richmond's Byrd Park; a fund raiser for the animals at Maymont Park, and the WRVA Salvation Army Shoe fund, a yearly Christmas Campaign that began in the late 60's that would go on to raise millions.

XIII

The Battle versus Holton face-off for Governor was in full tilt that fall of 1969, making page one headlines in the national papers and drawing network television crews to Richmond like flies. One morning in mid-October, I was surprised to find Huntley-Brinkley's National Political Correspondent John Chancellor working the phones in the newsroom. He and his producer were lining up interviews for a piece on the contest. I went down to Capitol Square with them to scout shooting locations.

We set up at the fountain near the Bell Tower on the western side of the square. The cameraman, I think it was Sozio, effortlessly tracked an oak leaf as it floated down for a soft landing in the fountain. The film provided visual cover for Chancellor's script: "For a century," he wrote, "Republicans haven't been able to get a drink of water in Virginia, but change is in the air."

Weeks tapped me to be one of the Anchors on WRVA's continuous election coverage along with Larry Dodd,

Wayne Farrar, who was with *The Roanoke Times,* Mary Jane Walsh and, of course, Joe. We joined forces with co-owned WRVA TV Channel 12 in Richmond, taking over the Roof Garden at the Hotel John Marshall downtown. The tote boards, radio anchor tables, engineering equipment and Channel 12's cameras and assorted gear took up about half of the huge room. The rest of the space was set aside for the public to come in and watch the returns.

The atmosphere was electric, as candidates and political Kingpins made their way through the standing room only crowd to the anchor desks for interviews and predictions.

It was the last time we broadcast election coverage from the Roof Garden. Subsequent election broadcasts would seem rather sterile in comparison, with anchors based in the Church Hill Studios and only reporters in remote locations. It was far easier to plan and execute but never as exciting.

Linwood Holton was elected by more than 65 thousand votes, becoming the first Republican Governor of Virginia in a century. Battle had won the Runoff Primary in August but Henry Howell's campaign had taken a toll, painting Battle, who was a moderate, as another Byrd Machine conservative because of the Byrd organization's endorsement.

Battle's news conference the next day at the Capitol was short. "I got beat," he said.

But the upcoming star of the Virginia Democratic Party, J. Sargeant Reynolds, had easily won the Lt. Governor's race. He would succeed Pollard, who had lost to Howell and Battle in the July party primary. Pollard had then sought to replace Reynolds in the State Senate but lost to a young lawyer named L. Douglas Wilder, the future Governor.

Everyone assumed that in four years Reynolds would be the next governor, but his career was cut short by an inoperable brain tumor. He died less than two years later.

The indefatigable Howell entered the race to fill the remaining two years of Reynold's term as Lt. Governor. Screaming the slogan "Keep the Big Boys Honest," "Howlin' Henry," as some pundits called him, was elected as an Independent.

While "Sarge" Reynolds' political career had been tragically snuffed out, the meteoric career of another local politician was just leaving the launch pad. In 1967, Thomas J. Bliley Junior, a Richmond funeral director, was elected Vice Mayor of the City of Richmond. A tall, thin man who wore glasses and bow ties, Bliley had been elected Mayor shortly before I arrived at WRVA.

Weeks would occasionally send me down to cover the city council, which then met in the classic Gothic revival "Old City Hall Building" on East Broad Street between 10th and 11th. When the docket was dull, I would have the clerk hand Bliley a note requesting a short meeting after the council session adjourned, an effort to get a unique peg for a story. Bliley usually agreed, humored my efforts and would sometimes offer a useful tidbit.

His nemesis on Council was Howard Carwile, a fiery and passionate trial attorney whose verbal theatrics had led him to politics. Howard was constantly in the headlines, lambasting city hall as a "political boondoggle" or "a horrendous heap of hokum." It was great fodder for Weeks' morning commentaries and more than a few times, Howard boomed into the newsroom in a barely under control, red faced rage demanding "equal time."

Carwile resigned from city council in 1973 and served a term in the House of Delegates. In 1980, he ran unsuccessfully as an Independent against Bliley for the 3rd district congressional seat.

Bliley, who was a Democrat, jumped to the Republican Party after his term as Mayor and went on to a long career in Congress. In the mid-90's, he was the principal author of landmark legislation that changed the American Communications Industry in ways no one had ever imagined. Some say it destroyed local radio, but all of that lay down the road as the 70's arrived.

XIV

WRVA lost its genteel charm as the 60's drew to a close. Larus sold itself foreign to Rothmans Limited of Canada. The TV Station was sold to Jefferson Pilot of Charlotte, NC, but not the call letters - Larus insisted they remain with the radio stations. WRVA TV became the tongue twisting WWBT. WRVA and WRVA FM, which had started life as WRVB, were purchased by Southern Broadcasting Company of Winston Salem, NC. The company would later recast WRVA FM as WRVQ bringing stereo rock and roll to the staid world of FM.

Under Larus, time had seemed to drift along at its own quiet pace, not quite sleepy, more of a purr. With Southern, the tempo was cranked up. Music, conversation, news, and commercials all became more urgent and more breathless by design. Everybody and everything was in a hurry as though time itself had become its own worst enemy. Everything, it seemed, took too much of it.

Alden Aaroe, who had been Program Manager, was replaced by Walt Williams, a Southern company man who had programmed the group's rock and roll station in Birmingham, Alabama. The company's National Programming Chief, George Williams, was also of the rock mold. Not surprisingly, the most noticeable and immediate change came in music. Ella, Sarah, even Frank along with the Count and Riddle, gave way to the likes of Tony Orlando and "Blood Sweat and Tears." Adult Contemporary became the new mantra.

One could almost feel the parlors crack in old Richmond when the quiet opulence of *Gaslight* was extinguished in the evenings. Its mannerly host Harry Wood wound up on Channel 6 as the Atlantic Weatherman. Several years later, Big John Trimble brought his overnight Country Music Trucking Show to the huge Jarrell's Truck Plaza north of Richmond from Shreveport, Louisiana, and "10-4" good buddy crackled into the Richmond vocabulary. Lou Dean's sedate all night show, which served up show tunes, pop standards and soothing post-midnight "chit chat," was sent packing. Lou himself was moved, horror upon horrors, to a day time slot. Was nothing sacred! Lou after sunup wasn't a hit and Walt Williams fired him only to rehire him on the same day putting him in charge of *Viewpoint* , a repackaged, more edgy version of the old *Open for Opinion* telephone talk show.

The long running *NBC Monitor* across weekends was ditched, along with the network's "Second Sunday Documentary Series," for which I had been a contributor. *The Metropolitan Opera* was cancelled. So was Garner Ted Armstrong and the rest of the nightly religion block.

A talking duck waddled onto the Alden Aaroe morning program, Chuck Noe, a retired Division One Basketball Coach, ushered sports talk into Sunday nights and disco music took over Saturday nights as the newly hip WRVA went after the "love beads generation."

The hour-long newscasts were chopped in half and quickly halved again. Milo quotes and theatre reviews missed the cut. Long form documentaries were suddenly obsolete. News field reports were chopped from a minute and a half to 50 seconds; then down to 35.

Immediacy became the next big thing. Brevity inched past Clarity second only to Accuracy. Substance and depth began to take a back seat. As time raced on, the King's English would be found deficient in conveying urgency. The past tense would be excommunicated from the airwaves. Consultants moved in. A false present tense that omitted verbs took root and "telegram speak" slowly became the new "news speak." The prophecy of Bob Dylan had arrived. The times were indeed "a'changing."

Part V

Millard The Mallard &

Morning Drive

I

Perhaps it was the sheer lunacy of a talking duck on the radio with the normally straight laced Alden Aaroe! Beyond that, I have no idea why "Millard The Mallard" caught on, but it did!

It had started as nothing more than a gag. I had popped in on Alden's top rated morning show after the 7:30 AM news one morning in the early 70's and let go with a few duck quacks in the background as Aaroe talked about some event sponsored by Ducks Unlimited. There was some positive listener reaction and, in pretty short order, the man at the top, John Tansey, was asking Alden," What's this about a duck on your show?"

I named him Millard T. Mallard, the "T" for his middle name which, of course, was "The." Millard talked via Buccal speech, a technique of blowing air from the cheek around the tongue while attempting to enunciate the King's English. It didn't work so well on words beginning with "L." Lose became "wooze," but in most cases, what came out, I hoped, was a more understandable version of the classic fractured quack sound.

Millard was the product of my aging imagination. His personality developed alongside my own as a kid growing up in Emporia. He called soft drinks "cold deliciouses," loved banana sandwiches, thought the Easter Bunny was an imposter, refused to soak in bathtubs without a string tied around his flipper (to keep him from going down the drain) and didn't like to go out in the rain without an umbrella. His favorite team was the Brooklyn Dodgers, never mind that they had long moved to the West Coast.

Nothing was ever scripted. Everything was completely off the cuff. There was only one iron clad rule, when I was in the studio to do a Millard bit, I was never John Harding. Almost from the first quack, Top Secret was stamped on Millard's bill.

John Tansey was a great believer in radio being a "theatre of the mind." He had been down this road before with a character called "The Capitol Squirrel," which got its voice from speeding up a tape recording. "Revealing your identity as Millard's voice would destroy the illusion," he said. I'm sure he also felt that it might damage what credibility I had as a reporter. Amazingly the lid pretty much remained intact for the next 30 years. The only exception was in Emporia. My Mother was well known for her loquacity. Asking her to keep Millard's identity to herself was like asking a duck to stay out of water.

"Millard" waddled into the studio around 6:45 every morning to toot the train whistle, a large hand-made aluminum whistle sent in by a listener. Audience research had determined that most Richmonders first turned on the radio at 6:45 in the morning. There really was some method to the madness. Once the train roared by, Millard would squawk about something or Alden would set him up.

Few of the early Millard spots were recorded for posterity; but, as the years wore on, each morning's bit was taped and used to promote the show in other day-parts on the station. A few became WRVA classics. One of my favorites involved Alden making the mistake of mentioning to Millard that he had shot a "birdie" on the golf course. Millard, of course, went on a tirade about Aaroe shooting song birds. Once Alden finally managed to calm Millard down over the "birdie" remark, he said he had also gotten lucky and shot an Eagle setting off Millard once again. "You can get into some big time trouble for shooting the Big Boss Bird Mr. Aaroe," he quacked.

Every year, Millard campaigned to save the Thanksgiving Turkey, begging listeners to have a banana sandwich instead. He had trouble figuring out which flipper that flip flops went on. He wore an Alden Aaroe "trick or treat" mask at Halloween, attended the International Soak Festivals in Goose Bay, sent long lists of Christmas "wants" to the Christmas Goose, wore galoshes when it rained, accused Ducks Unlimited of saving ducks so "they can shoot us later," and on and on....

The Millard spots seldom lasted longer than a few minutes at most. After about three or four minutes of duck talking, my tongue would go numb, so from the moment we began, we were looking to end it. We were playing with no net and no idea about how it was going over with the audience. No matter. Just about every morning after the bit, Alden shrugged and said, "Well, at least we think we're funny."

II

By 1972, Millard was showing up as a viable personality in the Arbitron Radio Diaries, from which the quarterly radio ratings were compiled. The gag had become serious business. Millard became the station mascot and, in a move aimed at getting more exposure for him, I began showing up every now and then on Bob Cory's afternoon drive show. The sit-ins with Bob, who had succeeded Wayne Lemon, also served to recycle listeners back to Alden the next morning. Cory, an English teacher in Ohio before going into broadcasting, wrote a clever article about working with a duck for *Richmond Magazine*.

Roy Cabell, who was on retainer as the station's attorney, told me he would like to represent Millard. I broached the subject of conflict of interest. He assured me it would not be a problem but said if I got uncomfortable at any point down the road, he would step aside in favor of his partner. I never did. Roy, who was held in very high esteem by the Richmond legal community, seemed to get a kick from telling people he was Millard The Mallard's attorney.

Roy decided the first thing that needed to be done was to set up a Virginia Corporation which would own all of the rights to Millard. It would keep my name behind the corporate curtain. He filed the papers and thus was born MTM, Inc. I was the sole stock holder. I listed my father as Secretary/ Treasurer. The corporation owned all copyrights to Millard, and, if we could get one, a United States Trademark.

A contract was drawn up between MTM Inc., and WRVA. The station would provide promotion, facilities for production and cover all legal fees associated with the trademark filing with the US Patent Office as well as filing fees with the State Corporation Commission. In return, WRVA would not have to pay a license fee for use of the character but would have to pay MTM, Inc. performance fees.

John Tansey quickly signed the contract. I asked Roy if it had been too easy, meaning, had the station gotten a sweetheart deal. He didn't think so. I had free use of the character outside of the Richmond Market and, subject to mutual agreement, within the Richmond Market in noncompetitive situations. Profits from the sale of Millard novelty items would be split 50/50 with MTM, Inc. Roy also said it was his opinion that Millard The Mallard's relationship with the station would cement my future there. Looking back, I'd have to say it probably did.

Using the good offices of the Dowell, Dowell and Dowell law firm in Northern Virginia, MTM, Inc. filed a successful application for a United States Trademark, which was registered on the 29th of July 1975. We also successfully filed for, and received, a Trademark from the State Corporation Commission.

As part of both applications, we had enlisted legendary Illustrator Jack Woodson, then with Carmine Graphics in Richmond, to come up with a graphic representation of Millard. Jack was well known. Among his credits was his painting of the Marlboro man on horseback replicated in magazines and the basis for those TV Commercials depicting a cowboy lighting up and riding off into the sunset to the *"Magnificent Seven"* motion picture theme.

Coming up with a graphic image of Millard was not an easy assignment. Jack had to steer clear of existing trademarks. What he came up with was a green duck with a sort of woodpecker bill who wore a brown suit and an orange sweater with the letter "M" on the front. Most think Jack simply drew what came to be the classic picture of Millard with headphones and a microphone. Actually, he took a picture of him. Jack created a 3 dimensional model of Millard about three and a half feet tall. He lit the model in his studio and photographed it in color. We had several thousand 8 x10 prints made of that shot and several hundred full-sized posters. A revised version was used in a market wide billboard campaign. Several were night boards, meaning they were lit up after dark

III

The first in what would turn out to be an ever increasing Millard novelty line was the Millard The Mallard "T" Shirt. The first run was for 2 thousand iron-on decals made from an eight color separation taken from Jack's original photograph. Over the next 25 to 30 years, thousands more were made. The decals were then professionally applied to cotton T shirts of every color imaginable and in every size, including infant. I knew we had arrived when Richmond's iconic department store chain, Miller & Rhoads, began running Millard "T" Shirt ads in the Richmond newspapers and selling the shirts in its stores.

Millard came to life off the air when a professional custom costume maker supplied us with a human sized Millard the Mallard outfit, complete with yellow "wing" gloves and yellow vinyl flippers. The costume was of a rather ingenious design. Included was a vest into which cold packs were inserted after being frozen. It was a life saver in the Richmond summer heat.

Some years later, we had a second identical costume made to use as a backup when one outfit was sent away for cleaning and the inevitable refurbishment. Millard's bill got a lot of abuse, particularly from little kids, which Millard attracted like flies. We began hiring college girls to wear the costume at WRVA events. They were better duck actors than guys, and they were better with little kids.

Millard in costume became a mainstay at WRVA remote broadcasts, community events sponsored by the station and, of course, parades. One of the largest was the annual Richmond Christmas Parade down Broad Street. Millard rode on a WRVA float decked out in a Santa Claus suit. One of the more memorable versions featured Millard in a sleigh being pulled by WRVA personalities wearing "Rain" Deer Antlers, red noses and yellow rain slickers. I was enlisted to sing, in duck, "Oh Christmas Tree" on an endless cassette, which was run through a sound system that had been rigged on the float by our engineers. The good news was I didn't have to listen to it for an hour or so as the parade snailed down Broad Street.

The longest running parade in Richmond was the annual Tobacco Festival Parade which was later reborn as the more politically correct Autumn Harvest Parade. WRVA entered a float every year. My favorite featured an oversized rowboat with Alden Aaroe and Tim Timberlake who had joined Alden on the Morning Show. They were dressed in hunting gear and were bound and gagged. Behind them with a toy shotgun was Millard The Mallard. A sign reading "It's Duck Hunting Season" had been crudely edited to replace the word "Duck" with "Tim and Alden," so it read, "It's Tim and Alden Season."

The WRVA Sales Department came up with the *Millard The Mallard Household Hints Book*, which went through two printings and sold out each time. Among the last novelty items created was a Millard the Mallard stuffed doll.

Alden and I produced a special Christmas Program entitled *Millard The Mallard's Christmas,* which was written by Alden's daughter Anna Lou. It became a tradition on Alden's program on Christmas morning. Anna Lou later published a small book with the same title, drawing all of the illustrations herself. We sold it and a companion book that she also wrote, *Millard The Mallard's Halloween,* with all proceeds from both books going to the WRVA Shoe Fund, which Alden had started in 1968. (The Shoe

Fund was later named after Alden in his honor but Clear Channel Communications removed his name in its remake of the station at the turn of the century and made the Shoe Fund a year round fund raiser.)

IV

Alden, Millard and I were paired for the rest of his time at WRVA. We became very close friends off the air. Alden and his second wife Frances vacationed with Jeri and me on the Outer Banks in the summers. Many a weekend found us at Alden's house in Hanover County lolling around his pool or fishing on the Chesapeake Bay.

After my wife Jeri and I moved into a new house we had built in Brandermill, a planned community in Chesterfield County, Alden and Frances dropped in often. One afternoon, Alden asked where our clothesline was. I told him Brandermill did not allow them outside. "Absolutely Un-American," he railed. When we left one weekend for a visit to see my Mother in Emporia, he and Frances snuck over one evening and erected a make-shift clothesline in our backyard. As soon as we arrived home, I noticed a line of extra-large bras and undershorts flapping in the breeze in our backyard. One pair of boxer shorts had a picture of Millard on the seat.

Millard's popularity was amazing. The Miller Morton Company produced a prototype tube of "Chapstick Bill Balm, Soothing Relief for Chapped Beaks." The U.S. Navy made him an Honorary Naval Recruiter, and The Air National Guard in Richmond painted his face on one of its jets. The C. F. Sauer Company routinely sent over cases of Duke's Mayonnaise to Millard for his banana sandwiches, and the Virginia State Fair contracted with MTM Inc. for Millard to front its promotion of the Fair's move from September to October. The state's annual wildlife calendar noted Millard's "Hatch Day"· September 2nd, and the Governor issued a blanket pardon for Millard during Duck Season.

People who knew me often asked how I felt about Millard's popularity while I remained anonymous in the background. I never looked at it that way. To me, Millard was another entity. Obviously, he was the product of my imagination. He was Captain Reynolds gone viral, but I viewed Millard's popularity as his own, not mine. Besides, remaining in the background as Millard's voice and alter ego allowed me to pursue my other job as a reporter. That's not to say it wasn't a challenge sometimes.

A few of my contacts were wise to my split personality. One happened to be Virginia's First Lady, Katherine Godwin.

Mrs. Godwin was a devoted Millard fan and a daily listener. She wrote often to comment about Millard's rantings and ravings. She sent Millard an autographed copy of her book *Living a Legacy*, about her years with Governor Godwin in the Executive Mansion. The inscription reads:

"To Millard The Mallard" with appreciation for the humor you bring to my life. With warm regards and best wishes.

Katherine Godwin

December 1977.

Mrs. Godwin was always wise to my identity as Millard, but she kept the ruse to herself, never telling the Governor even after he left office after his second term. "It is our secret," she said.

Mrs. Godwin died in 2015. The Governor had passed away in 1999.

V

The 70's arrived on Ingleside Avenue with a death. Lyman Harrell died suddenly two days after New Year's. Mother had called me with the news at work. I was stunned. I had just talked with him over the Christmas Holidays and he seemed well.

I owed Mr. Harrell a great debt. He had gotten me into college when I had SAT numbers as low as what you get for just signing your name. He had held my feet to the fire, demanding progress reports on grades. When I graduated from junior college, he called with congratulations but said, "you're only half done." When I got my degree from AU, he was as proud as my parents.

It was Lyman who got me interested in state politics. We had many a late night political talk in his den, often running into the wee small hours, ending only when his wife Duane started blinking the lights. I had stuffed envelopes during his campaigns for re-election to the House of Delegates. Only a broken promise from a Kingmaker had prevented him from running for the State Senate. When I first drew an assignment at the State Capitol, Lyman saw to it that I knew all of the major players and was well schooled on what was cooking on the legislative stove.

After the funeral, Duane gave me Lyman's brass buttons from his US Navy Dress Uniform as a keepsake. I wore them on a succession of blue and black blazers over my working life as an ongoing tribute. Upon Duane's death, I sent them to Lyman and Duane's son, Randy.

Several weeks later, we got word that Father's lung disease had returned. It had shown up on an X-ray during a checkup. This time it was diagnosed as a fungus, leaving little doubt he had been misdiagnosed in the 50's. "Tuberculosis," the doctors had said back then. Now, we were told it was a fungus contracted from the carrier pigeons he had raised as a boy. It was not contagious and not hereditary. No mattresses and sheets were burned in the backyard and, this time, no one wore patch tests.

We were all stunned. It seemed to be some kind of fateful double cross but Father seemed rather stoic about it, as though he had expected it. From all appearances, he seemed to take it in stride.

He was sent back to the Blue Ridge Sanitarium near Charlottesville, scene of the horrors of the 50's. Every week, I would drive from work to Emporia, pick up Mother, drive her to the Blue Ridge Complex, then take her back to Emporia and return to Richmond. He returned home in about six weeks. There was no surgery this time. He only had one lung. At age 62, he took early retirement from Swift and Company. I suspect he knew when he came home that his condition was terminal, but he kept it to himself for the next five years.

Late that spring, I spent a week in LA with June. As soon as we walked out of the terminal at LAX, my eyes became water fountains, assaulted by the infamous southern California smog. The thick, dirty beige vapor smelled of gasoline and exhaust fumes and permeated everything, even seeping into automobile air conditioning. June's small house was nestled on a hilly, wooded neighborhood in Echo Park. The view from her tiny backyard was breathtaking. On light smog days, one could see Sulphur Canyon in the distance and make out Dodger Stadium far below in Chavez Ravine.

We did the usual first timer circuit; Disneyland in Anaheim, a concert at the Hollywood Bowl (Dylan's backup group, "The Band" was the headliner), the beach at Santa Monica, the LA Farmer's Market and a trendy eatery called "The Pantry." I went to work with her several days at Universal where she was doing a series called "Matt Lincoln," with Vince Edwards of "Ben Casey MD" fame. There were hundreds of people on the set. I was amazed they managed to get anything done. June would wait around for hours to do a scene. The days were incredibly long, from before dawn to long after dark. Then, a late night at home, to learn lines for the next day's shooting. I was glad to be in radio.

VI

The position of news director at WRVA became something of a parlor game in the early 70's. Joe Weeks left to become the Assignment Editor at WNEW TV in New York. He was succeeded by Mike Dewey, who was brought in from the Washington area; but eight months after arriving, Dewey was out. Weeks had been telling Tansey what a huge mistake he had made in leaving. His mentor, who had hired him at WNEW, had jumped to ABC, leaving him with no support. He wanted to come back. Tansey finally agreed.

Joe returned as News Director and, for a while, he was his old swashbuckling self; but soon his health went into decline. He was suffering from emphysema. Oxygen tanks were brought in and set up by his desk in the newsroom. I was working alongside Joe on the same shift, and I sometimes wondered if he was going to blow us all up lighting his pipe while on oxygen. He soldiered on, but the disease was slowly robbing him of his vitality. His flamboyant style began to fade. He was eventually forced into retirement and later died in a Richmond hospital.

Both Merrill Hartson and I paid tribute to him at his funeral. Merrill succeeded him as News Director. It was a popular appointment.

I was brought inside - "Air Conditioned" in newsroom parlance. I was assigned as anchor of the afternoon Six o'clock News Roundup, which was then an hour long news block. My window was about 25 minutes. Sports, weather, reviews, commentaries, and such filled out the hour.

Anchor work was very different from field reporting and, while I missed the thrill and freedom of chasing down leads and nosing out tips, I was surprised to discover I enjoyed the writing and producing of an entire news strip. A little over a year later, I was named anchor of the 7 and 8AM News broadcasts where Joe had presided.

I was quite nervous about it, but I was lucky. The newscast was bookended by Alden's top rated program. The station probably could have put the sound of a dishwasher running on the air at 7 and 8AM without a blip in the ratings. It was an enviable situation to be in. I quickly discovered my brain worked better in the morning, and I enjoyed the solitude.

The anonymity of radio had always appealed to me; but when I started working morning drive, which necessitated a 3AM wakeup, I discovered a special attraction to working while most of the city slept. Even after moving to the suburbs years later, I found the challenge of silently sneaking out of the house, with the stealth of a seasoned burglar, rather exciting. I never ate anything when I first got up. I was always overdosing on adrenalin prior to work, so there was no chance that the tinkling of a glass or clang of a skillet would awaken my wife or our cat Harry.

The nineteen mile commute from our house in Chesterfield County to Church Hill went quickly. Seldom was there any traffic to speak of, and most of the traffic lights, which seemed to require having a birthday before changing during the day, were on blink overnight.

Once ensconced in my little "Electronic Clubhouse," as Tim Timberlake would later call the studio, I went about the process of finding out what had happened overnight.

VII

The WRVA Newsroom was a multiplex of urgency · a combination situation room, command and control center and data dump where raw information poured in around the clock waiting to be processed in a place where there was never enough time and deadlines ruled. To the uninitiated, it was a mindless cauldron of confounding, incredibly noisy confusion with lights, bells, alarms, buzzers, squawks, monitors, and printers run amok. For those of us who subjected ourselves to it every day, it was simply background noise.

Over time, one learned to tune out all of the extraneous noise and static and key on the sounds, words and signals that alerted our ears to breaking news. There was an unmistakable, grinding growl that signaled a multi-alarm fire call. Several of the police radio codes carried immediate urgency: shots fired, an armed robbery or a serious traffic wreck with injuries. A call for the M.E. (medical examiner) always stood out as did a call for the homicide squad. The ear jarring bells of a wire service bulletin or flash required immediate attention as did the pulsing buzz and flashing light of the network hotline box. If there was ever a calm nanosecond, it was somehow a cue that something bad was about to happen.

When I first arrived at WRVA, I had a girlfriend who was a flight attendant. She and her fellow crew members were constantly being reminded of the need for situational awareness, the discipline of always knowing what is going on around you as you go about your work, to be alert for the unexpected. The same could be said of the newsroom.

Often, if I had to use the restroom across the hall and I was alone in the newsroom, I would push a button and route the output of the emergency scanner radios to a reel to reel tape recorder so I could "catch up" when I got back. I was always running on adrenalin in the newsroom, wired, on edge, keen not to miss anything, all the while racing to meet broadcast deadlines. I loved it, but after 8 to 10 hours of it, my senses seemed to dull.

When I got home at the end of my shift, I would sit alone in the quiet stillness to wind down to where I could relax and grab a quick afternoon nap, the best sleep of the day. After dinner, I would try for another 4 hours sleep, but often my brain would not turn off. I quickly learned that no sleep is better than too little. If I was awake at 10:30, I'd just call it a night and get up.

My Doctor Bob Chaplin, a fellow Emporian, prescribed stress tabs for me early on and constantly hammered me about the need to quit smoking and find a hobby that would take my mind off "News."

Kicking the smoking habit would take years, but the hobby came quickly. When Millard came along, his illustrator, Jack Woodson, introduced me to the world of ship modeling. Jack, one of the most talented people I have ever known, was himself a master craftsman. I was instantly attracted to the ancient hobby and found it to be wonderful therapy to release the pent up stress and angst I brought home from the newsroom.

VIII

Working morning drive news at WRVA was akin to pushing a reset button as a new news cycle began. I often equated the process with climbing a mountain of information. Once it was scaled, it was simply a matter of boiling it down to a newscast.

Aside from rush hour traffic accidents and the occasional house fire, breaking news often took a holiday in morning drive. Other dayparts were quite different, requiring us to continually adjust to stay on top of the mountain, which constantly grew through the day.

I'd scan the morning papers, *The Richmond Times Dispatch* and the *The Washington Post,* to see what they knew that we didn't. Often, a compelling enterprise story required us to pick something up with attribution. My goal was always to use the papers as a tip service and try to work a new top or angle that would make it ours. As a consequence, many a public official would get a rude wake-up call in the early hours of the morning.

A quick flip through the news "cut sheets" from the day and evening before alerted me to all of the news sound that had been taken in. Many pieces had been "turned" for morning drive with a new top or lead, part of the ongoing tradition of one news shift laying the groundwork for the next.

It was then a matter of working the phones, making beat calls to the various police, fire and emergency services dispatchers, hospital workers, power company spokesmen, forecasters at the National Weather Service and others who went about their mostly unrecognized jobs disguised as official sources. The voices on the other end were usually familiar to me and I to them. Talking with them was a daily morning ritual ideally performed at the same time each morning. One of the more productive things I did was to visit many of the dispatchers where they worked, so we could put a face with our voices.

I was closest to the officers and support staff with the Richmond Police Bureau. My first cousin, Norman Harding, was a Detective Sergeant in the city homicide detail. Norman, Norman Junior to my sisters and me growing up in Emporia, introduced me to many of his fellow officers in the city, including Captain Tom Shook, the overnight watch commander in Richmond, who became a good friend.

There was also a sense of camaraderie with the engineers who were always at our beck and call to keep things working and make us look good, or to be precise about it, sound good. When I arrived at WRVA, the Chief Engineer was Ted Chezik. Tall as a transmitter tower with the build of a bomb shelter, Big Ted was a quiet, unassuming man who went about his job without a lot of fanfare. He and most of his staff had come over from the Hotel Richmond Studios.

G.W. Garthright was the Technical Supervisor at the Church Hill Studio Building.   His given name was Garland, but he only responded to his nickname "Mike." Irish to the core with the red hair to prove it, Mike was a World War II Veteran who mustered out as a Tech Sergeant.   He was always making the rounds of the studios, putting out fires while taking time each morning to chat with Alden and me. Mike and I shared a hobby - we were both into photography and had many a long conversation in the snack room about film and cameras.

Julian Huckstep, who, like Garthright, had come over from the hotel studios, often answered our panic calls for help in the Newsroom. Once when one of the huge, rack mounted Ampex tape decks refused to cooperate, "Huck," as we called him, arrived with a ball peen hammer in hand. He promptly opened the rear cabinet door and gave something a whack with his hammer. "Just a stuck solenoid that needed a little convincing," he said.

His colleague Harry Long was a tall and lanky man with a very dry sense of humor. A Ham Operator, Harry's Amateur Radio call sign was displayed on his Virginia License Plate. He was my "go to" guy for schizophrenic solid state electronics. I called him one morning about a tape cartridge recorder that was having a seizure. "Go around to the back of the console, remove the back and unplug the machine," he counseled, "then count to 30 and plug it back in. If that doesn't drain the stupidity, call me back." It almost always did. Harry went on to a long career with our sister station WRVQ, as Q-94's Chief Engineer.

IX

The News Air Studio in the Church Hill Building faced the city, which was laid out below and beyond. It would be my view for the next 25 years or so anchoring the 7 and 8 AM news. I would gaze out of the huge picture window watching the city come to life while waiting in blissful silence for my cue to go on the air. The News Air Studio was the only place in the radio station where I heard nothing but what I wanted to hear.

Sometimes on very foggy mornings, our view was smothered by a veil of vapory mist that gave me the sensation of floating on a giant cloud with only the top edge of the city skyline visible in the distance like some giant, fogbound ocean liner. Most mornings I could see the traffic on the Interstate 95 bridge, which crossed the James River to the far left in our view, and, just beyond, a keen eye could grab a glimpse of the 14th and 9th street bridges in the distance.

The grand, Second Renaissance Main Street Station with its landmark Clock Tower and train shed dominated the view just left of center. Interstate 95, the "super slab," as truckers called it, was always thick with traffic during the morning rush. It sped across our view, darting under Broad Street Hill and around the Medical College of Virginia complex, anchored by the old hospital building at the crest of Broad Street Hill with its signature rooftop light beacon. If you looked closely just to the left of Broad Street and the Highway Department Building, you might catch a glimmer of the Governor's Mansion.

It was almost the same perspective as that photographed by the famed Civil War Photographer Mathew Brady shortly after the war. A colorized panoramic print composed of several photographs stitched together had been a gift to the station from the Sisters Of The Visitation Of Monte Maria Convent next door to the Studio Building. It was displayed in the WRVA Lobby at almost the exact vantage point where Brady had taken the original photograph.

Alden always jerked me out of my pre-air daydreams with a heads up on the "Loud Mouth," the ancient studio intercom brought over from the hotel. "Take it out of the spot, John," he barked. (Spot was radio speak for a commercial.)

I'd pop the news sounder on the air and key my mike always thinking, *maybe this time I will get it right.*

I always harbored a rather terrifying nightmare that was very high in the nightmare rotation. It was always the same. I had lost my news script and never realized it was missing until I was live on the air. I would awaken immediately in a cold sweat. It never happened, but I was always obsessed about misplacing my script.

The grand panorama of that million dollar view of Richmond afforded by our Church Hill studio windows seemed to ground us to the city as though we were plugged into its circuitry, hardwired into its collective vibe. Similar perhaps to the sensation one gets when seeing their home city from an airplane when returning from a trip out of town.

In later years, we would use the on-air slogan "WRVA IS Richmond." It wasn't original. A station in the Midwest had a similar line, but I thought it rang more true for us. After all, as Lou Dean often said on his all night program, WRVA meant "Wonderful Richmond, Virginia." I always thought it was the most appropriate slogan we ever came up with to describe WRVA and its special relationship with Richmond.

X

My hours got a bit closer to the normal world when I started anchoring the 8AM broadcast, and I began to run into other humans at my apartment building. River Towers was a haven for young adults - young professionals, medical students and the like. It was there that I first met Jeri Kennedy in late 1968.

Jeri and her roommate Judy Shoemaker and another resident, Zon Gordon, hopped into one of the lobby elevators with me one afternoon just as the doors were beginning to close. I had met Zon before. Everybody knew Zon. He was a salesman for a New York fashion house and was renowned for the twice yearly sample sales he held in the building. Zon had that "always on" salesman's personality. He could sell a drowning man a case of bottled water. He quickly introduced me to Jeri and Judy.

Jeri, short for Geraldine, which she hated, was petite with long auburn brown hair and emerald green eyes.

She had attended East Carolina but finished school at the Medical College of Virginia. Certified in Cytology, a branch of Pathology dealing with the interpretation of cells and tissue to detect disease, she worked in a private lab in Richmond where she was primarily involved in cancer detection. Judy, her blond apartment mate, was the Office Manager at the Department of Neurosurgery at MCV. They had paired up while at the University of North Carolina Medical Center in Chapel Hill. Jeri grew up on a small farm in Eastern North Carolina. Judy was from the Charlotte area.

They started inviting me up to their apartment for dinner every now and then. Jeri made a mean eye of round, and Judy was the best bartender in the building. Her Peach Daiquiri was pure liquid art. Their talents were put to good use when our crowd would jam into their apartment to watch *ABC's Monday Night Football* back when the show was as much in the booth, with Howard Cosell, Dandy Don Meredith and Frank Gifford, as it was on the field.

My love life had been rather schizophrenic since I had come to Richmond. Soon after I arrived, I had hooked up again with Tracey, the dangerously cute blonde I had met while both of us were in school. After graduation, Tracey had gone to flight attendant school. We had been seeing each other for going on two years. It wasn't meant to be.

Constantly suffering from what airline crews call "place lag," from her daily cross country "there and backs," she signed on with another ride that based her in Chicago for long haul International runs. Our relationship ran out of lift somewhere over the North Atlantic when she met a sales rep.

It was the second breakup after a lengthy relationship and left me questioning whether I was infected with some sort of genetic, psychological quirk that doomed me to selfdom. After a few weeks of disgusting self-absorption, I rebounded. I dated a pretty reporter at another station for a short while. Then, several meet ups with a young woman who worked at the State Department of Education, followed by a lengthy fling with a stunning woman I had met at a party the building threw for tenants and guests.

Slim with long black hair, and a flawless Mediterranean tan, she had a figure that would tempt the Pope. But the relationship had no substance, no depth and, like the Peggy Lee tune that became a boomer anthem at the time, we both were asking ourselves, "Is That All There Is?"

I had taken Tracey to the WRVA Christmas party the previous year and Weeks had virtually slobbered all over her; but we were history, so I thought I would ask Jeri if she would go with me. I knew she was well aware of my recent escapades. There were no secrets at River Towers. I was fully expecting an, "I'm sorry, I have other plans," so I was surprised when she said she'd love to go.

As soon as we walked in, I spied Weeks heading for us with a lascivious gleam in his eye. He gave Jeri a wicked grin,

"You're the airline stewardess, aren't you?" I was mortified but Jeri didn't miss a beat saying, "No, Mister Weeks, my name is Jeri Kennedy and my feet are firmly on the ground." Weeks howled with laughter and Jeri and I became an item.

XI

Television came calling in the 70's. I had gotten a few offers from stations in the Midwest and South over the years, but they were lateral moves, meaning there was no additional money involved, just a chance to go to a larger market and be famous on TV, which really had no appeal to me. Brinkley's comment about television robbing you of your privacy was always in the back of my mind, but the offer I got from WAVY TV in Portsmouth/Norfolk was worth considering.

For one thing, the contact came from John Wilson, the main anchor at the station. I knew John rather well. An alumnus of WRVA Radio, his voice was still heard on the station every Sunday introducing the legendary gospel group, "The Silver Stars." He had gone over to WRVA TV to anchor their major evening newscasts. He had since left for WAVY. He asked me if I had ever thought about television. I told him of my taste of TV news with NBC in Washington. He was aware of my work and said he was convinced I would be a perfect fit at WAVY. He wanted me to come to Portsmouth and be WAVY's City Hall Reporter three days a week and main anchor across weekends. "Come on down and let's talk," he said. I said I would get back to him.

The following weekend I drove to Portsmouth to look over the station and do an on-camera audition. It wasn't hard to write to pictures. I was fully capable of not saying orange when the picture was of an apple. I checked my script for sense and walked into the studio to tape it, remembering to sit on my coat tail, a tip from the NBC days. It prevented your jacket from creeping up your neck giving you the look of wearing a horse collar. When

I was done, I went into the control room to look at the playback. Aside from hating how I looked and sounded, I was pretty sure I could not do it any better so I told the engineer to spool it up and give it to the news director. The offer was promptly put in writing, and I went back to Richmond to mull it over.

I ran into Jeri in the lobby at River Towers when I got back from Portsmouth. She had missed seeing me at the Friday Night Social and asked where I had been. I told her I had left very early to drive down to Portsmouth to do an audition for WAVY TV and that, if WRVA could not better what I had been offered, I would probably be leaving Richmond. "I'd rather you didn't leave, John," she said. A signal, perhaps, that our relationship was not a flash in the pan.

The following Monday morning, I told Merrill, the News Director, about Wilson's offer. He promptly sent me to see Tansey. I told him I was inclined to take WAVY's offer. I said the money was far better than what I was making at WRVA and, while I loved radio, I thought I could do well in television. John told me he was sure I could do well in TV but, he said, "You'll do better here."

He promptly met Wilson's money offer and raised it by another 5 percent. Additionally, I would be promoted to Senior News Editor, go on a straight five day week, with no on-call duty on weekends, and I would receive a third week of vacation. It was an incredible counter offer. I asked him to give me a day to think it over.

I called my Father that night. "Always take the sure thing when you can, John, not the good thing," he said. "Television is a good thing but WRVA is closer to the sure thing."

"You've got a lot in your corner there," he said, "not the least of which is Millard The Mallard." He advised me to think long and hard before walking away from it.

"Don't forget," he said, "the fact that Mr. Tansey made such an attractive counter offer should tell you that you are quite valuable to the franchise." He also told me that if the TV station did not at least meet the counter offer, I'd have an excellent read on where I stood.

I called Wilson and told him WRVA had made a very lucrative counter offer. He made no move to sweeten his offer. I took my father's advice and stayed with WRVA.

My parents never visited me at WRVA, though they were frequently in Richmond. Occasionally, Mother would phone me at the station and ask if we could meet for lunch at Miller & Rhoads or the Hot Shoppes Cafeteria she often frequented when in the city by herself.

Aside from Norman, my police detective cousin who was a regular visitor, I only recall one other relative ever coming by the station, Father's older brother Vance, who had assembled my pirate radio transmitter when I was 13. I gave him a tour of both the Church Hill Studio Building and the station's enormous transmitter plant at Deep Bottom in southeastern Henrico County on the James River.

Captivated by the big 50,000 watt transmitters and the huge towers out back, Vance was like a kid in a candy store, grinning from ear to ear, as happy as I had ever seen him.

XII

"It is June of 1972. The sky is so blue it almost hurts to look up, but the James River is on an angry rampage." So began my journal entry about the infamous Agnes flooding that swept into Richmond early that summer.

The picturesque Falls of the James from Bosher's Dam West of the Huguenot Bridge to Mayo's Bridge downtown, a distance of some 7 miles through the center of Richmond, had been transformed into a thundering, muddy, trash moving torrent, transporting everything from the carcasses of cows to uprooted trees downstream. It was the work of Hurricane Agnes, which had dumped torrential rain over the foothills of the Blue Ridge Mountains in the Upper James River Basin. It was a replay of the 1969 Camille flooding, only much worse.

Two hundred blocks of Richmond were flooded. The Shockoe Valley, the low lying area between downtown and Church Hill, was quickly under thirteen feet of water and, for the first time, Broad Street was cut in two. There were massive power failures. The National Guard cordoned off the downtown area, which was completely blacked out. No one was admitted without a military escort.

The Richmond Water Filtration Plant was flooded and knocked out of commission. So was the City's Sewage Treatment Plant. There was no drinking water. Raw Sewage began flowing into the James River.

On the 23rd of June, flows on the James River peaked at 70 times normal, topping out at 36 and a half feet. It was more than enough to force the shut-down of many of the City's bridges. The Robert E. Lee Bridge near my apartment was reduced to two lanes. The city had parked loaded tractor trailer trucks back to back in one lane each way across the span to add stability.

The WRVA Traffic Helicopter was pressed into service bringing critical employees to Church Hill. There was no other quick way to get there. There was quite a show at River Towers when the chopper landed in a nearby parking lot to pick me up. I had my toothbrush and a change of clothes with me. I would spend the next two days at the Church Hill Studio Building.

Crossing the river in the air, the scene below was mind boggling. There was water everywhere. Mayo's Bridge, more popularly known as the 14th Street Bridge, was completely under water. Only the light stanchions on the bridge were visible, seemingly levitating above the roaring river. An abandoned railway trestle to Belle Isle in the middle of the river was an early casualty. I had seen it crash into the raging water from my window at River Towers. Huge oil storage tanks had broken from their foundations on the south bank and were floating in the flood water. The city was totally paralyzed.

We managed to get reporters to strategic points along the river and at the city's two command posts. The WRVA Helicopter stayed in the air throughout each day, with Howard Bloom reporting on flood conditions in Richmond and upstream, landing only to refuel.

My 8AM newscast, normally a quarter of an hour, routinely ran almost a half hour before I gave it back to Alden, who would launch into an almost endless list of closings and cancellations. Governor Linwood Holton came up to the studios and helped man the phones, which never stopped ringing.

Several days into the disaster, a very well dressed gentleman came into the newsroom and said that John Tansey had told him to report to me, that I could use some help. "What can I do?" he asked. I put him on the phone bank taking closings and postponements. I later learned that he was John G. Johnson, The President and CEO of Southern Broadcasting Corporation, which owned WRVA and our sister station, WRVQ.

XIII

There was another shuffling of News Directors at WRVA in 1973. Merrill Hartson left the station to join the Richmond Bureau of the Associated Press. I was appointed Acting News Director until a full-time replacement could be found. It dawned on me then that, if I stayed, I might have a big decision to make somewhere down the road.

John Tansey again went back to the Washington Area to troll for a replacement. The recruit this time was Larry Matthews from WWDC. Larry was a likeable, knowledgeable and highly competent guy, who brought some much needed reforms to the newsroom but I always sensed Larry favored field reporting over supervision.

It was Matthews who brought Bill McGowan into the fold. McGowan had some impressive writing credentials and would succeed Matthews as News Director. Bill's forte was documentaries, and he produced two notable long form investigations during his time at WRVA. The first was an in depth examination into the Kepone

Environmental Disaster in 1975, which poisoned the lower James River and Chesapeake Bay and forced the Governor to close both to commercial fishing. The documentary won several major news awards, including the national Sigma Delta Chi Award. The other was an award winning investigation into abuse of the elderly.

The New Year brought a rare call from my father. He wanted me to come down to Emporia that coming weekend because he had something he needed to discuss with me; and he did not wish to do it over the telephone.

The news was not good. He told me he did not have long to live, perhaps a year, maybe less. It was the fungus condition in his lung that had been diagnosed roughly five years earlier. There was no cure. He said he was putting his and Mother's joint assets in Mother's name except for a mutual fund, which he was signing over to me with specific conditions on use of the earnings for her care after he was gone.

I thought it might create ill will with my sisters, who were older, and suggested that he should assign it to one of them but he said no. "They will never come back to Virginia," he said, "and I know you will be nearby to look after your Mother when the time comes." Always thorough, he typed up our agreement, signed it and sent me two copies, one to be signed by me and sent back to him.

Jeri and I were returning to Richmond from a similar visit to Emporia later that spring when I remarked that if we were serious about each other (and after several years of dating, and for the immediate past, living with one another, it was obvious we were), it was probably time to make things permanent and legal.

She was completely surprised. "John Harding are you proposing to me?" "Yes, I am," I replied. "Ohhhh Yessssss!" She said. When we got back to the apartment, she called her mother with the news, and I called Emporia. The announcements were printed in the respective hometown papers, and we set the date for September 14th.

XIV

Howard Bloom was a big man with a full beard that gave him the look of a modern day Old Testament Prophet. Blessed with a booming voice made for radio, he was the workhorse of the WRVA newsroom. In morning and afternoon drive, he was the station's traffic reporter, broadcasting continuous traffic updates every five minutes or so from the WRVA Helicopter. When he wasn't in the air or on the air, he was out chasing fires and what not. He ate and slept news. He had quickly become a close friend.

Shortly after I arrived at WRVA, Howard had shown up unannounced at my apartment one Saturday morning to install a burglar alarm in my, new to me, AMC Javelin. I had mentioned in the newsroom one day that the battery had been stolen one night in the parking lot at my apartment building. "You need an alarm, John," Howard barked. "I suppose I do," I replied. Nothing more had been said about it until Howard showed up that morning.

Bloom had, of course, designed the system himself. He gave me pause when he punched a hole in the car door just below the door handle to install a key switch but his self-confidence and take charge attitude put my misgivings to rest. After about 15 minutes, he inserted the key, armed the system and instructed me to try to open the hood. When I did, the horn immediately blasted for a solid minute, then again and again until it reset itself. An attempt to open a door set it off again. He refused to even let me pay him for the parts.

It was classic Howard. You never had to ask Howard for help, he sensed it and just went to it. Howard was loud, could be bossy as hell, and sometimes overbearing. He was also the best friend anyone could ever hope to have.

I had worked the morning news shift at the station, then filed a piece for Howard's 12 o'clock News, an hour long strip he produced and broadcast each weekday. I had run some errands after work, grabbed some lunch and gotten back to the apartment around 2:30 that afternoon. Jeri was at the lab working. We had been sharing the apartment for about a year. I fell on the bed for the best sleep I got every day. It was a Friday afternoon, May 24th, 1974.

My clock radio awakened me at 5:25PM. I had learned to never sleep more than three hours in the afternoon or I would not be able to sleep at night. On the radio, Howard had been called in for a traffic report. The sounder that was always his cue tailed off, but there was no Howard. I didn't think anything of it. He had probably missed a cue or there was radio trouble. It happened sometimes. Then the phone rang.

It was John Tansey. Hearing his voice, I was instantly on edge. "John, the helicopter is down," he said. "We cannot raise Howard on the radio. We fear the worst. How close are you to West 31st Street?" I said I could be there in about five minutes. Tansey said, "Go!"

I pulled on some jeans, T shirt and a pair of sneakers and headed for the elevator. I punched the big V8 in my new Firebird and roared West on Semmes Avenue, then took a left onto West 31st street and headed south to Moody Street. I saw it immediately: a small house with a huge hole in the roof. Sooty smoke was billowing skyward. There was no sign of the helicopter. It wasn't a quantum leap to figure the chopper had plummeted through the roof.

The Richmond Fire Department had just arrived and was laying hoses. Police were cordoning off the scene. I got out of the Firebird with my hand held 2-way radio and glanced at my watch. It was 20 minutes to 6. I radioed the station and told Tansey what I had seen and to be prepared for the worst.

I started walking toward the Richmond Fire Battalion Chief who had command of the scene. I had taken maybe four or five steps when Norman, my detective cousin, grabbed me in a bear hug. He had responded when he heard the call on his police radio. "You don't need to see this, John," he said, "they're all dead." I went limp. He said Howard had been killed instantly. So had the substitute pilot and a young boy who was in the house.

I had barely processed what Norman had told me when he and John Finnegan, the Richmond Fire Chief, practically carried me to Norman's car, stashing me in the back seat. I yanked my notebook from my hip pocket, interviewed Norman and the Chief and scribbled a few notes. The news was devastating.

Police had identified the victims as Howard, the substitute pilot, Walter Cottrell Junior who was an off duty Richmond Police Officer, and 9 year old Michael

Wilson, who was killed inside the house when he was struck by debris. Police had cordoned off the scene and Richmond Fire and Rescue Crews were entering the house to retrieve the bodies. The enormity of what I had just reported tipped the reservoir of internal emotion and I began to well up.

The next thing I remember was Norman stopping me from getting out of the car. He wouldn't let me drive back to Church Hill. I rode with him and he had an officer follow with my car.

Everyone was in John Tansey's office. When I walked in, everyone just looked without saying anything. We sat together for a long time in the quiet. John said it was better for us to be together than be alone. He was right, of course. We just sat, gazing out of the huge window as the sun sank over Richmond, and we tried to comprehend what had happened.

Several hours later, when I got back to the apartment, Jeri met me at the door with a stunned look of disbelief on her face. She had heard the news.

Just the previous weekend, she, along with Howard's wife Patt and the regular pilot of the Helicopter, Willie Windham, had flown in the same machine to the Camptown Races in the Varina area of Henrico County and back to the airport as part of WRVA's sponsorship of the event. Days before, we had all been together at Howard's house in Mechanicsville, just north of the city, for a crab feast.

I was devastated by Howard's death and had great difficulty coming to terms with it. For the longest time, I could not talk about it.

Less than a month after the crash, the station put a new helicopter in the skies over Richmond with Tim Timberlake signing on as the station's new traffic reporter.

Four months later, Jeri and I were married in the small country church she grew up in, not far from her father's small farm in Lenoir County, North Carolina. It was a very small ceremony. Our parents and several of Jeri's aunts attended, along with my sister Barbara and my nephew Paul. Jeri's elder sister Marjorie was her Maid of Honor and my father was my best man. June, who was working in Los Angeles, could not attend. The reception was held at Jeri's parents' home on the farm, with her many aunts floating among the guests like clouds, bearing dainty homemade pastries and watercress sandwiches.

We had decided in the summer that a cruise to Bermuda that August would be our honeymoon. We saved what little money we had to put toward a house somewhere down the road.

Back at River Towers, we moved into a large two bedroom apartment on the 12th floor with a small terrace overlooking the James River and Downtown Richmond. The view was sensational, particularly at night, with the lights of the city beyond reflecting in the river below.

We were so proud of our apartment that we decided to host a New Year's Eve Party. We invited everyone we knew and most came, including Mother and June. The next morning, I learned my father had died that night.

XV

When I look at the last photograph we have of Father, taken over the Christmas Holidays in 1974, it is obvious he is not well, but the slow deterioration of his health had not registered with us. Almost forgotten was our conversation the previous February, when he had summoned me to Emporia to tell me he did not have long to live because of the fungus condition on his lung. He had not said another word to me about it. He had died in his bed on New Year's morning. Mother found him when she and June returned to Emporia from our New Year's Eve Party.

My memories of that New Year's Day are limited to short flashes like heat lightning in the summer: the surreal pool of brilliant white sunlight that flooded the foyer of the house on Ingleside, spotlighting the out of place lectern from the funeral home with the bright red leather bound guest book; the silhouettes of the people in the living room, who all turned in unison like the crowd at a tennis match when we walked in; the silhouette of Mother alone in the den at the back of the house looking out at her garden in the backyard; and me, sitting alone in my father's basement studio, with his tools, paints, and unfinished projects.

Father was very much an enigma to me, a puzzle with missing pieces. Aside from his two brothers and a sister, I knew nothing about his side of the family. Mother said he never talked about it because his childhood had been so horrible. He had been forced to quit school in the 7th grade to go to work to help support his family during the First World War. I was an adult before I knew the names of my paternal grandparents. Father had never mentioned them.

We had never been close when I was growing up. I can only remember one outing with him. He had taken me on a Redskin's Booster Train trip to Washington to see the Redskins play the Detroit Lions at the old Griffith Stadium. I don't ever remember confiding in him or seeking his help on anything, without going through Mother until I was an adult out of school and working. We had then begun to get to know one another, but he had run out of time.

Mother seemed to carry on without much trepidation after Father's death. It wasn't long before she started making deals and finding people to take care of things, such as cutting the grass or washing her windows. I was amazed at how much she could get done by baking someone a pie. Her buddies rallied around her. Grace, Doctor Allison's wife, was her BFF. They were always involved in something, from buying yard tools at antique auctions to making flower arrangements to sell for the Hospital Auxiliary.

Whenever Jeri and I drove down to see her, which was just about every weekend for a time after Father died, she would greet us at the door usually decked out in her yard patrol getup · a mishmash of not yet ready for the Goodwill outerwear: an old flowery print house coat, one of Father's threadbare jackets, suitably camouflaged with plant food stains, a very worn pair of black-rubber galoshes · the kind that had metal clips on the front, and an ancient straw hat.

It was pretty much the same "outfit" she wore when she and Margaret Lucas would trek down to the local USDA Office for the free cheese handout · Mother said the idea was not to look too well to do. I told her she looked absolutely homeless.

Mother had always doted on her garden but after Father died, it became a sanctuary for her. She would often sit on the vintage park bench from the courthouse square that he had restored for her, deep in her thoughts. Mother was religious, but she never wore it on her sleeve. She had a strong sense of self and seldom minced words. One Sunday after the service, the Minister thanked her for "coming to be with God," she replied, " Reverend, I don't need to come to church to be with God. I'm with him every day when I'm in my garden. I come to church," she said, "because I like to dress up and see my friends." Mother was a bit vain but she was never a hypocrite.

She would assume the role of a plantation overseer pointing and directing as we went about mulching, weeding, feeding, transplanting, pruning and dragging piles of limbs and yard waste to the street, where it would be picked up by the city the following week. Mother always believed manual labor improved one's character.

In the afternoons, Jeri would drive her on her rounds: to Ruby Southall's Beauty Parlor, to the library with books that needed to be returned and unread ones picked up, or to check out those new shoes at the local department store where she liked to nose around for bargains. Dinner was at "Johnny's New York Restaurant," the primary eatery for Mother's crowd, though the menu had little to do with New York. Johnny's specialty was southern soul food: collard greens, black-eyed peas, fried pork chops and the like. Then it was back to the house for an evening of PBS, followed by long philosophical talks on into the wee small hours.

On the rare weekend when we weren't in Emporia, I always called Mother on Sunday afternoons. It was a command performance. My sisters and I each had assigned time slots in which we were to call. You couldn't make this up! BB had the 2-3PM hour, 3-4PM was my hour and June from 4 to 5. If one of us was late, we got the standard "What on earth could possibly be more important than talking to your Mother" monologue. And the answer is yes, she consumed the entire hour.

She seldom visited us in Richmond. Mother did not like being away from her house. She said traveling was too much trouble. She had to pack up all of her daily potions, pills, salves, vitamins, fiber supplements and drops, all of which she carried in an old Miller & Roads shopping bag. And, she didn't like our schedule. Mother was a night owl. She seldom went to bed before 2 or 3 in the morning, long after Charlie Rose, Carson, and Tom Snyder were done, and she slept until 10 most mornings. When she did visit, she was like a fish out of water. Often it would come down to her dealing the "I'm the only Mother you are ever going to have" card, which translated meant, "You come to see me, not the other way around." And so it went for the next 20 years until the ravages of old age settled in, and she became even more intransigent about leaving her house.

XVI

WRVA marked its 50th Anniversary in the fall of 1975. The station was in an unparalleled position. *TV Radio Age* had published rankings that August, putting WRVA at number 3 in the country in morning and afternoon drive and number five in the USA's top 50 radio markets from 6AM to Midnight, Monday through Sundays.

The station celebrated with a huge open house spread over the course of several weekends at the Church Hill

Studio Building at North 22nd and East Grace Streets. The lines stretched for blocks. Off duty police officers were hired to handle the traffic and parking. It seemed the entire city had turned out for the celebration. The station published a 50th Anniversary Booklet commemorating the milestone and produced a special long playing record album filled with the sounds of the previous 50 years.

The biggest attraction seemed to be "Millard The Mallard's Closet." Temporarily converted from a janitor's closet just off the main Lobby, it had been decorated with all of Millard's stuff: a Brooklyn Dodger's Pennant, empty cans of "Cold Deliciouses," and Flip Flops. Photographs of Millard's relatives were hung on the wall, along with a large portrait of a Banana Sandwich, an Alden Aaroe Halloween mask and vintage Millard "T" shirts.

A door bell had been installed at kid height beside the screened door with a crude sign: "Press Here." It triggered a recording of Millard blabbering about having to go downstairs for a "Cold Delicious" or some other excuse for not being there.

Lou Dean recalls an episode involving a little kid, 4 or 5 years old, who was heartbroken when Millard wasn't in his nest. He had started to cry. "You noticed him and spoke to him in Millard's voice. The kid brightened up immediately with a big smile. Even though he never really saw you, you were a hero that day."

Listeners got a tour of the building, including the newsroom and studio spaces. Outside on the lawn, Jeri manned The Millard The Mallard booth, selling Millard "T" shirts and copies of *A Millard The Mallard Christmas* with proceeds going to the WRVA Shoe Fund. The WRVA

Traffic Helicopter had been flown in. Kids could put on the flight helmet and sit in the pilot's seat.

The immense popularity of WRVA and Millard was reflected in an exhaustive study of the Richmond radio audience that the station had commissioned. Every personality on the air in Richmond was tested. Almost every respondent associated Millard The Mallard with WRVA, including a majority of those who were not regular WRVA listeners.

Mother remarked, "To think we move heaven and earth to get you into school, where you get a degree, and you make the big time as a duck!" It wasn't enough. I didn't want Millard The Mallard to be my magnum opus.

My urge to write sent me into the print world in the summer of 1976. I had seen the giant ocean liner "United States" in storage at Norfolk International Terminals when Jeri and I departed on our cruise to Bermuda. Our small Greek Liner, Queen Anna Maria, was tied up across the quay. It looked like a toy beside the Superliner. The "United States" had been withdrawn from service in 1969, and I thought it would make for an interesting photo essay and story.

I called First District Congressman Tom Downing, who was Chairman of the House Subcommittee on the Merchant Marine, to see if he could get me access to the liner. He did. Jeri went along as my assistant. A Maritime Administration guide met us on the dock.

The "United States" epitomized the stately majesty of the pure bred transatlantic liners from another era. Its layup had left only the SS France in transatlantic service. (The new Queen Elizabeth 2 had been built as a dual liner and cruise ship.) The "United States" had the look of a thoroughbred anxious to jump from the starting gate. It was almost hard to believe anything that big could move. Just ten feet short of a thousand feet long, the liner was seventeen stories high. Without the guide, we would have been lost for a week.

We entered through a shell hatch on "B" deck. Nothing was off limits, not even the two engine rooms which had been classified for years because of the liner's blazing top speed, which was just over 40 knots or in excess of 46 miles an hour.

It was like stepping back in time. Everything had been left exactly as it was after the last transatlantic crossing in the fall of 1969. It was eerie, as though someone had waved a magic wand and all of the passengers and crew had vanished. The beds in the staterooms had been left unmade. The bars were still stocked with liquor, newspapers were still in the racks, sheet music was still on the bandstand in the First Class Ballroom and charts were laid out on the navigation bridge.

The only sound was the soft din of the dehumidification system that had been installed. There was enough natural light to see where one was going, but every photograph required a flash or a time exposure. I shot a half dozen or so 35 mm exposure rolls of Kodachrome and sold a multi-page photo essay and article to *Sea Classics Magazine*. It was published the following March. Scores of other photo essays would follow, laying the groundwork for what would become my second career when I left broadcasting.

Part VI

Management

I

John Tansey was something of an oddity among radio general managers. He had not come up through the sales ranks. He was a reporter. His roots in the news trade were deep. He had hawked the *Miami Daily News-Record* on the streets of Miami and was a carrier for the *Miami Herald*. He had edited his high school newspaper, *The Vacuum Cleaner.* "We scooped up all the dirt," he said. His first radio job was with WRUF at the University of Florida, where he graduated with a degree in Journalism. He found his way to WRVA and spent World War II in the Navy, serving in the Pacific. After the war, he rejoined WRVA as a field reporter.

Among his early assignments was the disappearance of four young boys from their homes near the McGuire Veteran's Hospital in Richmond. Their bodies were found two days later in a large refrigerator in an abandoned building, only yards from one of the boy's home. It was a gruesome story for genteel Richmond and a state police officer tried, to no avail, to prevent John from reporting the tragic discovery.

Tansey became Program Services Manager, then became General Manager of the company's FM station, WRVC, in Norfolk in 1954. Two years later, he succeeded the legendary C.T. Lucy as manager of the company's flagship WRVA.

As General Manager, Tansey set the tone for the radio station; and it was decidedly tilted toward news. News was his passion. Like Bob Kintner at NBC during the heyday of Huntley Brinkley, Tansey was always pushing for more, and more was never enough. Constantly driven to beat the newspapers in their own backyard, nothing escaped his attention. Everything mattered. Nothing was insignificant. John would come back from cocktail parties, vacations, civic club meetings, conventions, community association meetings, and backyard-over-the-fence chats with neighbors, filled with tips and suggestions. Had we seen the story in the Post this morning? Were we looking into this or that?

By late 1977, Tansey had gone through another pair of news directors. Bill McGowan, who had replaced Larry Matthews, was replaced by Larry Dodd. It had been a popular choice. After going outside the station three times to find leadership for the news department, Tansey promoted from within. Dodd was the obvious choice.

Larry Dodd was an old WRVA hand who had returned to the station in 1969 after serving two years as Assistant Chief of Staff in the office of Richmond Democratic Congressman David E. Satterfield III. Upon his return to WRVA, he was given the title Director of Public Affairs. Larry hosted the long running *Open For Opinion* telephone talk program at mid-day, and he was the station's editorial writer. He was also a frequent news anchor in the morning and was an anchor for WRVA's election coverage. Upon McGowan's departure from the station, Dodd added News Director to his title. When he left in early 1978 to go into private business, my name popped up.

I had seen it coming and spent a lot of time thinking about it, long before Tansey pitched it to me; but I had no interest. Management was a foreign zip code. There was nothing I wanted to do less. The first time I was offered the position, I turned it down, saying management was not my cup of tea and was not why I had gone into broadcast journalism. I liked what I was doing. When Tansey pressed the question again, I told him I didn't want to be another revolving door department manager; but he was unrelenting. I was summoned to his office almost daily for long spiels on why I had to take the job. All the little voices in my head were telling me to say no; but over the next few weeks, my resolve began to crumble. Reality was closing in. I was 32 years old and at a crossroads. I had maxed out at WRVA. Either I went into management or I had to leave for a bigger market. There was no other avenue to a fatter paycheck. Every fabric of my being told me not to do it for the money; but I caved. I took the money! John Tansey's memo appointing me News Director was issued to the staff in February, 1978.

II

Everything changed when I moved into management. I traded my reporter's notebook and the fun and excitement of chasing and writing news for the more lucrative, but mundane, work of middle management. I had become one of the cheap suits in the organization chart. My days would now be spent dealing with personnel problems, manipulating people to do things they didn't want to do, recruiting, strategy, scheduling, making budgets, tracking expenses and trying to please the big cheeses. It was depressing as hell, and the odds were not good that I would have any success.

I was well aware that John Tansey had gone through a total of 7 News Directors at WRVA in less than 9 years, one of them twice. I mentioned it as a major concern in my journal where I had posed the question: "Why do I have any reason to believe I won't be number 8?" The only person I knew who could roll back the curtain on Tansey's in-your-face management style and understood how to handle it was Brick Rider.

Brick, short for Brickford, his middle name, had been program manager at WRVA for many years under John. In those days, the Program Manager also oversaw the News Department so Brick knew first-hand what I would be opening myself up to. He had left the station before I arrived in Richmond to become a Public Relations officer for the City Manager of Richmond at City Hall. He later worked in a similar capacity at Reynold's Metals. We had become friends.

He told me, "You'll be fine, John." "But," he added, "every so often you'll have to have a "G** Damn It John" session with him because he will keep meddling with what you are doing. "If you don't confront him," he said, " he'll just grind you up, have no respect for you, and move on to the next victim." Eight months would pass before I had that encounter.

The *Times Dispatch* and the afternoon *News Leader* ran articles about my appointment. Friends and acquaintances called or mailed their congratulations. Mid Weeks, Joe's wife, wrote me: "It's about time, John." I was basking in the spotlight of being the new kid smiling in the school cafeteria; but when I thought of all that awaited me, I was overwhelmed, and I sensed the honeymoon with Tansey would be short lived.

There was little structure, no documented procedures, few systems and, aside from news scripts, no records. For starters, there was no policy manual. Nothing was in writing. There was no source rule, no bulletin rule, and no recently updated manual for covering disasters, such as major plane crashes, floods or hurricanes. Aside from a vast collection of ET's (Electrical Transcriptions or very large vinyl recordings) that dated from the 30's, 40's and 50's, there were few archives for news audio. At the end of every day, culled news sound was simply erased. There was no posted news personnel schedule each week. I was starting from a blank page.

Getting everything in place and functioning would take months, and on top of all of that, we had to cover the day to day. I wrote in my journal, "Don't set too many priorities." It was the best advice I ever gave myself.

I knew I had to have help - a competent, aggressive, super loyal number 2, someone I could trust and count on to run the place when I wasn't there or was tied up elsewhere. I called John Ennis, who was running an all-news station in Providence, Rhode Island, for the Providence Journal.

John had been the long time Military Reporter for Jim Mayes at WTAR Radio and Television in Norfolk. We had first met at the State Capitol, where he was subbing for WTAR's (now WTKR) Capitol Reporter.

I told John what I was looking for, that I had to move fast, that the salary was open and would depend on experience. He told me he thought he knew the perfect candidate and would have him call me the next morning. He did. " I'm the guy," he said. "The only thing colder up here than the weather is the people. Let's talk."

We flew him down to Richmond, and I was quickly convinced that Ennis was indeed the guy. John would be my right hand man for the next 15 years. He was aggressive, could write the hell out of anything, made good decisions and got no gruff from the staff.

I began sketching out a News Department Policy Manual. Emergency coverage guides were written. I didn't want us to forget how we had covered the Camille and Agnes Floods and other disasters.

John Tansey's Administrative Assistant, Debbie Ashley, the most organized person on the planet, was instrumental in helping me put it all together and keeping it updated. In a matter of weeks, she had the completed policy manual all printed, arranged by subject, alphabetized, cross indexed, color coded and copied for every member of the news staff.

Every successful enterprise has a Debbie. Officially, she was John Tansey's Executive Assistant, but in reality she wore multiple hats. Like Barbara Little at WEVA in the 60's, Debbie was practically indispensable. A world class multi-tasker, all the myriad of things that would have fallen through the cracks at WRVA didn't because Debbie was always there to catch them. She was devoted to the station, and decades later, she would step up to save its archives.

My news department wish list was long. For starters, I wanted to refit the newsroom. The building may have been ultra-modern, but aside from a custom made editor's console fitted with a push button switcher that eliminated using patch cords to input news audio sources, the news department was a flashback to the 50's and 60's.

Several years into my tenure, I drew up plans for two fully equipped anchor work stations to replace desks that dated back to the Hotel Richmond days. Wilson Yarbrough, our ace master carpenter and cabinet maker, brought them to life. Our Chief Engineer, John Francioni, and his crew, meticulously fitted them out. They also planned and built a news production booth and a backup news air studio.

It was a very ambitious plan, but I had no intention of just being a caretaker. I was determined to go all out, to give it my best shot. My goal, as I wrote in my journal was, "to put in place the structure and systems, and acquire the resources, to build a respected and trusted news organization."

III

By the time I became News Director, John Tansey had removed News from the Program Department. The News Director reported directly to him. The change made John a sort of General Manager-Executive Editor. He relished the role.

Unlike any of his successors, John viewed WRVA as a news organization. As a trained journalist, he grasped the essential truth of the news trade. There is no substitute for being there. And he understood that being there required people and money.

He gave us the money and, just as importantly, he gave us unimpeded access to air, moving control from the announcer or personality on the air to the line news editor/ anchor in the newsroom. He ordered the installation of a bulletin interrupt switch in the main news air studio. When activated, on air programming was instantly interrupted for the immediate broadcast of bulletins and special reports.

Tansey wanted WRVA to be noticed, to have impact. He expected us to push the envelope with fair, aggressive, compelling reporting and let him worry about the consequences. If a client threatened to pull their advertising off the station because of a story, and quite a few did, John showed them the door.

Right or wrong, he always backed us to the hilt. When we were wrong, he demanded an immediate on-air correction at the top of every newscast and an investigation to determine what had happened and why; but I don't recall anyone ever being fired for making a mistake. "If we don't make a mistake, we're not doing anything," he said.

When we were right, he was lavish with praise. It wasn't unusual for reporters to find a congratulatory "Tanseygram" in their station mailbox, complimenting them on a job well done.

He insisted that we participate to the fullest in the broadcast journalism news awards programs. He expected us to win, but he never belittled us if we didn't, judging us not on the results but rather on the quality of our effort. And to that end, for the first year of my tenure, he asked to hear the entries before they were submitted.

I handled all of the awards' production myself so as not to tie up reporters, anchors and editors. Every spring, I went to work for several months putting entries together. Archived sound from our daily news morgue, which I had put in place, and "Air Check" recordings of major breaking news coverage were used extensively, each entry becoming, in effect, a radio documentary.

Each year, we participated in all of the major broadcast journalism awards programs. We did not do well in the early years but as our "beat system" evolved, opening the door to more original reporting and extensive coverage of breaking news, we began to win.

IV

There had been some departures when I took over. One staffer left because he had been passed over for News Director, another jumped to television and one left to go into academia.

Finding replacements wasn't as difficult as I had anticipated. In the late 70's and on into the 80's, there was a steady pool of young, talented reporters in smaller or similar sized markets who were looking to move. Once the positions were filled, we were able to set up the beginnings of a beat system with reporters assigned to localities in the Metro area and the State Capitol full time. It was the best way to lay the foundation for enterprising news instead of practicing what Weeks' had called "hand out journalism" or cribbing from the newspapers.

One wily veteran stayed and became the core of our rebuilding effort. Dave Miller had joined the station in the early 70's. He had gained the spotlight with his coverage of a sniper incident in downtown Richmond, managing to get an interview with the suspect on the phone in the Hotel John Marshal before the man took his own life. Miller was soon a fixture at the State Capitol, where he became the best broadcast reporter on the beat. I always thought of him as Richmond's version of Gabe Pressman, the iconic newsman in Miller's hometown of New York.

We brought in Georgeann Herbert from WTAR in Norfolk, Dale Gauding from WFIR in Roanoke, and, Randy Webster, also from Roanoke. Eugenia Halsey joined us as a general assignment reporter and Margaret Branham came on as an anchor and reporter. Mike Raff, another New Yorker, took over the so-called animal beat chasing breaking news, earning him the inevitable nickname "Riff." Jim McAndrew, out of Boston College, brought big sound to our evening anchor desk.

Peter Vieth, also from WFIR became our man at City Hall. Renee Ridley joined us from Northern Virginia. Pam Prouty, a UNC Graduate with the instincts of a veteran, joined the staff as our Chesterfield Reporter.

Deanna Malone arrived in the early 80's to cover Henrico County. Tom Calmeyer, a seasoned anchor and editor, came on board, as did Ron Horne and Jim Carter. Bill Gordon became our go to street guy, replacing Mike Raff. Ellen Reinhardt stepped into the Chesterfield beat without missing one. We recruited Charles Taylor as a general assignment reporter, and Kathy Culpepper came up from WCMS in Norfolk. Later, Veronica Robinson, Monique Braxton, Craig Butterworth and Mike Frontiero joined the staff as Anchor Reporters. Tammy Jones signed on to handle the overnight watch. Dean Lane took over the evening desk.

Scores of part-timers came and went with frustrating regularity. Mercedes Sprouse and Ray Swiderski brought much needed stability.

V

I don't recall the issue that brought John storming into the newsroom in the fall of 1978 in a holy rage; but I vividly remember his tirade. Almost purple faced with anger, he proceeded to thoroughly dress me down in front of everybody, then wheeled around and managed to slam the heavy oak, soundproof door to the newsroom that had a very strong damper mechanism, supposedly designed to prevent sudden closure. I was stunned. So was Ennis and everyone else. The "G** Damn It, John" moment that Brick had predicted was at hand.

I went into my office just off the newsroom, picked up my keys and ID cards and told Ennis I did not know if I would be back. He said something about giving Tansey time to cool off but I was adrenalized.

John seldom closed his door. I walked in without knocking on the door frame and tossed my keys on his desk. I recalled the episode in my Journal that October of 1978.

"I quit," I said, and turned to leave.

"Talk to me," he said.

I told him he had every right to say whatever he wanted to me but that he should have at least had the decency to do it behind closed doors. "Dressing me down in front of my staff," I said, "only trashes what little credibility and authority I have managed to build. If that's the way you do business, you can do it with someone else." I was really angry and started again to leave.

"You're right," he said. "I was out of line."

He apologized on the spot and said he would personally apologize to the news staff right away. He did. He also gave me his word that, from that point forward, our disagreements would be handled in a civil manner and in private. They were.

News Director was a package deal as far as Tansey was concerned. In addition to administering the News Department, I was to continue working my morning news shift, which included my role as Millard The Mallard on Alden's morning program, and I was to be the station's editorial writer.

John was an old hand at Editorial Broadcasting. WRVA had broadcast its first station editorial in 1961, taking a position on the proposed Richmond-Henrico County merger. John was for it. (The Annexation Judge decided in Richmond's favor; but he set the price so high the city refused to pay and allowed the case to expire.) For the next 35 years, WRVA regularly took stands on controversial issues of local importance.

I began meeting with him every week to identify worthy issues and hash out positions. John was by nature a very pragmatic and passionate man and while our exchanges were always lively and often loud, it was a matter of emphasis, not anger, and never personal. I never met anyone in my life who enjoyed a good argument more than Tansey.

More often than not, we saw eye to eye. John was, as he described himself, a "fast" moderate on social issues while conservative on fiscal matters, which dovetailed nicely with my own views. I would usually write a draft, which John would then edit. The editorials usually ran no more than a minute or so and were broadcast during all of the major newscasts beginning in morning drive.

They usually struck a chord. By far, the great majority of the issues we addressed were specific to the Metropolitan Richmond area and our position often generated requests for "equal time" to respond. "Equal Time," a reference to the Federal Communications Commission Equal-Time Rule, was widely misconstrued by the public as applying to any controversial view expressed over the air. In practice, it only applied only to political broadcasting. The rule afforded opposing political candidates an equal opportunity to respond. The FCC's Fairness Doctrine, which would later be revoked in the deregulation frenzy of the late 80's, often did apply. It required broadcast stations to address controversial issues equally. It was never a problem for us. As a news and information station, putting opposing views on the air was what we did. Even so, we afforded representatives of bona-fide groups and organizations who wished to respond to station editorials the opportunity to do so. Individuals who wished to respond were directed to the station's "Open for Opinion" telephone talk forum or its later successor "Viewpoint."

When John retired as General Manager in 1982, he stayed on as a consultant and continued his role in editorial broadcasting. When he finally left the station permanently in 1992, after the Clear Channel upheaval, I continued the station's editorial broadcasts until Clear Channel ended editorial broadcasting by WRVA in 1996.

Always looking to increase the diversity of opinions on the air, Tansey recruited Darrell Rollins, a black Libertarian theologian, in the early 70's to join the daily commentary rotation, which included those of us on the news staff.

The rotating assignments worked out to one opinion piece for each of us every week.

The commentaries, or "Profiles" as they were called, each ran about 90 seconds. The usual rules prevailed. Personal attacks were off limits. So were endorsements of causes, products or political candidates; and all scripts had to be pre-approved by the news director.

Rollins, who had a professorial air about him, was later succeeded by The Reverend E. E. Smith Junior, or "Jeep," as he was widely known. "Jeep," a big man who had the physique of an armored personnel carrier, brought a degree of street hipness to the commentaries. When he left a few years later, we recruited Jack Gravely, who was the Executive Director of the Virginia NAACP.

Every week, I looked forward to the give and take I had with Jack while editing his scripts and showing him the ropes of broadcast production. He was a quick study. Jack's gritty passion was his signature and he became a hell of a communicator. His always lively and provoking, twice weekly "On the Black Side" commentaries ran until he left in 1987 to pursue other interests. He returned in the late 90's to host a Saturday night talk show that was a hot ticket in Richmond. The show ran until 2001 when Clear Channel pulled it off the air and replaced it with a syndicated program.

VI

There was always pressure not to report things and sometimes it came from within, bubbling up during the weekly department head meetings held in Tansey's office. I was updating our progress in putting together an investigative series on crime in the city, along with a supporting editorial series. Sales which frequently saw news as being at cross purposes with its task of bringing in revenue, objected, warning that what we were doing could anger clients and hurt the bottom line. John waved their complaint aside with what became a familiar refrain, "We'll just have to make the bucks another day."

We obeyed the law, but we did not withhold information. Once we had information and confirmed it to our satisfaction, we would usually report it at the earliest opportunity. Embargoes were particularly irksome.

When the Federal Reserve was preparing to move from its location at 9th and Franklin Streets to its new skyscraper headquarters overlooking the James River in 1978, the media was invited to a briefing on the move, at which time details of the logistics involved were to be revealed. There was a catch. In order to attend, news organizations had to agree to an embargo on the release of any information. We did not attend and, thus, were not bound by it.

We worked our sources and soon confirmed what was about to happen, including the deployment of armed troops along the route of the move. We decided the public had a right to know and we reported it.

Every now and then, we had to make a deal. The case of Raymond Royall comes to mind. Royall was a Richmond City Councilman who had faked his death in a boating accident. The fact that his body was never found aroused our suspicion. When the story shifted out of state, Tansey okayed the hiring of a private investigator. We eventually tracked Royall down in St. Louis, where he had surfaced with a new identity. Authorities asked us to withhold the story until Royall could be arrested and charged. In return for having an exclusive beat on the story, we agreed. Royall pled guilty to loan fraud and tax evasion and we got the scoop on his capture.

After my appointment at News Director, I seldom, if ever, got out into the field to chase down a story, confirming the old axiom in journalism that the higher one climbs in the profession, the further away from real reporting one gets. I was anchoring newscasts in morning drive, and while I would work the phones to flesh out a pickup from beat calls, my position chained me to the newsroom. Every now and then I would phone in a piece on a fire or an accident I'd happen upon, but the rare times I got to do any substantial field reporting was when something popped up while on vacation.

Jeri and I had taken two weeks off in the late summer of 1979 and booked a small oceanfront cottage in South Nags Head on the Outer Banks of North Carolina. Shortly after we arrived, storm warnings went up along the coast. We had been to Maine to visit June the year before, but this was our first real vacation by ourselves since we had been married and we decided to stick it out.

The little cottage was rocked by the storm, quaking each time one of the big breakers slammed into its pilings. The wind turned the blinding rain sideways, pounding the windows so hard that the water seeped around the glazing to puddle on the floor.

There was a phone booth on highway 12, just up from the cottage. Jeri thought I was crazy to go out, but I had to try. I was amazed to get a dial tone. I phoned the station and did a quick on-scene report.

When I called back several hours later, Ennis told me to call the NBC desk in New York. The editor asked if I had any sound. I said "sure" and held the receiver outside the phone booth where the roaring Atlantic, not 40 yards away, coupled with the howling wind and driving rain, sounded like a constant sonic boom. I filed several reports and quite a few more over the next several days. Back at the cottage, Jeri remarked, "You're really enjoying this aren't you?" I was and there was a plus. The network fees more than paid for our vacation.

VII

There probably wasn't a kid alive from the 50's on into the 90's who wasn't praying on snowy mornings for Mr. Aaroe to announce their school was closed. WRVA was the first thing people thought of when the flakes began to fall. One joke had it that when the word "snow" showed up in the weather forecast, Richmonders headed to the grocery store to stock up on bread and milk and tune to WRVA, not necessarily in that order.

WRVA was known far and wide for its snow closing system, which we shamelessly promoted in every way imaginable, including an easily removable refrigerator sticker (magnets would not "stick" to stainless steel). It pictured Millard The Mallard on skis duded up in a bibbed ski outfit with matching goggles. Printed below was the slogan "When it Snows - WRVA." Cases of them were mailed or handed out.

Organized with military precision and utilizing special codes, unlisted phone numbers and teams of staff members assigned to man the phone banks around the clock, if necessary, the station's emergency closing system was most often activated during snow events in the city. But it also went into operation during natural disasters, such as floods and hurricanes.

The Church Hill Building had been designed to accommodate staff around the clock. There were showers downstairs and full kitchen facilities. Bunks were set up in the studios. Food was brought in; and 4 wheel drive vehicles and, if necessary, the station's helicopter were used to transport staff members to the studios.

Many of us would come in the night before in advance of bad weather. The station took on the atmosphere of a college dormitory. Most of us were good friends and enjoyed one another's company. Many a WRVA employee would spend a snowy evening watching the flakes fall over Richmond from that spectacular view atop Church Hill. I don't imagine many got any sleep at all. What little I got was on the corduroy sofa in John Tansey's office, which always gave my face the look of a waffle by morning.

Alden was the face of the system. He became a sort of unofficial School Closing Czar for Central Virginia. If Aaroe said your school was closed, you could bag it. Once, in the heat of a snowy morning, I got a call from the Superintendent of a Southside Virginia School District who complained that WRVA had mistakenly closed his school system. I responded that I would get Mr. Aaroe to correct the mistake immediately. The superintendent paused, then said, "Well, if Mr. Aaroe closed our schools, they probably need to be closed. Just leave it as it is."

The closing list grew to the size of a small city phone book. In addition to public and private schools, colleges, universities, businesses, industry, corporations, government offices and agencies, non-profits, museums, and churches all had closing codes. All used the closing system.

Over the ensuing years, school closings crawling across the bottom of a TV screen, then, computer screens and, still later, text messages to smart phones would largely replace radio as the primary source of closing information. It was clearly more efficient, but I never thought it was as exciting as waiting to hear it on the radio.

VIII

The letter had all the warmth of a tax due notice. Formal and cold, it was from Leonard G. "Bob" Jones, a Vice President of our parent company, Southern Broadcasting Corporation.

Jones had grown up on a farm in North Carolina. After the Second World War, he paired up with John G. Johnson, a former FBI man, to form Southern Broadcasting Corporation. They purchased a small station in Winston Salem, North Carolina and subsequently added stations in Raleigh, Birmingham, Phoenix and other markets. His short, strictly to the point letter read like a telegram.

"I want to congratulate you on your appointment as News Director." STOP "This is a very important and demanding position, as you know." STOP "I look forward to meeting you on my next trip to Richmond". STOP

I wasn't looking forward to it. Mr. Jones had a reputation, widely telegraphed, as a humorless, hard-nosed, no- nonsense numbers cruncher. He made the rounds of all the company's stations at budget time to conduct reviews, which were described as the equivalent of being put on a medieval rack.

I had a feeling of impending doom as I went in for my first session with him. Even his old school briefcase was intimidating. Leather with big buckles and straps, I visualized it being packed with the remains of those who had been carved up in similar meetings. That I escaped relatively unscathed was mostly Bob going easy on me in my first encounter.

Subsequent reviews would be far tougher. There were no pleasantries, never any small talk, and no levity, just hard cold numbers. The human factor never entered the equation. Bob was always impenetrably polite, but the atmosphere was always incredibly tense and the grilling was brutal. To Jones, a crumb was equivalent to a seven layer cake. After every session, I felt as though I had been thoroughly pressed and dry cleaned.

In August of 1977, WRVA was purchased by Harte Hanks Communications based in San Antonio. The station had been owned by Larus for well over 40 years, but then, a variant of the seven-year itch seemed to kick in. Roughly 7 years after acquiring WRVA from the tobacco company, Southern Broadcasting was taken over by Harte Hanks.

Harte Hanks' President and CEO Robert Marbut, with his entourage of suited handlers, zoomed onto Church Hill in the WRVA Helicopter like a "Rock Star." After a cursory look around, with everyone acknowledging his presence by affording him additional CEO "space," he zoomed out. I never saw him again. Bob Jones who had been a Vice President with Southern, became head of Harte Hanks

Radio, providing some semblance of continuity over the change in ownership.

Our beat system of assigning reporters full time to each of the metro area localities began to pay dividends in the early 80's. Story budgets were beginning to include a respectable amount of enterprise, or original reporting, including in depth, investigative work. The journalism awards began coming in and, with them, came the lawsuits.

The first on my watch involved the Henrico County Sheriff. I've forgotten the particulars, but when the documents arrived, panic raced up my spine like rats abandoning a sinking ship. When I walked into John Tansey's office, he immediately stood up, smiled and said, "Congratulations." I thought he was being facetious, but he was quite serious. "If we don't get sued now and then," he said, "we're not doing anything."

A week or so later, a flamboyant attorney flew into Richmond from Harte Hanks Headquarters in San Antonio. He was hard to miss. Tall and thin, wearing a ten gallon cowboy hat, western shirt, blue jeans, cowboy boots and a leather sport coat, he offered a handshake as soon as he saw me with my WRVA sign in the terminal building. In his best Texas drawl, he said, "Howdy Partner."

On the drive to the station, he asked me to bring him up to speed. When I finished, he slapped me on the knee and said, "This is just a little ole cow tick boy," adding, "we don't lose cases like this." I relaxed. True to his word, the lawsuit eventually went away.

IX

There was an undercurrent of unease rippling through the halls over who would succeed John as Vice President and General Manager. The great majority of the staff had never worked for anyone other than John. He had been the boss since the mid 50's. Everyone assumed the job would go to the current sales manager Hal Barre, so it was a shock when the announcement came that Bob Jones would be the new General Manager.

Jones was then President of Harte Hanks Radio, our parent company. It was said he wanted to finish his career at WRVA. He brought in Carl McNeil from South Carolina to take over as sales manager, replacing Barre who was given a settlement.

One of Tansey's last acts as General Manager had been to appoint Lou Dean as Program Director to replace Walt Williams, who had left to assume the same position at WSB in Atlanta; but Lou and the rest of us would be working for Jones, the incoming General Manager.

Lou recalls interviewing Jones "more than he interviewed me." Lou wanted to know if Jones had a philosophy similar to Tansey's. "By way of an answer, Jones showed me his Rolex watch," Lou said, "to him a symbol of quality."

Jones was right at home in the fine wine and small portion set. He had the deference and moneyed reserve of old Richmond even though he was a relative newcomer to the city. Soon to join the exclusive Commonwealth Club, he drove a pricey BMW, dined at the best restaurants in the city and was heavily into the stock market. He struck me as rather aloof and almost paralyzed with formality.

My only exposure to him had been in those incredibly tense budget review sessions. I could not imagine trying to work day in and day out in that kind of environment. I finally talked myself into submitting my resignation. I recorded the encounter in my Journal.

When I dropped my resignation letter on his desk, Jones opened it immediately and, with no hesitation said, "John, if I wanted to replace you, you would already know it." Then, waving my letter, he added, "I have absolutely no intention of accepting this."

I thanked him for his vote of confidence and turned to leave his office.

"And John, one more thing," he said, "from now on, it's just Bob." I think it was the first time I had ever seen him smile.

John Harding News Director 2.0 was a different ballgame. Jones' management style was vastly different from that of John Tansey. Bob was not a hands-on manager and he sometimes seemed averse to making a decision. Jones had kept Tansey on in a consulting capacity and I assumed he wanted to get John's thoughts, particularly on news and editorial matters, before making a decision. Soon, he brought in Bob McNeill as "Station Manager," ostensibly an Operations Manager, to oversee programming, news and engineering.

McNeill had worked his magic at WRVQ, Q94, our sister FM station. He knew the market and WRVA as well as anyone and better than most. Bob was a tremendous innovator. He was decisive, a superb facilitator and a great advocate for the news department.

With Tansey and McNeill having Jones' ear, I figured we were in pretty good hands in the front office. It wasn't quite the same thing as having a GM who wore lawsuits as a badge of honor, but it was probably the best we could hope for and things ran smoothly.

Jones had his own unique talents. He was the consummate negotiator. He had a gift for maneuvering people toward a consensus without feeling they had been used or deceived. A master at setting up a no-escape situation to increase pressure and soften up those involved, he had the patience of Job. It was not unusual for him to wait out a party for a week or more until the inevitable concession arrived. Once when I told a wire service rep on the phone that Bob Jones and I would like to review a proposed contract face to face, there was an audible groan.

As he settled in at WRVA, Bob began to loosen up. The formality faded; suits were replaced with open collared shirts sans necktie. He began spending more time out of his office, interacting with the staff. Alden, and I began inviting Bob and his wife Joan to the Outer Banks with us for a week in the summers. Jones, a collector and connoisseur of French Wine, always brought a case or two along. Shop talk stayed in Richmond.

On my 40th birthday, Bob came into my office to pass along best wishes and to ask what I was giving myself for my 40th. I told him I had vowed to quit smoking. A reformed heavy smoker himself, Jones quickly whipped up the evangelical zeal of a modern day Billy Sunday. "Nothing is more important than this," he preached. "Nothing." He began calling me on weekends imploring me not to fall off the wagon.

With his unrelenting encouragement and that of Bob Chaplin, the best doctor anyone could ever hope to have, I kicked the habit. I remember asking Dr. Chaplin if I would ever stop dreaming about cigarettes. He told me it would take a long time. "But," he said, "one day you'll realize you had not thought about a cigarette that day, and when that happens," he continued, "you'll be free." It happened exactly that way.

X

The last thing I wanted or needed was something else on my plate, but when John Tansey retired, he also stepped down as Chairman of the Virginia Emergency Broadcast System. The Federal Communications Commission nominated me to replace him and the Director of the State Office of Emergency Services quickly concurred. I had little choice but to accept. The position brought with it another, Chairman of the Virginia State Emergency Communications Committee.

WRVA was the entry point for Virginia in the statewide EBS, and, as such, we had very close ties with the Department of Defense, which had installed emergency generators and other "site hardening" equipment to keep the station on the air during a national emergency. It had done much the same, albeit on a smaller scale, for other regional EBS stations around the state.

It was handy leverage when the new owner of a key EBS participant in the Norfolk area called me to end his station's participation. I told him that could be quickly arranged, that I would immediately get on the phone with the FCC's Defense Commissioner who would arrange for the Department of Defense to come down and retrieve its equipment, which included a very expensive emergency generator. The manager quickly changed his mind.

The bread and butter of EBS was local and regional disasters, such as hurricanes and floods. It was activated more than 20 thousand times before it was updated in the mid 90's, but never for a national emergency. After the fall of the Soviet Union, the threat of nuclear missile attack receded in the national consciousness, but with the rise of international terrorism in the wake of 9/11, the threat entered a new dimension and the country's collective anxiety returned. EBS has since been replaced by the Emergency Alert System, but the mission is the same.

I served as State EBS Chairman and Chair of the Virginia Emergency Communications Committee for eleven years until the station was sold to Clear Channel Communications and my position at the station changed. When I resigned in 1992, Governor L. Douglas Wilder presented me with a Certificate of Recognition for my service.

After arriving at WSB in Atlanta, Walt Williams made a play for Dick Hemby, whose afternoon drive antics with scores of characters like his engineer "Rusty Knob" and "Councilman Chuck," were wildly popular in Richmond. Tansey, Jones and Lou Dean attempted to make Dick a better offer so he would stay at WRVA. Lou remembers Tansey, in considering how much more money to offer Hemby to stay, asking how much a rating point was worth. Ultimately, with WSB and WRVA competing for Dick, the only result was to raise Hemby's worth when he went to Atlanta.

His last show on WRVA featured a priceless bit of all of Dick's characters boarding a bus for Atlanta. It was what radio was all about; but things did not go well in Atlanta. Jones eventually okayed bringing him back to WRVA for a time but it didn't work out. An absolute master of radio's "theatre of the mind," Dick was one of the wittiest, most original, creative people I ever met in radio.

After the almost requisite 7 years of Harte Hanks ownership, WRVA was sold to Edens Broadcasting in 1984. Gary Edens, an executive with Harte Hanks Radio, and a group of investors purchased many of the old Southern Broadcasting Corporation stations from Harte Hanks, then added stations in Hampton, Virginia and San Diego, California.

As with the sale to Southern and later to Harte Hanks, there was a carryover of executive talent in the hierarchy of the new owner. Bob Jones was one of the principal investors. So was Phil Goldman, the General Manager of our sister FM station WRVQ. It made for a seamless transition.

XI

I met Tim Timberlake shortly after coming to WRVA. He was working part time doing nights and weekends while attending Randolph Macon College in Ashland. After graduation and a stint at a smaller AM station in Richmond, he got on full-time at WRVA.

Timberlake's hometown was Staunton, where he had gotten into radio at WTON. He had stepped up to be

WRVA's Traffic Helicopter Reporter following the death of Howard Bloom in the Spring of 1974.

Tim was living in Church Hill then, and some mornings he would call me on the news desk to say he was running late and that the helicopter pilot was going to pick him up on the back lawn of the station. By 1978, the twice daily traffic grind had burned him out, and he left the station to freelance.

Five years later, Alden Aaroe pitched him on becoming his partner on the morning show and eventually taking his place when he retired. WRVA, like most stations in the south, was then a so-called "combo operation," meaning the person on the air ran their own controls. There was no "board operator" or engineer in the studio to do it for them. The system worked well for the typical disc jockey, running tunes and commercials, but the morning program on WRVA had become incredibly complex. There were live weather feeds, live helicopter traffic reports, information taken over the phone, such as lost dog reports and school closings, satellite feeds and remote news reports. It was more than any one individual could efficiently handle and still be a viable personality on the air. Bringing Timberlake on board would free Aaroe to be Aaroe and, later, to retire. Timberlake said yes.

Tim began running the big control console on the morning program in 1983, but he did not debut on the air with Alden until two years later. At the time, I think Alden was genuinely thinking about retiring, but Tim's arrival seemed to give him a second wind. He didn't retire until shortly before his death in 1993.

It was Timberlake who set up the legendary call from President Ronald Reagan on Aaroe's 70th birthday in May of 1988. Aaroe was totally gobsmacked when the President came on the line from the White House. He quickly recovered and launched into an extended conversation with the President about their days in the Army Air Corps during World War II, even managing to step on the President's comments now and then. The event instantly became one of those priceless moments that would be resurrected whenever the history of WRVA was recounted.

Chuck Noe was a retired Division I basketball coach who was doing a lot of motivational speaking when Walt Williams brought him to WRVA to do a Sunday night sports call-in show and weekday sports commentaries.

Chuck was a natural for radio. He had a knack for communicating, for cutting through all of the "psycho-babble," as he called it. His three daily commentaries cut to the bone of an issue, won a ton of awards and served as fodder for his Sunday night sports call-in show, "Let's Talk Sports."

It wasn't really a show. It was a happening. Thanks to WRVA's big night time sky wave, people across the country dialed in and called in. Chuck's lovely wife Barbara wrote the caller's names and where they were calling from on sheets of paper, holding them up for the Coach to read on the air. When he'd welcome them to the program, many were so excited they could hardly talk.

Chuck had a way of making you think you were the most important person in the world when he was talking with you, because to him, you were. It was a rare gift. All the great communicators have it. Chuck did.

For a string of summers in the 80's, a bunch of us from WRVA would head for the Outer Banks of North Carolina. We would get a solid week of the Noe Full Court Press. I have a photograph of Chuck, Alden and me sitting on the beach at Duck. Chuck is all jazzed up doing his "X's and O's," giving us his half time sermon. I would come back from the beach so pumped up I couldn't sleep at night.

When he died in late 2003, Barbara asked me to speak at his Memorial Service. In my remarks, I said I could only imagine the good that Chuck did for all those young hearts and minds at the University of South Carolina, VMI, VPI, and Virginia Commonwealth University. I know, I said, that his 20 plus years with WRVA made many a would-be quitter stay in the race. Chuck made us all believe in ourselves.

XII

In 1986, word came that Bob McNeill's expertise was required in Phoenix at the company's KOY. It was announced that McNeill would keep his position as Station Manager at WRVA in addition to tending to KOY; but I suspected early on that, as talented as Bob was, holding down two positions on opposite ends of the country would not last, and that sooner or later, upper management would appoint someone to replace him at WRVA. Several encouraged me to put my hat in the ring, including John Tansey, who was still with the station as a consultant.

After talking it over at length with Jeri and with Tansey, I decided to go for it. If I got the job and had some success, it might put me in a position to succeed Bob when he retired as General Manager. Nothing ventured, nothing gained.

After word got out that I had pitched for the position, when and if it became available, Gary King, the Program Director, also applied. (King had succeeded Lou Dean as Program Director after Lou had been named Manager of Community Services.)

Jones' vetting process was excruciating, a marathon inquisition that took days. First, he had to be convinced you really wanted the position. Second, that you were the best person for it and most importantly, that you could be counted on to always do the right thing.

We spent an entire day discussing the station's future. I had long held the opinion that WRVA would have to evolve to a personality talk-news station with a heavy emphasis on local news. The operative word, I said, was "evolve." "With a legacy AM station like WRVA, one didn't make sudden or kneejerk moves." Jones agreed, then, asked whether I saw WRVA as an all-news entity? I did not.

My view was that going all news was counterintuitive to running a quality news organization, particularly in a market like Richmond. Feeding the beast, or filling the time, would become the first priority and without additional staff, which I didn't think the market could support, would likely require the dismantling of our full-time beat system which was critical to original or enterprise reporting. It was a question of quantity versus quality.

The memo announcing my appointment as WRVA Operations Manager came out in December. (Gary King accepted a similar position at a sister Edens station in Hampton/ Norfolk. Tim Farley succeeded King as WRVA Program Director.) I retained the position of News Director while adding the new position as Operations Manager. I would be directly responsible for the News and Editorial Department, and oversee Engineering and Programming on the station. Most of my day to day continued to be spent in News.

Under Edens, the yearly budget review sessions were quite different from the intense one on one sessions with Bob Jones when Southern Broadcasting owned the station. Many of the officers of Edens Broadcasting sat in on the process, including Jones, who was a principal in the Company, but it was the CEO, Michael Osterhout, who presided.

Osterhout, who had flaring eyes and sported a short red beard, was the General Manager of Edens' wildly successful cash cow, rock and roll station in Tampa. He was hammering me over my persistent defense of an operating budget item earmarking funds for some modules needed to activate an unused console for use in the main news air studio. We were going to a dual anchor arrangement on the major morning news strips and needed the flexibility of the larger control console.

Osterhout kept insisting that the items were, in effect, a capital project and did not belong in an operating budget. I argued that the items were simply parts needed to activate an existing piece of equipment we already owned. Moreover, I wanted to keep it as an operating expense because capital projects were prioritized, and small items like what I was proposing would likely never see the light of day (which I assumed was Osterhout's strategy).

As the argument became more animated and heated, I noticed Bob Jones' neck turning beet red, a sure indication of a coming eruption. Suddenly, there was a thunderous whack as he slammed his hand down on the conference room table, so hard I was certain the thick glass top had shattered. The entire room was stunned into silence, including Osterhout. "Enough!" Jones shouted. He then proceeded to defend the budgeted items and demanded that we move on. We did. I was a nervous wreck when we walked out of the meeting, but it occurred to me that Bob had thoroughly enjoyed himself.

XIII

Alden was then nearing his 40th year with the radio station. It was a remarkable milestone, and the station put on a massive celebration. A huge tent was erected on the back lawn overlooking Downtown Richmond. Food and wine were served. VIP's, politicians, media, advertising and corporate executives, clients and community leaders were invited.

Governor Gerald Baliles proclaimed it "Alden Aaroe Day" in Virginia. The Mayor of Richmond followed suit. At the Virginia General Assembly, resolutions honoring Aaroe were adopted by the House and Senate.

Aaroe's popularity was astonishing. First among equals, he was the face of WRVA. His morning program with Tim Timberlake owned the market with a quarter hour cumulative audience rating of nearly a quarter million people. It put morning drive on WRVA into some pretty fast company around the country.

State Capitol Reporter Dave Miller remarked that Alden was "the meal ticket." There was a lot of truth to the remark, and I suspect all of us had overtly "piggybacked" on Alden's fame in one way or another.

I received a call one morning from the distributor of a religion program, aiming to secure a time slot in morning drive on the station. In closing his pitch, he said, "Mr. Harding, we have God on our side!" I replied that while we didn't have the Almighty himself on the air, we did have the next best thing: Alden Aaroe.

Bob Jones loved the story, but Alden was clearly embarrassed. He was always quick to say that his popularity was because he was on WRVA, not the other way around; but we all knew that whenever Alden left us, WRVA would be a far different place.

At the time though, things could not have been better. The ratings were consistently good. The station won the Spring Arbitron Radio Audience Survey, the Spring Book as it was called. We would repeat the win in the fall.

The news department had begun collecting scores of news awards, giving a little credence to our adding additional anchors and reporters bringing the staff up to 16. I had also hired veteran Washington reporter Hanna Guttman to keep tabs on the state's congressional delegation.

In September, Millard The Mallard marked his 15th 'Happy Hatch Day.' Jones, who was always looking for something to celebrate, ("Celebrate the good times because the bad times are coming"), threw a huge catered party in the lobby for the WRVA and WRVQ Staffs. A big cake was brought in with Millard's picture in colored icing on top. Aaroe ate his bill.

Millard was a guest on the popular "Q Morning Zoo" on our sister FM. WNBC called to set up the first of several Millard appearances on the Don Imus Show in New York. The Virginia Department of Wildlife got in on the celebration by duly noting Millard's hatch day on the official State Wildlife Calendar, and Governor Gerald Baliles called in that morning to wish Millard a Happy Hatch Day and to grant him a blanket pardon from duck hunters.

Even with the successes, Bob and I sensed we needed to do another audience research project. We contracted with a research firm to conduct a comprehensive study of WRVA's place in the market, its strengths and vulnerabilities. There were no exploding cigars personality-wise. Tim Timberlake had become the most recognized person on the station; Millard was a close second and Alden a very close third.

Teaming Tim up with Alden had been a brilliant move, but there were concerns.

Television had become our biggest competitor in news, information and community service. WWBT, the old WRVA TV, had added helicopter traffic reports and was making inroads on such WRVA strongholds as our Emergency Closing System. It wasn't unexpected.

The word "synergy" had been thrown around a lot in the front office to describe the station's budding romance with the long divorced Channel 12 during the late 80's. "Synergy" soon morphed into "cross pollination." We started using the TV station's weatherman on our air. Timberlake was doing a Noon News gig at WWBT after wrapping up with Alden in the morning. Bob Jones had even okayed the TV station putting cameras in our main air studio while we broadcast snow closings.

At first blush, it seemed as though Bob was giving them the keys to the kingdom. I mused in my journal whether, "it was akin to McClellan having a mole in A.P Hill's tent at Beaver Dam Creek," but television clearly had the upper hand. It could run closing information as a crawl across the bottom of the screen without pre-empting regular programming. We could not. Perhaps Jones was taking a page from baseball great Branch Rickey with the old Brooklyn Dodgers, trying to get us something for one of our big players while we still had a bit of leverage.

XIV

Emporia marked its 100th birthday in the spring of 1987. Part of the celebration was the re-dedication of the city seal which had been designed by my father decades earlier when Emporia was a town. Mother insisted we all come home for the event, which was held in the Emporia Auditorium, still the prime venue in the city.

Mother, BB, June, Jeri and I all trooped on stage for the ceremony. Bill Pruett, who was a co-chair of the Centennial Committee, asked me to talk a bit about Father's design.

I recalled having suggested to my father that the centerpiece ought to be what we called "The Old River Bridge," the steel truss bridge that connected Lee Street and Hicksford Avenue for many years before it was replaced. Father dismissed the idea saying that he was surprised I had not suggested the Emporia Diner as the focal point of the seal since I spent more time there than at home.

He instead chose the old French designed Main Street Bridge over the Meherrin River, which had been built in the mid 1920's but had long since been replaced with a nondescript, modern span. To Father, the old bridge symbolized the coming together of the Villages of Hicksford and Belfield to form Emporia.

The seal had been displayed on official Emporia stationery, police cars and so forth when Emporia was a town, but when Emporia became a city, it was put on the shelf. I told the crowd Father would have been honored that his design, the original painting of which now hangs in our den, had been resurrected.

While home that weekend, I had noticed tears in Mother's eyes when she started to get up out of her chair in the den. She had long maintained that her hip didn't hurt bad enough to go through surgery, but when I asked her this time, she said she thought it was time. The surgery was performed at St. Mary's Hospital in Richmond. She came through fine with no complications.

She stayed with us in Richmond to recuperate. St. Mary's sent rehab nurses to the house to help her with post op exercises, but she refused to do them. She did not get out of the bed for nearly a week. When we took her home, her Doctor told her she had to get out and walk, but she remained anchored to her chair in the den. It left her with a permanent limp and marked the beginning of a long, slow deterioration of her health.

XV

The seemingly unthinkable idea of abandoning the Church Hill Studio Building bubbled up in the late 80's. The landmark building had been designed for one radio station back in 1968. (WRVA FM, the old WRVB, simply duplicated WRVA programming during the day and ran automated country music at night.) The advent of WRVQ had consumed all of the remaining space in the building. The station had since been forced to move its administrative offices to leased space in the Shockoe Slip splitting the operation between two locations. It was clearly an unacceptable situation.

When a months' long search turned up nothing suitable in the way of existing space elsewhere, the company decided to lease space in a new, yet to be built, building at Stony Point, a new development just south of the James River in Richmond's near west end. As the idea took root, Bob asked me to develop some proposals for the news and studio spaces.

I had drawn the plans for our house in Chesterfield, and I had designed the new work stations in the WRVA newsroom but configuring studio and news spaces in a commercial building was clearly beyond my skill set. Undaunted, I took up the challenge with the zeal of a neophyte. I contacted several stations similar to WRVA around the country, which had recently gone through new builds and renovation projects. Many were very helpful. With their input, I set to work in my loft at home at night and on weekends. Over the next few months, I put together several proposals.

Even to my untrained eye, the major stumbling block of the proposed location was the substantial distance from the WRVA/WRVQ transmitter plant on the James River in the Deep Bottom area of Henrico County, southeast of the city. A tall tower would be required for an unobstructed microwave "shot" to the transmitter site. Moving the transmitter location closer in was a nonstarter. Both stations were grandfathered to the site and going elsewhere was the equivalent of unscrambling an egg.

When the Stony Point project went before public hearings, the proposed microwave tower became a lightning rod for opponents. Neighbors complained property values would suffer. Many expressed deep concern over the environmental impact. There were comments that the tower and signal would harm delicate wildlife habitats along the James River. There was particular concern for Bald Eagles, which were thriving along the river. There was talk of the microwave signal "frying owls."

When the outcry made headlines in the *Richmond Times Dispatch*, Bob Jones quickly pulled the plug on the project saying, "We're not in the business of pissing people off!" Plans to move the stations were tabled. Both would remain on Church Hill.

I had put a lot of work into the project, but, privately, I wasn't displeased with the outcome. Moving to Stony Point would have cut my commute time considerably, but giving up that million dollar view on Church Hill would have been hard to swallow.

XVI

No one seemed to notice when the Federal Communications Commission voted unanimously in 1987 to repeal the long standing Fairness Doctrine, which required broadcast stations to address controversial issues equally. The vote opened the door for an unknown, right wing radio host named Rush Limbaugh to take to the airwaves in California.

With radio stations no longer required to broadcast opposing views, Limbaugh quickly morphed into a nationwide phenomenon. By 1990, legions of "ditto heads," as they called themselves · mainly young, white males · became devoted followers. So did Republican office holders on both the national and local stages. Soon, Limbaugh would be proclaimed as the titular head of the Republican Party. His show was picked up by a small Richmond daytime station, which began making inroads into WRVA's midday audience. It was enough for Bob Jones to call a special meeting to address the situation.

I jotted down some thoughts in my journal in advance of the meeting. First, picking up Limbaugh made perfect sense. It would immediately plug the ratings drain and boost, what for us, had always been an anemic part of the day.

On the other hand, putting Limbaugh on WRVA would take us away from the station's longstanding policy of super serving the Richmond Metropolitan Area. All politics might be local, as the saying went, but Limbaugh wasn't.

I was also concerned that another daily three hour dose of conservative talk (we were already running local conservative talk at night) would skew the station further to the right and would tarnish our reputation for fairness in addressing controversial issues. Fairness was no longer a condition of license, but it was our bread and butter.

Bob; Carl McNeill; Tim Farley, the Program Director; and I met in Bob's office. Revenue and quick ratings carried the day. It's hard to argue against success. The midday ratings rebounded, and then some, but I had a bad feeling about it and continued to view it as a watershed moment for the station.

I was stunned to see our call letters in a front page story in the *Washington Post* on the 6th of August, 1991, quoting Governor Douglas Wilder as saying that a listening device had been discovered in a tree outside of his office at the State Capitol.

The Commander of the State Capitol Police disputed the Governor's claim. He said the only device he knew about was a small antenna mounted in a holly tree about two floors below the Governor's office that was used by WRVA Radio to beam news reports back to the station's Church Hill Studios.

The Governor's Chief of Staff insisted it was a bug and called in the State Police Bureau of Investigation to remove it. The State Police quickly confirmed it was not a bug. I had searched our files and quickly turned up written permission from the Capitol Buildings and Grounds Superintendent to install the antenna and transmitter some years previously to replace a very costly broadcast line we had been leasing from the phone company.

A *Post* reporter called me. "It's not a listening device," I said. "It's a transmitter that connects our State Capitol Bureau to our Newsroom. In the event of a statewide emergency, the Governor himself would use the link to activate the Statewide Emergency Broadcast System."

The newspapers continued to have fun with it at the Governor's expense. So did we. Millard the Mallard began swatting bugs on the morning show. Gary Brookins published a cartoon in the *Times Dispatch* depicting the Governor and his Chief of Staff spraying insecticide at a small antenna in a tree at the Capitol. The Governor is saying, "Get it Jay! It looks like a bug to me." Off to the side is Millard The Mallard, who has a bewildered look on his face. Bob Jones asked Gary for the original panel, which he had framed and presented to me.

"Millard The Mallard" 1972

"Millard The Mallard" 1970's

With Alden Aaroe. WRVA 1993

Jeri manning the Millard Booth at WRVA 50th Anniversary.
November 1975.

Richmond Christmas Parade.
1980's

Part VII

The Unraveling

I

As the 80's faded, the financial condition of Eden's Broadcasting had begun to slide. The company's biggest revenue producer had long been WRBQ in Tampa, Florida. The rock station had enjoyed 20 years of ratings dominance, but it cracked when a cross town rival launched a huge ratings war, running billboards reading "Screw The Q!"

Eventually, the corporate revenue shortfall resulted in orders to cut personnel at WRVA, and news was the primary target. Jones admitted that firing a couple of reporters and anchors would not begin to solve Eden's problems, but the banks underwriting the company's debt were demanding heads to show the company was serious about reducing costs.

I was forced to eliminate two of our most experienced people. I appealed but news had no standing. We were word people, and the numbers people were running the show. The dictate was firm. Across the board pay cuts wouldn't fly. The positions had to be eliminated. John Tansey, who was still with the station as a consultant, shared my disgust about the cuts but told me on the phone one night, "John, this probably won't lessen your anguish but remember, if you don't do it, your replacement will." The great shame of it was, it was all for naught.

Forced to pay down debt, the company sold WRVA, WRVQ and Hampton station WWDE in September of 1991 to Force II Communications of San Diego, California for 28 million dollars.

Force II's CEO flew into Richmond and made the standard speech about few if any changes being made. None were. Force II became a phantom owner. Nothing happened! One of Force II's principal backers had reportedly pulled out, and the deal ultimately went south.

It triggered a relentless search by Bob Jones to find an in-state buyer for WRVA. He had become firmly convinced that local ownership was the absolute key to the station's survival, perhaps proving once again that one's perspective changes with one's position.

Over the course of several weeks, Jones worked the phones late into the night, trying to put together a deal. I'd often run into him leaving when I came into the station. Then suddenly, with no leaks and no advance warning from the rumor mill or the usual tipsters, it was over. In the Spring of 1992, Edens dealt WRVA and WRVQ, along with the Eden's stations in Tampa, Florida, to Clear Channel Communications, a huge media conglomerate in San Antonio, for 18.2 million dollars.

Clear Channel's CEO, Lowry Mays, dashed into Richmond to claim his newly acquired prizes. While driving him to Church Hill from the airport, I asked him for his take on the broadcast business. I was stunned by his answer. "John," he said, "Clear Channel is not in the broadcast business. We're in the business of selling Fords."

Bob Jones, who had no respect for Clear Channel or Mays, retired and left broadcasting. Carl McNeill, the sales manager, put his hat in the ring to succeed him.

Carl loved his job, and he was terrific at it. A true salesman, the life of the party, Carl craved success and while he obviously had the inside track, I thought my experience as Operations Manager and News Director had prepared me well for the position. After all, one of the reasons I had gone after the ops manager position in the first place was to hopefully gain additional management experience, perhaps have some success and be in a position to take a shot for the top spot.

When I told Bob I was going to apply for the job, he said he had made a deal with Carl when he recruited him to come to WRVA from South Carolina in 1982, assuring him he would be the next General Manager. He said he had to stand by his promise but said he hoped I would go for it anyway. I thanked him and said I understood his position.

After talking it over with Jeri again, I decided to go for it. I had read somewhere along the way, "Isn't everything worthwhile a gamble?" I told Carl I was tossing my hat in the ring. I wished him good luck, and he did the same.

Lowry Mays flew in to interview us. From the start, I got a very strong vibe that Mays had his mind made up before he left Texas. He was just going through the motions. He listened with what seemed vacant detachment to my pitch, expressed no interest in what I said, asked no questions, and made no comments. Then, with not a whiff of hesitation, he promptly confirmed my suspicion. "Carl is the guy," he quickly announced. He said that "Clear Channel was sales oriented and that all of its General Managers were sales people." I wasn't.

II

To say I wasn't disappointed would be disingenuous; but privately, I never thought I would get the job, perhaps giving some certainty to the old saying, "If you aren't completely sold that you will win, you will likely lose." I did! Father would have told me not to go for it because it wasn't even a good thing, let alone a sure thing; but I knew it was my only shot, and I had spent the last decade pushing the dream uphill. I never regretted shooting the moon. I had no issues with Jones' "behind the curtain deal" with Carl. I never thought it was a factor. Mays would have chosen Carl anyway. I wished him well.

Some days later, I ran into Phil Goldman. Phil was still the General Manager of WRVQ, our sister FM. Unlike Jones, who had left, Phil had a contract and would stay on with the station into the first year of Clear Channel Ownership. As one of the principals of Edens, he was also the seller of the station. Goldman didn't like the way Clear Channel was running things and would later leave after he had heart surgery. We talked downstairs. "You know, John, from what I'm seeing," he said, "I think Mays did you a big favor." It was another of those blessings in disguise. It was well disguised at the time, but as the years tick-tocked by, I came to agree with Phil. I would not have to preside over the unraveling of a great radio station.

As soon as Bob Jones had cleared out of his office, Carl, as I suspected, sent me packing as Operations Manager. He said Clear Channel did not permit a layer of management between the GM and department heads and that I would have to give up the job. I was to remain News Director, and my on air duties would not change.

My first inclination was to update the resume and start looking to move on. I was then under a non-compete contract with WRVA, which pretty much precluded me from seeking work at any other station in Virginia or, at least the few that appealed to me.

My thoughts returned to Washington. I had a lot of good, solid contacts in broadcast news circles there, and I knew the city, but Mother's health was in decline and I felt the need to stay close. I had promised my father I would. Washington was then a good three to three and a half hours distant from Emporia. It was simply too far. If Mother were alive and read this she would be absolutely furious; but there it is. I decided to ride out the immediate future with Clear Channel.

From the beginning, there were subtle signals that Clear Channel had little regard for WRVA's long history in Richmond or for those who had made it such a valuable property.

The company never made an effort to replace the vandalized John Tansey Memorial, marking the overlook of the city at the dead end of East Grace Street, next to the studio building. When that section of East Grace was renamed "Alden Aaroe Drive," executives who showed up for the dedication said the street would be insignificant because WRVA was going to be moved away from Church Hill. Perhaps, but I thought it was a tacky comment to make at a dedication ceremony.

Only the enterprising efforts of Debbie Ashley, who had been the Executive Assistant to Tansey his last few years and had served in the same capacity for Bob Jones and would do so for Carl McNeill, had saved the station's archives. She had arranged for their transfer to the Library of Virginia, where they now reside.

A month or so into the Clear Channel ownership, the company sent Tim Farley, the Program Director, and me to WHAS In Louisville and WOAI in San Antonio for a quick primer on the Clear Channel way of doing business. Both stations had been under the Clear Channel umbrella for a number of years, WOAI since the 70's, so the visit gave us an up close glimpse into the company's long term play book.

Under Clear Channel, stations had little, if any, autonomy. Edens and the previous owners of WRVA had allowed General Managers substantial leeway in running their stations. They were, in fact, local businesses with local bank accounts. Not so with Clear Channel. Everything was run from San Antonio. Clear Channel was all about centralizing control, maximizing efficiency and minimizing costs through consolidation and downsizing. Programming was tightly formatted and more national in scope, with satellite-delivered programs replacing local content. But programming was just the pitch. What the company sold was audiences. Clear Channel's customers weren't listeners but advertisers. It really was about "selling Fords."

III

In January of 1992, Alden Aaroe went to see his doctor, complaining of what he thought was a bad case of bronchitis. It was lung cancer. He underwent surgery to have it removed, recovered and returned to the morning program.

Every three months over the next year, Alden went in for a check-up. There was no sign the cancer had returned. That winter, he and Frances embarked on a cruise through the Panama Canal.

In February of 1993, our attention turned to Jeri's mother. Ruby Kennedy had been hospitalized at the University of North Carolina Medical Center in Chapel Hill. She had been battling chronic leukemia for more than twenty years. The cancer had spread to her brain. There were so many small tumors that surgery had been deemed out of the question.

Jeri and I drove down to be with her. We booked a room at the Carolina Inn near the hospital and saw her the next morning. Ruby was in good spirits, but wanted to go home. There was no reason to keep her in the hospital. It was the last time I would see her. Jeri went to the farm to stay with her. She died peacefully on the 23rd of February. I drove down for the funeral two days later.

In April, Alden went for another check-up. The cancer had returned. It was terminal. He and Frances drove up to the station late one morning and phoned me to come out to the car.

"I guess you know the score," he said.

I nodded.

"Of course, I had to turn down chemotherapy," he said. "I want to keep working for now. It's an escape from all this and I don't want you to spread the word. Keep it to yourself."

I nodded.

"I'll make the announcement myself when the time comes," he said.

I managed an "Okay." He shook my hand with a look that went deep into my soul.

"Come out to the house once we get everything worked out."

I said I would. Alden started the car, I got out and they drove away. I noted the conversation in my Journal that night. I walked over to my car, which was parked nearby. I needed to compose myself before I went back into the building.

When I got home, I was visibly upset, and Jeri picked up on it.

"It's Alden, isn't it? The lung cancer has metastasized?"

I nodded.

She cursed.

"How long does he have?" I asked.

"With no intervention, three months, maybe four," she said.

The next day I started working on a documentary tribute to Alden.

Aaroe turned 75 on the 5th of May. The station threw a huge catered Birthday Party on the back lawn. Invitations went out, reading "Come Celebrate a Radio Legend." Few knew about the cancer. For those of us who did, it had the air of a wake.

The entire party from 8AM to 10AM was broadcast live with Tim Timberlake serving as MC. Hundreds of people turned out. Alden was so weak he had to sit on a stool during the broadcast. He worked the remainder of his birthday week. His last show was Friday, May 7th. He never came back.

Frances set up hospice care at their home in Hanover County north of Richmond. Every morning when I finished my news shift, I drove out to sit with him on his back porch for an hour or so. We talked about the good times and the bad, the many trips to the Outer Banks, the fishing expeditions to the bay, and the countless cut throat "hearts" and "nine ball games."

One morning in late May, he said he needed to talk seriously with me. I recounted our conversation in my journal.

"I want you to take my place on the air with Timberlake," he said.

I was stunned. I told him I wasn't a disc jockey or a personality. My background was in reporting, writing news, and in management. There was also the politics of it. "I'm not sure taking your chair would sit well with Tim long term," I said. After all, Tim had been brought on board to succeed Alden when he retired.

"Tim is good people," he said, "but you know the station, what makes it tick and the importance of news here," which he thought would assume an even greater role on the program.

I started to say something, but he held up his hand closing off the conversation. "It's done John, I've already told Carl."

I tried to view it as a new adventure, but I was very anxious about it and would remain so.

Alden faded quickly. On the 24th of June, in a taped interview with Lou Dean, he announced his retirement from WRVA. *The Richmond Times Dispatch* paid tribute to him in an Editorial on the 25th. Cartoonist Gary Brookins noted the occasion. The panel shows a couple at the breakfast table. The man is holding a copy of the newspaper with the front page headline, "Aaroe Retires." He tells his wife, "I could handle the closing of the John Marshall and even the demise of Miller & Rhoads, but no more Alden in the morning?" Frances sent us framed copies.

He died at home in the very early morning of Wednesday the 7th of July. I had recorded a special Editorial Tribute to him that was broadcast that morning. The half hour documentary I had produced, *A Tribute to Alden Aaroe,* ran at 7PM on the night he died. It was the subject of Ray McAllister's Column in the *Times Dispatch* the next morning. He gave it a good review, and told readers they should write the station and ask for reruns. The station rebroadcast it at least six times over the following week. We offered free cassette copies of the program for anyone writing in. Scores of people did.

The day after his death, Alden's daughter Anna Lou came to the station to see me.

"I want you to deliver the eulogy at the Memorial Service, John · only I don't want it to be a eulogy," she said. "I want it to be a personal remembrance. I want you to depict him as you knew him and don't be afraid to make us laugh. Dad would want that."

I told her I would do my best. When I got home, I noted our conversation in my Journal and started working on what would be the first in a long string of eulogies or personal remembrances I would be called upon to do for colleagues I would lose over the next 15 years.

The Memorial Service was held at historic St. Paul's Episcopal Church in downtown Richmond. The church was packed. WRVA broadcast the service live. I titled my piece "Reflections." It ran for maybe four minutes. A quote from Mark Twain seemed appropriate: "Few things are harder to put up with than the annoyance of a good example." "Alden," I said, "was WRVA's good example."

IV

Less than a year after purchasing WRVA and WRVQ, Clear Channel had gone on another buying spree in Richmond, adding three more properties to its bulging "cluster." WRNL AM, which in its heyday had been owned by Richmond Newspapers, WRXL, yet another FM rock station, and the Virginia News Network. It had news in its name but its bread and butter was University of Virginia play by play sports. WRNL and the network were to be moved into the Church Hill Building until the new "warehouse" facility in Henrico County was completed. Carl would be managing WRNL and the Network, along with WRVA.

That April, just as I was learning of Alden's cancer, Carl called me into his office and said he was appointing me Director of News Operations for VNN and WRVA. (WRNL, a sports talk station, programmed no news.) He said I had enjoyed great success with WRVA News and was confident I could take VNN and WRVA News "to new heights." I couldn't see any upside.

Bringing the VNN into the fold only assured the weakening of both news organizations and, from my perspective as News Director of WRVA, we had the most to lose. The acquisition, of course, had been a corporate call, not Carl's; but I wanted no part of it. I responded with a twist on an old saying, "If at once you do succeed, don't try it again."

Reading it in my Journal all these years later, it's clear I was stupidly trying to hold onto what was left of the station and to fight what was happening. Obviously, I was not the person for the job, but Carl insisted. I didn't see that I had any choice. The memo came out on the 21st of April, 1993.

The title looked very impressive on the organization chart; but its immediate effect was to cut off Kevin Hall, who was the News Director of the Virginia Network, from reporting to Carl. Hall didn't like the arrangement and made his feelings quite clear to me.

Two months later, on the 28th of June, Carl followed up on Alden's suggestion and announced my move to the Morning Show with Timberlake. I was to continue as the WRVA News Director, but the appointment to also oversee the VNN News Department seemed to fall by the wayside. I had no complaints.

I sensed Timberlake was glad to have my company on the morning show in the immediate days after Alden's death. It was a difficult time, and not a little awkward, carrying on without him. The presence of his absence was overwhelming, and I was dealing with a bad case of "un-belonging." Tim had come on board with the understanding that, when Alden finally retired, it would be his show; yet, here I was sitting in Alden's chair. The fact that I had not sought it was of little consolation, and I had the feeling that many at the station thought I had lobbied for it.

At times, I felt like a fish flopping around in a boat trying to find water. I was unsure of my role, what I was expected to do. No one but Alden himself had ever even hinted that the show needed to be more news intensive. Neither Carl nor Tim Farley, the Program Director, had mentioned it. I assumed Carl was just honoring Alden's last request. I was certain it was only temporary.

Tim appeared to pick up on my unease, giving me housekeeping chores to tend to, like reading the lottery numbers, lost pet notices and birthday greetings. I was crowned "Mr. Birthday" and "Lottoman." I began interviewing Charlie Curry, the Henrico Extension Agent, who was a regular contributor of gardening tips, and I began talking in tunes, introducing music, DJ work - something I had not done since campus radio at AU.

"Millard The Mallard" had taken a hiatus after Alden died. I was unsure of whether to continue with the character. Not knowing what to do, I had Millard flap up to Goose Bay for a long soak. We needed time to decide if he should come back on the air. If we decided to bring him back, how would he handle the absence of Alden? Millard and Alden had been together for 23 years. Should he react with sadness? Should he inquire what happened to "Mr. Aaroe?" And what if we decided it was time for Millard to just flap away? Would we say anything? If we did, what?

After several weeks, Millard returned from his sabbatical. We had him note Alden's passing, but we didn't dwell on it. Millard became Tim Timberlake's feisty foil on the reconstituted WRVA Morning Show for another 8 years, ranting and raving about all things "Unduck." *Richmond Magazine* listed him among the top 100 Richmonders everyone should know.

The old rule still held. When Millard came on the air, John Harding took an exit. It seemed to work well. Millard had such a presence about him, no one noticed I was gone.

As the months rolled by, music was ditched, and we began booking guests - stars coming to town for concerts or touring shows, NASCAR drivers. Jimmy Dean, the country music singer turned Sausage King, was a regular. So was Richmond Chef Jimmy Sneed and comedian Brett Leake, among others. We received some positive reviews in the *Times Dispatch,* and the ratings were pretty good.

Nine months after moving to the morning program, Carl told me he was announcing that I was being promoted to full time co-host of the program with Timberlake and naming Deanna Malone as my successor as WRVA News Director. He said he wanted the Morning Program to be the sole focus of my efforts.

I appreciated where he was coming from, but I was leery of walking away from the news position because, Carl's memo notwithstanding, I still viewed the Morning Show as a temporary assignment and was certain that, sooner or later, for whatever reason, he would pull me off the program and send me back to news. I still thought that would be the case, but looking at it through a wider lens, I could see the current situation was unfair to the News Department. Carl asked me to write the memo. I did.

V

Moving out of the News arena had opened the door to the perks of the programming department. Two free cruises fell into my lap. The first was a trip up the inside passage to Alaska. Ambassador Travel in Richmond asked me to lead the tour. In return for doing the on air commercials on WRVA, leading the group on the ship, and serving as Master of Ceremonies at shipboard gatherings of those who signed up, I would get free passage. I would only have to pay for Jeri's trip.

It was quite a deal, and, given my anxiety about my status at the station, it was the only way we would have ever been able to afford such a trip. Our financial wagons had been pulled into a defensive circle soon after Clear Channel purchased the station and I was demoted. The President of Ambassador Travel, Diane Harris, had already gotten Carl McNeill's blessing for my involvement.

Another cruise fell into my lap in January of 1996, an eleven day Caribbean · Trans Panama Canal adventure that took us to San Juan, St. Thomas, Charlotte Amalie, Santo Domingo, Curacao, the Panama Canal, Caldera, Costa Rica and Acapulco. The deal with Ambassador Travel was the same as before.

As soon as we walked in our house, my sister BB was on the phone from Emporia. She was with Mother, who had suffered what the doctors called several mini strokes.

Mother was back home. There had been no discernable after-effects from the episodes; but it was obvious that she needed to be in an assisted living center. She refused.

Rapidly running out of options, BB arranged through Home Health Services for a woman to come sit with Mother during the day, to shop for her and to cook; but Mother fired her on the first day. The woman had refused to scrub her floors!

There was nothing left for us to do but to start making regular trips to Emporia. BB, Jeri and I began rotating weekends in Emporia to do the shopping and tend to the house. BB would go one weekend, Jeri and I the next.

June set up an account with a cab company in Emporia to take Mother to her doctors' appointments, the drug store or wherever. She refused to use it, telling me she expected us to take her. Jeri started driving to Emporia just about every Wednesday.

Mother became even more obstinate about not accepting any kind of help. I had a help line installed in the house, which had a tiny transmitter she could wear around her neck. With the push of a button, she could summon help. Perhaps it was just me trying to find some kernel of peace of mind, but it was pointless. She refused to wear it.

In the fall of 1996, we took the morning show back to Disney World for the Park's 25th Anniversary Celebration. As with the previous trip, it seemed a natural for Millard so I was sent along to dole out the quacks. The talent, who did the voices of Disney Characters, came to our location and, in character, carried on lengthy conversations with Millard during the show. When the guy who did the voice of "Mickey" finished his stint with Millard and Tim, he told me, "Your duck talks better than "Donald!'"

Shortly after I returned to work, Carl, as I had long anticipated, pulled me off the Morning Show, though I was to continue with the Millard The Mallard character. I resumed anchoring the 7 AM and 8 AM broadcasts. John Ennis had wisely retired and moved to Florida.

I was back in my comfort zone, but the station's slow slide to mediocrity had taken a toll. WRVA was no longer staffing the newsroom at night. For my own self-respect, I tried to cover the hole by coming in shortly after midnight every night to catch up with what we had missed so that, at the very least, we could report the news everyone already knew.

That October, Carl reappointed me Operations Manager for WRVA and VNN News. I didn't want the job any more this time than I had before, but, as before, I didn't see I had any choice.

Predictably, the two news directors (Deanna Malone had replaced me as WRVA News Director) were less than thrilled with my presence. I was being positioned to deal with what everyone had to know was coming - the merger of the two news departments with the inevitable downsizing to follow, including one of the two news directors and, in all probability, my own position. The first step was to begin laying the groundwork for the cross training of the staffs. The writing was immediately on the wall, and I knew I was in for a very rough time of it.

VI

The jolt literally knocked me out of the bed. I thought an airplane had crashed into our house. Dazed, I stumbled down the steps to be greeted by a beeping, flashing, smoke alarm which flew by in front of me and crashed into a wall. The house had been struck by lightning. It had blasted a large hole in the roof and another in a side wall in the attic just above the downstairs bathroom. Jeri had been watching TV in the den, not ten feet away. She was running into the bathroom just as I was coming down the stairs. She said she smelled smoke. I looked into the attic and felt rain on my face. I smelled it too. I called the fire department.

The Midlothian Volunteer Fire Department was at our house in a manner of minutes. By some miracle, there had been no fire. The fire crews installed a large tarp over the hole in the roof and secured the side of the house with plywood. I had no idea they carried such materials with them on calls. They were an absolute godsend. The next day, I drove to the firehouse in Midlothian and wrote a healthy check.

The house was intact; but, aside from the refrigerator and stove top, every appliance, including our brand new replacement heat pumps, had been fried and would have to be replaced. The stately oak in the side yard, which had been the conduit for the surge, had been destroyed. It would have to be taken down limb by limb.

We had been invited down to the Outer Banks for a couple of days the following week. With the house secured, we decided to go. I thought we needed a break. Our neighbor

Herb said he would keep an eye on the place and watch our cat Harry.

On the way back, we stopped in Emporia to see Mother. I had just seen her several days before, but when I saw her this time, she looked much worse. Precariously thin, she had withered down to maybe a hundred pounds, if that. She insisted she was fine, but clearly she wasn't.

The situation had worsened considerably over the summer because, on top of everything else, her vision was deteriorating. She was practically blind in her left eye, the result of blood or fluid buildup. We had taken her to two specialists and both agreed there was nothing to be done. Her right eye was corrected to about 20/60. She had become quite despondent because she could no longer read without using a very large magnification panel.

I had made repeated attempts throughout the summer to talk with her about going into an assisted living center or at least having home health services come in to sit with her, but she adamantly refused. Mother was still a heavy smoker, and I had seen cigarette burns on her chair in the den. I was afraid she would burn herself up. Though she was rather feeble and weak, mentally she was still sharp as a tack. There was nothing to be done except to continue to look after her as best we could.

Most of the load was falling on Jeri, who was then plagued with almost constant migraines. I began making several of the trips during the week myself to give her a break. I'd take off for Emporia after a two hour nap when I got home from work, then drive back that evening. Sometimes I stayed the night in Emporia and left at midnight to drive straight to the radio station.

VII

We had driven down to see her after I got off work on Friday the 29th of August. As soon as we arrived, she told me she had decided to leave the house to June.

"Is that all right with you?" she asked.

I told her it was her house and she could leave it to anyone she wanted.

"But is that all right with you?"

I said it was as far as I was concerned, but I asked where that left BB.

Mother nodded but said nothing.

We left Sunday morning, the 31st. Even though I had just seen her, I felt compelled to call her that afternoon as I always did. I told her that we would be back down the middle of the week but told her that, if she needed us sooner, to just call. It was the last time I heard her voice.

Around 11PM on the 2nd of September, Jeri flashed the light at the top of the stairs to our bedroom several times, our long prearranged emergency signal. I was instantly awake. I knew it had to be Mother. "Peggy Vincent called," she said. "Virginia has had a stroke and has been taken to the Emergency Room in Emporia."

Peggy and Ronald Vincent had purchased the old Tillar house across the street from Mother. Peggy had made a practice of looking in on Mother when she did not see her outside. She had found her unconscious on the floor in the den and called 911.

Jeri and I left for Emporia. She drove. I was making lists in my head, what I had to do when we got to the hospital, a way of keeping emotion at bay. We arrived just after one in the morning. The attending in the ER told us that Mother had suffered a massive cerebral hemorrhage and that, at most, she had only a few hours to live.

I seemed to go on automatic pilot. I called the radio station, then both of my sisters. The rest could wait. BB arrived at 4:30 that morning from North Carolina. June would come all the way from New England. She was at Mother's bedside by one o'clock that afternoon.

The scene in Mother's room was surreal. While she was unconscious and close to death, people poured in, talking and telling stories. We cleared the room. Mother died around four that afternoon. We were all with her.

The next day, we went to Echols Funeral Home and made arrangements. Mrs. Echols, who was a good friend of Mother's, was visibly upset.

By Wednesday, nerves were fried. Everyone was on edge. Tempers were short. There were angry words on the side porch. Jeri was very upset. She said it would be best if she went back to Richmond, leaving me and my sisters to sort things out. Besides, she reminded me, someone needed to be at the house. I had completely forgotten that the tree removal company, the contractor and the insurance adjustor were all coming by that Thursday. I took Jeri back to Richmond that afternoon.

She called me that night. "How are things?"

"Tense," I said.

"I'm sorry," she said. I told her she had nothing to be sorry about. She had done more for Mother than the rest of us combined. She drove down for the Funeral on Friday, still quite distressed.

"I just miss her, John," she said. "Virginia was such a powerful presence. Now that she is gone, the void is overwhelming."

Visitation had been held at the Funeral Home the night before. I'd never thought much of the practice, but Mother had it all planned out in her notebook of "Instructions." Every aspect of her "deportation," as she had called it, had been written out in meticulous detail. There were two pages on just preparing the dining room · where the custom-made pads for the dining room table were to be found, which table cloth was to be used and the precise arrangement I was to use as a centerpiece. It was already made and sitting on a shelf in the basement. Who was I to interfere!

The graveside service was held Friday, the 5th of September. We had given the minister at Monumental, who did not know Mother, copious notes and he captured the essence of her quite well in the committal service. There was a large turnout. More than thirty of my colleagues from WRVA came by the house to pay their respects. The station sent a large wreath.

VIII

I went back to the house several times over the next few weeks to pick up the things Mother had left me. Everything else had been disposed of. June and BB had wrapped up their work there in early October and gone back to Maine and North Carolina, respectively.

Even after the house was completely vacant, I had trouble letting go. I drove down on weekends, ostensibly to check on the house, which June had put on the market. Mostly though, I just walked around the empty rooms. Without the personality of the art and furnishings, there were only faint whispers of our lives there.

Jeri insisted I had to stop going there, that I was only prolonging the dream. It came each night with regularity. Mother would meet me at the front door, but strangers were walking behind her in the foyer. They would always stop and look at me, and one would come up alongside Mother and ask, "Who are you? Why are you here?"

After the house was sold, Duane Harrell wrote and asked that Jeri and I stop in Emporia on our next trip to North Carolina. We had a long visit. She told us the old neighborhood was alive again, reinvigorated with young couples and children. Life goes on. 522 Ingleside has sold several times since Mother died. All of the beautiful gardens in the backyard have long been stripped away, along with Father's hand cast patio; and the front of the house has a new entryway. Everything changes. The dream went away but the memories linger.

That Christmas, we drove to the farm in North Carolina to be with Jeri's father and her sisters. We always stayed in his house when we came down. Joel had moved his room to the den on the first floor so he would not have to climb steps. I had a long talk with him late Christmas Eve afternoon. He told me he was so sorry to hear about "Virginia." "We're the same age you know," he said.

He and Ruby, who had died four years previously, always stopped in to visit Mother on their many trips to Richmond to see us. He asked me what I had been building lately. Joel appreciated people who were good with their hands. We had always had a warm relationship.

After about a half hour of conversation, he told me he was very tired and was going to sleep. I told him I was too. I had been up since midnight and had gotten no nap.

I went upstairs and quickly fell asleep. The house was very quiet. Jeri was at her sister's house, no doubt wrapping Christmas packages. At around 5:30 that afternoon, I was awakened by a noise downstairs and went to investigate. Joel was on his bed, where I had last talked to him, but a cup had been knocked off his bedside table. He had died in his sleep. I had been the last person to see him alive. It was as though he didn't want to go until he talked to somebody on his way out.

The Funeral was held the Friday after Christmas. It had rained all day, but cleared just before the graveside service. I took the following Monday off from work. I needed a day to gather myself before going back to face God knows what.

IX

Carl wore the face of a funeral director when I was summoned to his office at the start of 1998. I was being "relieved" as News Operations Director for WRVA and the Virginia Network. I had gotten "bad grades" in an employee management survey.

I wondered in my Journal if it was Clear Channel's version of the "Rank and Yank" management strategy that had gained traction in the 80's. Supposedly aimed at weeding out "dead wood," the net effect seemed to rob companies of collaboration, reducing the workplace to some sort of ongoing every man for himself "hunger game." Carl spooned a little saccharine on it saying my job performance had nothing to do with it, but he had to act. It was not a surprise to me. I was the face of Clear Channel and thus, persona non grata! The negative vibes in the newsroom were palpable.

Many on the staff seemed to be under the mistaken impression I was their supervisor, perhaps the result of a "Dilbert" situation that was created when I was appointed. There were conflicting lines of authority. As a WRVA news anchor in morning drive, I was reporting to Deanna Malone as my superior; but as Operations Manager, she reported to me. It was not a recipe for good will.

Even so, some of the staff's anonymous comments that were quoted back to me stung. Anyone who says they don't care what people say about them is lying, but relieved was the right word. I was just glad to be out of it.

Short of stopping people in the halls for advice, top management seemed to have run out of ideas. A new perspective was sought so "the powers that be" did what they always do to give themselves some cover - they brought in consultants.

The first was Mike McVay of McVay Media. He monitored the station in a series of visits beginning in the spring of 1998. His report on perceived areas of concern and suggested programming changes showed up under my office door in a plain brown envelope. To this day, I don't know who leaked it.

Stressed out over my own fate, I read it as though I was a condemned man praying for a stay of execution and a new trial. The gods of radio shined upon me. McVay liked my work. He said the best thing he heard on the station were the morning drive newscasts. He asked for copies of my 8AM news script to share with another client. I quickly scanned the whole report and put it in my Journal for safe keeping as though it was some form of DNA evidence proving my worthiness. My expiration date had been extended.

I was summoned to Carl's office to sort through the McVay Report, specifically the suggestion that I begin "dropping in from time to time" to, as McVay put it, "increase the news presence on the morning show." I didn't think Timberlake would go for it, and I had little interest in a rerun of reading lotto numbers and birthday announcements; but Carl wanted to try something. I said I would go home and see what I could come up with.

My "info snacks," as I came to call them, were long on satire and skepticism with a touch of what I hoped was witty cynicism. I was heavily influenced by Piers

Anderton's classic commentaries on KNBC-TV in Los Angeles in the 70's. I took about two hours every night at home to write them before I went to bed.

The "dropping in" idea, as McVay had suggested, didn't make the cut. Instead, everything I had written for the morning was bundled up into a five or six minute package, which was done live after the 6AM news. Tim, who had a thing for "handles," called it "Snackman." The initial feedback was pretty good. Tim began recording it and rerunning it later in the program. It ran until the show folded in 2001.

X

The radio station celebrated my 30th year at WRVA that June by hosting a large dinner party at a trendy downtown seafood restaurant. Carl's assistant Debbie Ashley put it together in her usually thorough way, and I was looking forward to it because I would make out the guest list. Of course, the need to massage egos, station politics, and those other always annoying, mitigating circumstances intervened and resulted in a couple of people being added to the guest list who did not exactly harbor warm and fuzzy thoughts about me. I was quite sure they only attended out of some sense of perceived duty. I wasn't exactly over the moon about their presence, but it turned out to be an enjoyable evening despite their glum faces at the far end of the table.

The "Old Guard" was back together for one night: John Tansey, his wife Shannon, Bob and Joan Jones, Chuck and Barbara Noe, Frances Aaroe, Roy Cabell and his wife and Lou and Sandy Dean, among others, were all there. I

can only think of one person who did not come, and that
was Jeri. When big events came up, she got stressed out
and went down with a severe migraine.

As the 90's faded, WRVA was hovering in 4th or 5th place
in the radio ratings among listeners 12 years old and up.
It was a pretty dismal performance. Were we really that
bad? In the eyes of the ratings company, we were.

Perhaps counterintuitively, radio ratings weren't so
much about people actually listening as they were about
randomly selected people writing down call letters in
diaries. Top of mind awareness was everything, but there
had been nothing much out there in the way of promotion
to reinforce what the station was doing. I suspected the
promotion budget had pretty much been eliminated.
Proof perhaps that what gets you into trouble is often
what keeps you from getting out of it. It was the perfect
storm to trigger yet another shuffling of the deck chairs.

Jim Jacobs' afternoon drive show had taken a hit in the
ratings. He was on the bubble and, for a time it appeared,
so was I. Carl's secretary Debbie Ashley had penned a
memo to him urging that I be placed in Jacob's slot. When
I found out, I was livid. On the commute home, I was
channeling Howard Beale's tirade in *Network,* screaming
at the windshield and pounding my hand on the steering
wheel drawing strange looks from other drivers.

Nothing came of the proposal. I stayed put in morning
drive news. Jacobs was replaced that spring by a two
person program with Tim Farley, the Program Director,
and Pam Overstreet, who had been doing a show at
mid-day. Jacobs, a competent, clever, witty and talented
guy, landed on his feet with a better gig across town.

Obviously, I had overreacted, an indication, perhaps, of how tightly wound I was.

A month or so later, I sat down with Carl for an employee evaluation. He had no complaints with what I was doing; but he volunteered that the station was in serious trouble ratings-wise and said another consultant was coming in and big changes were in store.

It wasn't just any consultant. It was Clear Channel's in-house guru for its news talk stations around the country. He checked into a Richmond hotel to monitor the radio station. Like the McVay report, a copy of the resulting "Monitor Notes" showed up under my door, presumably from the same, still unknown, source. Jeri remarked the place was becoming a John LeCarre novel.

It was pretty much a rewrite of the McVay Report. There was praise for my anchor work and a recommendation that the station make more use of me. Such accolades are usually kept behind the curtain in the halls of management so it was a much welcomed boost in a rising tide of gloom. It was nice to read, but I had been around long enough to know that praise is only temporary and to just enjoy the moment.

Clear Channel wanted more "Relateables," consultant speak for celebrity gossip, entertainment news, fuzzy human interest stories, health news and so on. In other words, cherry picking content that had more entertainment value, which would translate to better ratings. A new moniker was put in place. "Newsradio 1140 WRVA" was born. If we said it enough, maybe listeners would believe it.

XI

As the powers that be searched for a miracle on North 22nd Street to stop the ratings hemorrhage, the company's radio division was pressing ahead with plans to shoehorn WRVA with the rest of its Richmond broadcast properties into one warehouse-like building in the near West End of Richmond. But the corporate people in San Antonio apparently were uncertain if the company would even own WRVA.

Clear Channel had purchased AM FM, the old Chancellor Media, and AM FM also owned properties in the Richmond Market. Within a week, there was word that the takeover would mean Clear Channel would have to spin off or sell WRVA. Loud cheers erupted in the building.

The rumor mill kicked into warp speed. Giddy highs swept the halls when news came that Jefferson Pilot, the owner of WWBT, the old WRVA TV, had put in a bid for the station, only to plummet to the depths of doom when the rumor mill cranked out word that a large, minority-owned broadcast group was also in the running.

If we had needed a reminder as to how far WRVA had slipped over the past 8 years, we got it on the 25th of January in 2000. Richmond awoke to six inches of snow on the ground. It would top out at nearly a foot and a half, the biggest snowfall the Metro had seen in decades. The city was completely smothered in white, covering all of the accumulated grime, debris and trash under huge snow drifts, some reaching more than four feet in places. Nothing moved. The area was completely paralyzed.

When I went in at my usual hour, the roads were already obliterated. Even the traffic cops, who usually staked out 9th Street hill on snow days looking to tag motorists running the stop sign at the bottom of the hill with a cheap ticket, were a no show.

As soon as I opened the parking lot door, I heard the din of phones jangling. Back in the day, we would have had people working all night. No more. Someone finally came in between 4:30 AM and 5AM to field the calls, which were mostly school closings.

We had no reporters to send out. Our assets, what few were left, were being concentrated in afternoon drive. I made do with an interview with a Highway Department spokesman and a few items from the overnight police blotter courtesy of Captain Shook, the police bureau's Overnight Watch Commander who had called around 3AM. Closing announcements pre-empted my other elements in the morning show; so after my news strips, I went home and slept like the dead for 12 hours.

The Quarterly meeting brought the news no one wanted to hear: there would be no stay of execution. WRVA was not going to be sold. The station would remain with Clear Channel. There were audible groans in the building; but things were looking up on another front, and I began to harbor some hope that I might be able to just walk away from all the drama before Clear Channel homogenized us out of existence.

XII

From the moment Lowry Mays told me in 1992 that Clear Channel was not in the broadcast business but in the business of "selling Fords," I sensed WRVA was on a very slippery slope. What I had seen at the company stations in Louisville and San Antonio only reinforced my gloom, but the other side of it was that Clear Channel was minting money. The company stock, CCU on the New York Exchange, was rocketing into the stratosphere. I couldn't ignore the paradox.

Within a month of the takeover, I decided to hedge my future at WRVA by investing in the company. Jeri agreed.

Using the payout I had received from the profit sharing plan Edens had set up for employees as seed money, I called a broker I knew at Thompson McKinnon Securities and loaded up on Clear Channel shares. I also put everything I had in the Clear Channel 401K plan in the company stock and upped my contribution to the maximum allowed.

I was betting Congress would continue down the deregulation road in broadcasting and Clear Channel would continue buying profitable stations, thereby growing the company and inflating the stock price. Buying in was the only way I could make the big gains required to walk away at some point down the road.

It turned out to be a pretty safe bet. The broadcast giants had Congress in their pockets and the government went on a deregulating frenzy that would culminate in the adoption of the 1996 Telecommunications Act, which opened the door for the big media conglomerates, Clear

Channel being the biggest of the big, to gobble up most of the broadcast properties in America. Clear Channel alone would top out owning more than twelve hundred radio stations in 300 cities and more than 400 television stations.

The stock hopped on an express train. It split more times than I can remember · 2 for 1, 3 for 5 · but, by the turn of the century, the stock started to take on water. Clear Channel's 24 billion dollar deal for AM-FM in 1999, which precipitated all the talk about WRVA being sold, had effectively ended the consolidation movement in radio, and the stock took a hit. By March of 2000, Clear Channel was trading in the 60's. It had peaked earlier, approaching 100 dollars a share. I had sold all of the CCU shares I owned in my self-directed 401K and most of the shares I owned outside the 401K in the high 90's, but what was left of my side bet was still in play in the market.

I called my broker. She told me her firm had a hold on Clear Channel. I told her I was convinced Clear Channel's growth would not come from operating what it owned but would still ride on future acquisitions, but from where I was sitting, there didn't appear to be much left on the table. In the end, I took her advice and held on; but I had Jeri keep a close eye on the stock.

Having been heavily invested in tech in her self-directed IRA, Jeri was then quickly diversifying in advance of the 2000 tech/ dot com bubble burst, which everyone and his brother knew was coming. In fact it would swamp the markets on the 10th of March that year. She was watching the CNBC stock ticker on the TV screen like a hawk and would call me whenever she saw significant moves in Clear Channel.

She rang me at work one morning, the first week in March, and said there was an article in Barron's with a quote from one of Lowry Mays' sons that the company was in the 7th inning of growth by acquisition.

As soon as I hung up, I immediately called my broker and unloaded all of my remaining shares. The stock never recovered.

Several weeks later, having checked off all of the little boxes in my head, I told Jeri I thought it was time for us to go see our accountant with an eye towards life after WRVA.

XIII

The summer brought what Clear Channel called a "Realignment." Carl was removed as General Manager of WRVA in favor of Reggie Jordan, who was running the company's "10 in a row, say hello," chicken rock station WTVR-FM, which went by the moniker "Lite 98." He became the manager of the company's "cluster" of stations in Richmond. Carl was named Director of Sales for the "Cluster." He met with Tim and me in his office just before moving out. Ever the eternal optimist, he said we were "bulletproof" and things would be okay with Reggie. I didn't share his sunny outlook.

A meeting was set for the next morning, presumably to introduce Reggie to his new subjects, but we would be on the air at the time. Timberlake stayed late to meet privately with him. Worn out and tired of all the drama, I went home to reset. I wasn't really sleeping, just detoxing enough to withstand another dose of mental chemo the next day.

Tim called me later. "He listened to my concerns, took notes and said the things one would expect him to say," he told me. Then, after a pause, he added, "Well, at least he said them."

Everyone in the building was wired, edgy, like tiptoeing through a minefield, hoping not to hear that awful click. That there was no immediate attempt to soothe the rampant concern people felt about their jobs led me to conclude it was either by design or the powers that be were just completely tone deaf, which was probably the case. Debbie Ashley, who was always a wealth of information, told us that Reggie Jordan always had an open door policy, but that at "Lite 98" he only had a dozen or so employees. Now, for the moment anyway, he was managing over a hundred.

It was mid-July before I finally met with him. I had gone over to the "warehouse" for a meeting to receive door combinations, email addresses, phone numbers, passwords and other information I hoped to God I would never have use for. Following a brutal presentation about phones, I popped in to see him, saying I was about to leave on vacation and wanted to say hello before I left. As with Tim earlier, he said the things one would expect and made a valiant attempt to be upbeat.

By mid-summer, with plans to abandon the Church Hill Studio Building finalized, Carl threw a big "Farewell To The Hill" party. Timberlake served as MC. Jeri went with me. The crowd was huge. Bob Jones and his wife Joan dropped in for a last look at that magnificent view of the city. We had talked on the phone several times, and he and Jeri had often traded stock tips, but I had not seen him since he had cleared out and retired.

He asked how things were going. I told him, "The station is dying from a thousand cuts. Their plan, if they have one seems to be making what's left of the staff as miserable as possible for as long as possible."

Jones shook his head. "I'm sorry, but I'm not surprised," he said. "What's your plan?"

"To leave as soon as my accountant and my financial advisor tell me I can," I said.

"Keep me posted," he said.

Grazing food had been laid out in the stripped down lobby. No one seemed inclined to eat much, but the wine and beer business was brisk. There were lots of macabre jokes about "slow suicide on the hill." Resigned to the inevitable, the party began to break up. As we walked around the building to our car, Jeri likened the evening to visitation before a funeral.

The following week everyone, except the handful of us left at WRVA in news and on-air, was packed up and moved to the new building. It was as though those of us left behind were an afterthought, like the players to be named later in a baseball trade. Tim and I would spend the rest of our days at WRVA lurking like mushrooms in the soulless building on Church Hill.

I began forcing myself to venture over to the new building after my news shift to train on the new news computer system. After the first couple of visits, I began having the strangest sensation when I drove across town, a kind of glorious detachment, as though it didn't matter, like I was beyond it but just didn't realize it yet.

XIV

The undoing of WRVA and other Richmond radio stations was ongoing fodder for the *Times Dispatch* at the turn of the century. Almost daily, it seemed, there were stories about firings and resignations, with quotes from radio executives who were becoming adept at using the new corporate-speak of "realignments," "restructurings," "right sizing," and so on, ad nauseam, often on the front page. The various broadcast associations had taken note and were handing out their hardware before people split town - a sort of public heads up that careers were on life support

My initiation arrived early in the radio consolidation game. WRVA was in a sort of twilight zone of ownership at the time. One deal to sell us had fallen through, and rumors were ripe that the station was going back on the block. Many of us were updating resumes and lining up references, the usual defense mechanism that kicks in when the uncertainty principle takes control of your life.

It was then that I got word I was to receive the Virginia Association of Broadcasters award for distinguished service in news. Named for longtime radio reporter George Bowles, it was presented at the VAB's winter meeting downtown at the Marriott. It was a welcomed distraction from the funereal atmosphere that hung over Church Hill like a death star. I began my acceptance remarks with a quip. I said I wondered what the VAB knew that I didn't. There was lots of nervous laughter.

Later, with the Clear Channel invasion and takeover of a large chunk of Richmond radio a part of the new media landscape, I was notified of my impending induction into the Richmond Broadcasters Association's Hall of Fame at their summer meeting. I prevailed upon Timberlake to introduce me. When I returned the favor the following year, the association had downsized its once formal dinner to a small lunch. Such was the state of Richmond Radio at the turn of the century.

The WRVA News Staff. 1980's

With Lou Dean and Bill Gordon.
WRVA Studios. 1980's.

Broadcasting from Disney World. 1990's.

Chuck Noe, Yours Truly, Jeri, Bob Jones, Frances Aaroe, Alden
Aaroe and Joan Jones at Duck, North Carolina. 1980's

Alden Aaroe's 75th Birthday.
With Alden and Tim Timberlake. May 1993.

Part VIII

Endgame

I

Depending on who was talking, Randal Bloomquist was either a fixer, a turnaround artist, though "artist" may be putting far too fine a point on it, a hired gun or, as the *Richmond Times Dispatch* called him, as a recipient of one of its "Raspberry Awards" for 2001, "a hatchet man."

Bloomquist was a rather tall young man with a healthy head of black hair who wore glasses and displayed a sort of sly, crocodile-like smile. He had worked for "Radio And Records" Magazine before reinventing himself as a nomadic, radio programmer for hire, hopping from station to station like the character in the old TV Western, *Have Gun Will Travel.* Bloomquist had just finished a four-year "fix" of WBT in Charlotte, North Carolina, when he was hired to steer Clear Channel's scorched earth supervision of WRVA.

I had gotten a heads up from Reggie Jordan at home. He phoned to say he had fired Tim Farley and was bringing in Bloomquist. The formal memo announcing Bloomquist's appointment as Operations Manager of WRVA, WRNL and the Virginia Network came out on August 14, 2000. He was introduced to the combined staffs two weeks later at the new warehouse building. He smiled and said nothing of substance.

I had my first face to face with the newly named "Fixer" the next day in the mausoleum-like Church Hill Building. My first impression was that of the kid in little league who had been coached to look real mean and swing real hard.

Bloomquist's first salvo was to declare that "Millard The Mallard" was "shot out of the sky," as he so eloquently put it. It was tough to hear, but I knew it was time for Millard to flap away into retirement. There was no place for any "theatre of the mind" in Clear Channel's pre-mixed "radio in a box."

Bloomquist offered a special "Farewell to Millard" program. I slept on it for a couple of nights, but I turned him down. I wasn't sure I could pull it off. There were too many memories. I could see myself wallowing in a sea of melancholy, remembering the time when radio was actually fun. I told him I would rather Millard just paddle away without any fanfare.

Bloomquist had no specific quarrel with my news work. He said the morning program would be more news intensive with more interviews of news makers, reporters and so on. He said he was waiting for Tim to commit to the change but said if he didn't, someone would be brought in. I knew Tim wouldn't go for it. Jockeying a news intensive morning program wasn't his thing.

The morning show might be more news driven but the newscasts were getting shorter. Bloomquist ordered the 7 AM and 8 AM newscasts cut back from 10 and 15 minutes to five, like the other hourly strips. The idea was to eliminate the second news shift in morning drive. It was all about the bucks. I would have to do all of the news strips solo, with no second anchor to share the load. I wasn't exactly lathered up over the idea but it was worth it to finally work alone in peace away from recurring newsroom temper tantrums which had lately gone viral with flying clipboards.

Orders came down to include catchy buzzwords and slogans in news copy. It reduced news writing to a kind of Sisyphean exercise. My personal favorite was "Team Coverage." I was ordered to use the phrase in connection with one story in every newscast, but the "Team," such as it was, was shrinking by the day.

Someone described the seemingly endless dismissals as "daylight terror bombing." Tim Farley had been fired as Program Director, Carl McNeil was removed as Director of Sales; Lou Dean resigned in January after being forced into semi-retirement. Former Governor Doug Wilder quit his morning talk show, saying he didn't like what WRVA had become. Two more WRVA news staffers departed. The evening talk show host Jerry Lund resigned and that was just the on-air people at WRVA. Scores of support people had been dismissed. It was the same at Q94, XL102, and WRNL.

I took time off to get my eye fixed.

II

Evan Leslie, MD, listened to Rock and Roll while he operated. "It has a calming effect on me," he said.

I was all for calm when someone was going to be cutting on my eye. He gave me several choices of rock bands from which to choose. "What's your favorite?" I asked.

"I like them all," he said, "but I'm partial to 'The Eagles.'"

"Then 'The Eagles' it is," I said. I wanted him to be really calm.

My vision had deteriorated to the point that I was driving to and from work from memory. I could no longer read the street signs. At work, I had the engineers put a big clock right in the news studio with me. I could not clearly see the clock through the window in the adjoining studio. Surgery had been put off because I had a very low cell count in my right eye. Now, my vision was so bad, I had nothing to lose.

The morning of the surgery, I was injected with a marvelous, mystery drug. Within five minutes, every molecule of stress evaporated and I began to float on a warm sea of detached reality. The surgery to remove a cataract and implant an artificial lens lasted roughly 45 minutes. I felt nothing, but what I saw was a colored light show that flooded every corner of my mind with brilliant, vivid, Kodachrome-like hues. Coupled with strains of "Tequila Sunrise," a pale, hazy, drowsy euphoria streamed through me. It was as though I had glimpsed some kind of secret grandeur. God, I thought, if death is like this, give me a ticket! I had never in my life experienced anything like it.

Later in the recovery room, I asked Doctor Leslie what it was.

"All I will tell you," he grinned, "is that it is very much a controlled substance. You'll get another trip in about a year when we do the left eye."

I was looking forward to it.

The bandage came off the next morning. The results were simply stunning. In one day, my vision had gone from muddy river water to near 20/30. Images were clear. Edges were crisp. Leaves on trees looked like leaves, not blobs of green. White no longer looked like dirty beige. Colors were ferociously vivid.

I spent the weekend walking around, looking at everything again for the first time. I was blown away. By year's end, my right eye was 20/20. The cell count in my eye was low, but had held steady despite the trauma of the surgery. My vision was near perfect. I would be back in a year to fix the left eye.

Jerri and I drove down to North Carolina to spend the Christmas holiday with her sisters at the farm. It felt very strange to drive past Emporia on Interstate 95 without stopping.

III

Timberlake seemed a bit down when I saw him that first morning back in January, 2001. He said he had resolved to find work elsewhere as soon as he could. He told me he wasn't comfortable with the format and frankly didn't think Bloomquist would ever like what he did. Some weeks later, he called one night at home and said he had "pulled the plug." His last day would be March 15th. "Keep it under your hat," he said. The story broke three days later on the front page of the Times Dispatch.

The undoing of WRVA was a running story in the newspaper. We had been very good at covering the demise of others, but we were lousy at it when it happened to us. Many of us had friends at the *Times Dispatch,* and we had been worthy competitors. Now they were writing our obituary. Bob Brown, the newspaper's chief shooter, brought his camera up to the hill on Tim's last day and snapped the two of us behind the main console. He sent each of us a color print. He titled it "Last of the Mohicans."

There was a huge send off, off premises! Bloomquist had dictated no going away party. Tim's pal Whit Baldwin, with Hawthorne Aviation in Richmond, who had been WRVA's Traffic Helicopter pilot and reporter before Clear Channel ended airborne traffic reporting, called to ask if I would introduce the man of the hour. Of course, I said yes.

An "SRO" crowd turned out. It seemed every person who worked in Richmond Media was there. I poked fun at Tim's reputation as a nice guy. It was widely held. *Style Weekly,* the Richmond Arts Newspaper, had plastered his sunny face on its cover some years earlier with the caption, "Richmond's Nice Guy." A framed copy had welcomed visitors to the water fountain in the Church Hill studio building for years. Tim was a nice guy. It was the foundation for his long success. It was hard to imagine WRVA without him.

Bloomquist began bringing in candidates to replace Timberlake for live, on air auditions. Among them was a guy from San Diego who had a pretty hard edge on the air. Bloomquist asked me what I thought. I told him I didn't think the hard ass act would play well in Richmond. The best of the lot by far, I said, was Jimmy Barrett from Detroit. I told Bloomquist that Barrett had my vote.

Clear Channel, meantime, continued to reach down to meet my expectations. The company sent another of its faceless Vice Presidents from central casting for an "un-pep rally," as a colleague remarked. It was held in the stripped down Church Hill Lobby, which had taken on the guise of a bunker awaiting the final assault. He was rather young, profoundly arrogant, condescending, and completely unzipped from reality.

On the way out, I stopped in the men's restroom and noticed a small, crudely made sign that had been posted - "Forgive them, Alden, they know not what they do."

Across the hall in the newsroom, equipment failure had become the new normal. Satellite receivers conked out almost daily, knocking out network audio feeds upon which I was becoming more and more dependent for "Team Coverage" because of the firings and resignations. Computer work stations and digital disc recorders crashed with maddening regularity, wiping out all of my processed news sound. Clear Channel was all about the new building. Those of us still on Church Hill were left to fend for ourselves.

Even Reggie Jordan had had enough. That spring, he abdicated as "Cluster King" to pursue other interests. There was a rumor that a holdover from the AM FM merger was lobbying to be the next contestant.

IV

I felt like a survivor of a radio coup and Bloomquist seemed to be on a mission to keep me. He told me that I was the premier radio news person in the market and would be working at WRVA as long as I wanted. After all the firings and dismissals, it seemed like a cheap compliment, but it no longer mattered. I was well beyond the tipping point. Mentally, I was already gone.

I had long since boxed up and removed all of my files, tapes, discs and flash drives. Radio people always have tapes or their digital equivalent. It's the only evidence that we ever did anything. My collection included copies I had made of all of the long form documentaries and series I had produced, the "Second Sunday" documentaries I had worked on for NBC, and a few editorial and commentary awards. When Millard was banished, I cleared out MTM Inc.'s corporate files, all of the graphics, photographs, costumes, tapes, "T" shirts and novelties. My life's work in a few boxes, keepsakes amidst all the detritus.

I was just waiting for a green light from Michelle and Rick, the gatekeepers of my future. Jeri and I had met twice with them: Rick Wilde, our CPA, and Michelle Mast, our financial planner. We had turned over all of our financial data and investment details for analysis by a team of accountants, tax specialists and lawyers. The preliminary results looked good, but there were still some blanks to fill in.

Everything else had clicked into place. Our completed house plans arrived that week from North Carolina. We were at the farm checking out our potential home site when I got a call that John Tansey had died at the age of 84.

We had last talked about a week earlier. Our conversations over the past few months had the tone of an exit interview. He had been quite despondent over what had happened to "my station." His voice was thin, but the old grit was still there. Finally he asked, "Are you and Jeri going to be okay?" I told him I was pretty sure we would be. "I am so sorry it came to this, John," he said.

The day after his death, his daughter called and said the family wanted me to deliver the Eulogy at St. Paul's near Capitol Square in Richmond. The historic church was filled to capacity for the service. The Rector complimented me on my remarks. So did the Tansey Family. They asked me to stand in the receiving line with them at the reception after the service. I was honored to do so.

In his time, John Tansey was among the best radio general managers in the country. He steered WRVA through the earthquake that was television and into its second golden age, taking the station to unfathomable heights in audience, prestige and national recognition. When he retired, he was at the pinnacle of his career. On his watch, WRVA had become one of the city's revered institutions, the crown jewel of Richmond radio. That he lived long enough to see it crumble was a cruel annotation at the end of a brilliant career.

I read somewhere that commercial radio in America reached its zenith in 1982. I don't know about radio in general but it seemed to fit as far as WRVA was concerned. In hindsight, it seemed as though the station had been on a glacial-like slide to also ran status ever since. Perhaps not coincidentally, 1982 was the year John Tansey retired from WRVA.

V

We got the last word on our retirement financing in early April. When we walked in, the big smiles on everyone's faces said it all. Michelle told me to get busy on that resignation letter. There were high fives all around, and we all went out for a celebratory dinner.

That night I slept the sleep of the blessed and that weekend I wrote my resignation letter. I thought about it all day that Sunday, and driving in early Monday I remember thinking, "This really is my final decision."

Deanna Malone, the WRVA News Director had seen it coming. Bloomquist appeared momentarily taken aback. A small victory perhaps, but overall he had treated me with a modicum of respect. I wished him well.

I left with a great sense of relief. I was out of the grinder, but there was a cloud of disappointment. I had never pictured my departure this way. I thought the station would always be there and just carry on in the grand tradition, but the dismantling of WRVA would go on. Everything but the call letters and the frequency would be obliterated.

The word got around quickly. Melissa Ruggeri, the Media Columnist for the *Richmond Times Dispatch*, called for a few quotes, newspaper "sound bites." She asked why I was leaving. "Remember the BB King song, "The Thrill Is Gone?" I asked. "Well, it has."

Bloomquist came by the following week and asked if I would stay on two or three more weeks. He was having trouble finding a replacement. I told him the train had left the station.

Clear Channel refused to pay me any severance and held me to working out my last two weeks, but the additional weeks served to reinforce my decision to resign. Gathering, preparing and broadcasting the news on WRVA had become rote assembly line work, following the same tired formula with the same mindless slogans hour after hour with machine-like precision. I had always told myself that when it wasn't fun anymore, I wanted to be in a position to walk away. It wasn't and I was.

Appropriately, my last day was a Friday. After my final newscast at 9AM, Jimmy Barrett, who had replaced Timberlake in the morning, told listeners that it had been my last at WRVA, that I was leaving the station after more than 33 years. He thanked me for my support.

Bloomquist, ever the Simon Legree, had decreed that there be no going away party for me and no parting gift. Not everyone had gotten the memo. Many of those I had worked with over the years came by or called. Breakfast pizzas from "Ukrops" were broken out in Studio A. Tim brought along a bottle of single malt. I thanked them all for coming - and I left.

Our house sold rather quickly. We went about packing our things, with time out for farewell calls, going away lunches and get-togethers.

Former colleagues held a "retirement" party for me at a Richmond restaurant in the near West End and presented me with a high dollar gift certificate from one of the Richmond area's better home furnishing stores. Bob Jones and his wife Joan, Chuck and Barbara Noe, Frances Aaroe and Shannon Tansey held a going away luncheon for us. (It was the last time I would see Chuck, Bob and Frances. Chuck died in 2003, Frances in 2006 and Bob in 2011.)

The week of our move in mid-June, I drove into Richmond to pick up a truck I had rented to move all of our books and art to the farm in North Carolina. The owner recognized my name, and lamenting what had happened to the station, grabbed a stack of new furniture blankets and put them on the counter. "Take 'em," he said, "to remember old times." I thanked him, and he said, "You know, John, I always knew it was you doing Millard The Mallard." It wasn't quite the epitaph I wanted to leave behind, but it was better than nothing!

Tim Timberlake's Last Day at WRVA. Bob Brown Photo. 2001

Jeri and I after retirement.

Postscript

It is late April of 2013. I am surprised to find an email from Dee Warren in my in-box. I seldom, if ever, heard from her, so I sensed it must be bad news. It was. Her mother had died that morning. "You were always one of her favorites," she said. The funeral was to be held later that week in Emporia. She said she just wanted me to know but certainly didn't expect me to make the trip. But, of course, I would.

Duane Harrell was the last of the great ladies of my time on Ingleside Avenue. She had tolerated my almost constant presence with reserved humor as I clumsily attempted to maneuver myself into her daughter's thoughts.

Duane had lobbied fiercely on my behalf, prodding her husband Lyman to use his considerable influence to get me into college. I had enormous respect for her and was grateful for her presence later in life as my wife and I dealt with my aging Mother. After Mother's death, Duane had us over to her home for dinner several times as we went about the sad task of closing the house. She was comfortable with the times, yet of another age · a very proper, elegant, classy lady with great style and just a slight touch of sassiness that added to her charm.

After my sister sold the house, Duane and I began an exchange of letters until she left Emporia for an assisted living center near Dee Warren. She was a special dame and a treasured link to the old neighborhood, and I would miss her.

Jeri was not up to the trip but told me, "You must go, John. I'll be fine." Her sister Marjorie immediately stepped up to look in on her while I was gone.

The drive to Emporia was about two and a half hours from our farm in southeastern North Carolina near the coast. I drove in silence with only the steady din of the traffic keeping me company. I seldom, if ever, listened to the radio anymore. It had ruled my life for more than 40 years but now I seldom thought about it.

The hours sped by, almost as quickly it seemed, as had the years. The exit sign for the small community of Skippers rocketed by, and within minutes, the familiar sign for Emporia loomed ahead.

As I drove into town, Emporia appeared to be thriving. West Atlantic Street, US Highway 58, once lined with private homes, was now a sprawl of franchise eateries - burger and pizza joints catering to the I-95 traffic. A huge Walmart Super Center anchored a nearby shopping center. The parking lot was almost full; but next door, a relatively new looking big box home improvement store had been boarded up, a sign the recession had entered. The only familiar landmark was the WEVA radio tower rising over the rooftops. It was where I had started in radio when I was 14, more than 50 years ago.

Only subtle hints of the glory days remained. A used car lot corralled by a chain link fence occupied the site of what had been the Emporia Diner, hangout extraordinaire of my youth. The once vibrant business district along Halifax Street was now a monument to lost enterprise. Bloom Brothers, once Emporia's Macy's, was gone without a trace. The Old Virginia Hotel had been lovingly repurposed as an antique shop, but most of the other stores, their names familiar to generations, had vanished.

A car horn jolted me out of my daydream. The lumbering CSX freight train that had brought down the crossing gates had passed. It was pushing 11 AM. I drove over the tracks and headed up Southampton Street to Monumental Methodist Church.

I must have been completely consumed by my thoughts as I walked down the sidewalk to the front portico of the church because I did not notice the woman who ran up, wrapped her arms around my neck and excitedly whispered in my ear, "Oh, My God, you have absolutely no idea how much I prayed that you would be here." It was Linda Harrell, Linda Bachman now. I had not seen her in decades, but I recognized her right away.

A sea of faces, some familiar, some not, milled about. "Where's your wife?"

"She's distressed she could not make the trip."

"Nice to see you again, John."

I made my way into the sanctuary and found a seat on my left. The church seemed much smaller than I remembered. Isn't that always the case? Echoes of Sundays long past floated through my thoughts · Richard Tucker's booming baritone, Duane's profile at the organ, my parents in their usual pew.

The church began to fill. The family came in. The service was lengthy but not overly so. Dee Warren had arranged for the last minister her mother had served as Choir Director to deliver the Eulogy.

Each of the children spoke. Dee Warren had the elegant air of her mother as she summarized Duane's last years.

She saw me as I walked down the steps at the entrance to the church after the service. "I was so hoping you would come, John. You ARE coming to the Keedwell house after the graveside service?" (The Keedwells were first cousins)

I had last seen her 8 years before at my sister Barbara's Memorial Service. The years had been very kind to her. I told her, "Yes, I'll be there."

The procession to the cemetery took an unexpected detour up Ingleside Avenue with a pause in front of the old Harrell House right across the street from where I grew up. It was a poignant reminder of those happy times in the old neighborhood.

The graveside service was short and to the point.

I remembered the way to the Keedwell house, but I had forgotten the name of the street. The house was packed. It was hard to circulate.

"My God, how long has it been? "

"A lifetime."

"You did that duck character on the radio in Richmond."

"I did."

She was in the living room with her husband Harvey standing nearby. A tall, lanky man, he had a rather blank look on his face so I introduced myself.

"Thanks," he said. "I remember your face but I couldn't place you."

She introduced me to her three grown sons. Suddenly I was obsolete.

After maybe five minutes of conversation, the strain of the day was evident on her face. I pointed to my watch and said I needed to get started on the trip back to Eastern North Carolina.

"We need to meet somewhere when there's more time to catch up with each other," she said.

I told her that would be nice, but I knew it was unlikely. Suddenly, in the wink of an eye, we were the oldest generation. It seemed time had broken the rules, speeding up our lives with each advancing year. It had all gone so quickly.

###

Acknowledgements

First, my thanks to you for reading it. It was my sister June who suggested I write it. She wanted to "catch up" with what happened to me growing up after she left for college and career when I was 10 years old. I had no thought of ever publishing it. I could not fathom anyone would be even remotely interested in my coming of age and working in radio. June convinced me otherwise saying "it's not just about you John, it's about about growing up in a small town and all of those marvelous people in the neighborhood and elsewhere along your path who helped you. I went to work polishing it up. That was 4 years ago.

My wife Jeri was an enormous help. Always the steady hand, she served as my sounding board, page proofer and coach.

A trainload of thanks to Elizabeth "Bet" Harrell Neale, who edited the book, and supplied untold anecdotes, recollections and suggestions. Without her help and expertise, the book would not have happened.

Thanks also to her sisters: Martha F. Harrell, Dee Harrell Roberts, and Linda Harrell Bachman. All were a big part of my life growing up. I am indebted to all of them for their support of the project, their many remembrances and suggestions and for allowing me to write in detail about their mother's funeral.

Former colleagues at WRVA were an enormous help. First and foremost, the late John Tansey. John was a

315

virtual encyclopedia of WRVA. His career at the station as a reporter, manager and consultant spanned nearly 50 years. He shared his recollections and thoughts with me during several conversations over the last few months of his life.

Huge thanks also to Lou Dean who wrote the Foreword to the book and who generously answered my many questions about his time and extraordinary career at WRVA.

Thanks to Tim Timberlake, my morning colleague on WRVA for more than 20 years, who penned a personal synopsis of the book for the back cover.

A special nod to Debbie Ashley for sharing her thoughts, impressions and remembrances of her long career at WRVA and for saving the station's history which now resides safe and sound in the Library of Virginia.

Finally, thanks to my financial planner Michelle Mast who made my life after radio possible.

The primary source for much of the book was my Personal Journal, which I maintained throughout my time at NBC and WRVA. It, along with my records and files containing memos, news releases, photographs, newspaper clips, and of course all of the MTM, Inc., corporate files along with numerous family scrapbooks provided a treasure trove of information and memories.

I have, with limited success, attempted to keep my opinions, observations and conclusions out of the book. Those which survived are my own and do not necessarily reflect those of WEVA Radio in Emporia, Virginia, The National Broadcasting Company, or WRVA Radio in

Richmond, Virginia, their current or former owners, operators, shareholders, employees or advertisers. I alone am responsible for any omissions and errors.

John Harding

Lenoir County, North Carolina

February 2016

About The Author

John Harding spent more than 40 years in broadcasting in Virginia and Washington, DC. He is the 1992 recipient of the Virginia Association of Broadcaster's "George A. Bowles Junior Award for Distinguished Performance in Broadcast News." He was honored by the Richmond Association of Broadcasters in 2000 with its "Lifetime Achievement Award. He was presented with a special Certificate of Recognition by Virginia Governor L. Douglas Wilder in 1992 for his long service as Chairman of the Virginia Emergency Broadcast System and Chairman of the Virginia State Emergency Communications Committee.

After leaving broadcasting in 2001, John went into freelance photography full time. He is also active in scale ship modeling and model railroading. This is his first book.

John and his wife Jeri live on their family farm in Eastern North Carolina.

John is on Facebook.

Made in the USA
Lexington, KY
30 October 2016